TIDES FROM THE WEST

A
CHINESE AUTOBIOGRAPHY
BY
CHIANG MONLIN

NEW HAVEN
YALE UNIVERSITY PRESS
LONDON · GEOFFREY CUMBERLEGE · OXFORD UNIVERSITY PRESS
1947

This book is issued by the Yale University Press in co-operation with the China Institute of Pacific Relations, of which Dr. Chiang Monlin has been Chairman.

PREFACE

THIS volume will try to tell the story of what has happened in China during the last hundred years, from the cession of Hongkong in 1842 to the blitzkrieg of Pearl Harbor in 1941, with emphasis on the latter half of that period. A century is a long time, but of China's more than four thousand years of history it is but a small fraction, less than one fortieth. Yet the change China has gone through in that brief span is unprecedented in her long life. And now more rapid changes on a still larger scale are about to take place.

Since the first exchange of gunfire at Marco Polo Bridge the attention of the world has been drawn to China. The heroic resistance at Shanghai, Taierchuan, and Changsha has evoked sympathy and admiration in the hearts of millions of China's friends throughout the world. The part China is destined to play in the affairs of nations will be of great interest to the world in the period before us. She has been appraised somewhat too high by her well-wishers and somewhat too low by those who do not know her. In either case the interest is there and the fact remains that she has fought almost singlehanded, for eight long, suffering years, a strong enemy sustained by religious-patriotic fanaticism, superior weapons, and efficient organization.

Neither by her friends nor by her own efforts could China be lifted overnight to the level of modern industrialized democracies; nor could she be exterminated by her enemies in a few years or even a few centuries. In the time ahead of us she will become a focus of attention for the world, since future peace—at least one of the major factors of peace—will depend much on a prosperous and strong China.

How is this great country to be made prosperous and strong? The problem must be solved by herself alone. Effective co-operation of friendly Powers will accelerate her success, but she alone must bear the responsibility of making herself worthy to be a leading partner of peace in the world.

China is a nation neither of angels nor of incompetents; she is a nation of common mortals with feelings, ideas, love and hate, hopes and despair, beauty and ugliness, accomplishments and failings, virtues and vices. It is hoped that the world will not expect from her people more than it does from other ordinary human beings. She has no panacea for all her troubles, nor any magic box by aid of which she can transform herself at will into what she desires to be. Whatever success she has achieved has been paid for with sweat in time of peace and with blood in time of war.

To the question "What is the trouble with China?" the author can only answer that there are a number of troubles waiting for solution in that vast country of teeming millions, more than she will be able to solve in any limited span of time. Some were created by enemies who tried to conquer her, others by herself during the time of metamorphosis; still others have been imposed on her by force of circumstance or as legacies of the past. Some of the more difficult problems have been solved or partially solved during recent years before the war; many others remain to be dealt with in due course of time.

Looking back over the last fifty years which he has personally experienced—over the past hundred years with which he is familiar, and even farther, down the long reaches of China's history which he has been taught—the author has traced to the best of his knowledge the threads of a number of problems, some lying deep in her past, others arising from the rapid changes which caught her unprepared. He has tried to tell, within the limits of discretion, what has happened in China, especially during the last fifty years. For those friends who desire to co-operate with her, with a view to solving some of the difficult problems of a more enduring peace, this moderate volume may be helpful in giving an insight into the life and problems of the Chinese people. For co-operation cannot possibly proceed without mutual understanding. To understand what is actually the background—the mental, emotional, and moral constitution—of the country, is essential for a lasting co-operation.

With the above ideas in mind the author has described ordinary happenings in some detail so as to acquaint the reader in some measure of intimacy with the mental, emotional, and moral make-up of the Chinese people as revealed through their life in peace and war. As small things often reflect major developments in a country, it is hoped that some sense of the meaning of greater events may be gathered from these apparent trifles of daily life.

CHIANG MONLIN

CONTENTS

PROLOGUE: FRONTIER CITY

DURING a world upheaval with bombs dropping from the sky and bursting all around, one is apt to wonder what caused these terrible things to happen.

What has happened in the world in the last decade is not something that merely dropped from the sky. Events have their causes. In the last years of the war, as I cast my mental view beyond the horizons of Kunming, where most of this volume was written, I saw how one event had led to another, with consequent social and political changes. Musing over the past in that scenic city on the Burma Road overlooking tranquil, historic Kunming Lake, with bomb-shattered houses standing around me like the remnants of Pompeii, the scenes of what had happened during my lifetime unfolded themselves like a dream clearly and vividly before me; and I set pen to paper to put down what I had seen with my own eyes during the last half century of rapid change in the life of my country.

As I began to write we were in the midst of heavy munitions traffic coming in by truck from Burma. The fighting planes of the American Volunteer Group known as the "Flying Tigers" droned over our heads. War profiteers and truck drivers roamed the streets by hundreds and thousands with their pockets full of bank notes, while the price of commodities soared sky-high.

A British friend remarked to a professor of our university that we ought to have controlled prices at the beginning of the war. "Well," said the professor with a tinge of humor, "we will know better in the next war." He went on to remark that if he had had the capital he might have followed the example of the Greek philosopher who cornered olives in ancient Greece in anticipation of a poor olive crop. When the crop failed, he was rich. But the professor had no capital and too little of that sort of foresight, and in addition, too much of patriotism in his way.

After Pearl Harbor came waves of bad news of the Allies. Hongkong, the Malay States, and Singapore fell one after the other. The enemy headed for Burma. China rushed troops there;

they retreated, after a stubborn resistance, through the mountains and swamps of Upper Burma, living on banana roots. They were greatly annoyed by the leeches that dropped on their heads from trees, suckers that hooked onto you and drank your blood. If you tried to tear one off, it carried away in its mouth a piece of your flesh. The best way of getting rid of these nasty parasites was to rub salt on them, but salt there was none. The next best way, in the circumstances, was to slap at them until they gave you up.

Chinese nationals in Burma left by tens of thousands and made their way back to China by the Burma Road. Enemy planes bombed and machine-gunned them. Three thousand people, men and women, young and old, died on the way. A torrent of refugees flowed along the road into Kunming. Streets were crowded with thousands of distressed people and public buildings were set aside for their temporary lodging. After two or three months they gradually melted into the neighboring provinces; many went back to their native provinces of Fukien and Kwangtung.

The Burma Road, built in eight months by the hands of some eighty thousand farmers, men, women, and children, was now cut at the other end and rendered useless. Kunming, once on the highway of international traffic, was now an isolated city, and only by air could one travel to India. The Yunnan-Burma Railway, under construction by 250,000 men, was to be finished within twelve months; it was partially built, then suspended. China was cut off from the world, with the enemy on three sides and only the faintest trickle of supplies remaining. In this isolation she held out, fighting for her national existence every inch of the way, until the end of the war.

Let us forget recent history for the moment and look back to the past to see what we can learn from it.

Part I

IN AN OLD EMPIRE

CHAPTER 1

HOW EAST AND WEST MET

CENTURIES ago certain wise men from the East, following a star, traveled to the land where a religion was born destined in centuries to come to play a great part in the life of Western nations. A religion based upon meekness was adopted in the course of time by these peoples of extreme vigor. This religion of meekness, which teaches "whosoever shall smite thee on the right cheek, turn to him the other also," won its way through the West slowly but persistently by braving Roman lions and enduring hardships, suffering, and persecution. A few centuries later it began to trickle into China with the same meekness.

The Nestorians came to China during the Tang Dynasty (618–905 A.D.), and the Tang emperors built churches for them. But they did not find China a fertile soil for their religion. Another few centuries passed; the Jesuits found their way into the court of the Ming Dynasty (1368–1643 A.D.). They brought with them Western astronomy, which caught the fancy of the Ming emperors.

The Western peoples, meanwhile, with vigorous blood in their veins, not only absorbed the new religion but also created science and made inventions which led to an industrial revolution in recent centuries. As a result they amassed an immense amount of capital, which had to find an outlet in other countries not as yet industrialized. It flowed to the East, first in a trickle, then in torrents, and finally in tides which flooded the Orient and almost swept China off her feet.

China had no trouble with Christianity, nor with any other religion. Only when it was coupled with commercialism supported by gunboats in the middle of the nineteenth century was the religion of meekness seen through Chinese eyes as that of an aggressor. For a religion seen arm in arm with force changes its color, and the Chinese were unable to dissociate the two. This naturally gave rise to the impression that while Buddha came to China on white elephants, Christ was borne on cannon balls.

Since we were knocked out by cannon balls, naturally we became interested in them, thinking that by learning to make them we could strike back. We could forget for the time being in whose name they had come, since for us common mortals to save our lives was more important than to save our souls.

But history seems to move through very curious ways. From studying cannon balls we came to mechanical inventions, which in turn led us to political reforms; from political reforms we began to see political theories, which led us again to the philosophies of the West. On the other hand, through mechanical inventions we saw science, from which we came to understand scientific method and the scientific mind. Step by step we were led farther and farther away from the cannon ball—yet we came nearer and nearer to it.

The story is a long one, but it all happened in the short span of a hundred years, the dramatic part of it in not more than half a century. I say a hundred years because in 1942 Hongkong was to celebrate its centenary as a British possession, and it was a coincidence that Japan, Britain's former ally, had snatched it from British hands in the previous year by lightning attack. I mention Hongkong without the least intention of rubbing an old sore, only because it will serve as a convenient landmark for the earlier part of China's westernization. As everyone will remember, this group of hilly islands—situated in the south sea not far from Canton, and nests for pirates a century ago—was ceded to Britain in 1842 at China's defeat in the so-called "Opium War." What actually happened was that China, having forbidden the importation of opium, Britain's principal export from India to that country, burned British opium at Canton. Britain retaliated with cannon balls and China lost the war.

Torrents of Western manufactures began to pour in through the subsequent opening, also stipulated under the treaty, of five coastal cities as commercial ports. These cities lay scattered at fairly regular intervals along the coast of the prosperous southern half of the country. Thus new frontiers were formed; China's frontiers had lain hitherto solely inland, to the north and northwest. This change in China's map was the turning point in her history.

These five seaports—Canton, Amoy, Foochow, Ningpo, and Shanghai—running from south to north in a chain, served as depots for Western manufactured goods which flowed thence into the richest and most populous parts of the country, the Pearl and Yangtze Valleys. Supported by gunboats the Western merchants squatted like octopuses in the ports, sending their tentacles into the interior of the rich provinces. China, an enormous country larger than the United States, was herself unaware of the penetration and blind to what was bound to happen later on. The life of her millions went its leisurely and contented way from the cradle to the grave without making the least effort toward modernization, while a section of the people began casually to pick up foreign manufactures, whether for use, for pleasure, or out of curiosity.

The gunboat policy of the Western Powers, however, carried with it not only manufactured goods and opium but also the healthy seeds of Western science and culture, which we did not see at the time but which were to germinate years later to the benefit of China—one of the ironies of history.

Meanwhile the westernization of Japan went on by leaps and bounds. Again, China was unaware of it. Half a century later, by 1894, the little Island Empire suddenly loomed large over the horizon of the China Sea, sprang a surprise attack upon the sleeping giant, and bit off a mouthful. The next to go after Hongkong was Formosa, an island province near the east coast hundreds of times larger than Hongkong. China now began to feel the pinch and rub her eyes in wonder. What was it that was disturbing her sweet dreams?

My original plan was just to write out what I know and feel about my own country. As I have let these mental pictures run their course, one after another, they have developed into a volume something like autobiography, something like reminiscences or contemporary history. Whatever it may be, it is all from the indelible images that unrolled in my mind as clearly and vividly as if they had been printed there only yesterday. In the rapid march of events I felt myself a tiny cog on the vast whirling wheel.

CHAPTER 2

VILLAGE LIFE

I came into the world as the youngest of five children, four boys and a girl, in a well-to-do family in a small village. The night before I was born my father dreamed of a bear coming to our house, the sign of a male baby. The next day the good omen came true: the spirits of our forefathers in heaven presented another son to the family.

Before my eldest brother was born, Father had dreamed of receiving a bouquet of orchids. So the child was named Orchid. My second brother was named Peach for the same reason. Naturally I was called Bear. As for my sister and third brother, Father had no dreams. My name was afterward changed from Bear to Unicorn when I registered at Chekiang College, because of events in the schools.

I was born a war baby, for the year in which I came into the world saw Britain cut off Burma from Chinese control; and the Sino-French War had just ended the previous year, by which China lost her suzerainty over Indo-China to France. The peeling of dependencies off China was a prelude to further invasion by foreign Powers. For China kept dependencies to serve as buffer states, not for exploitation. She never interfered with their internal administration.

When the peel was gone, germs began to make inroads into the orange. However, people in China were not aware of it. These wars on the southwest frontiers were far away and mere ripples on her vast ocean. The villagers were the least concerned—in their profound isolation they gave less attention to such news than they would to ghost stories. Yet China drew a part of her defense forces from among just such villages, not interested in war.

When I came to know the little world around me I noticed that people spoke more realistically of the Taiping Rebellion, which had destroyed a part of the village some thirty years before. The chief of the elders of the Chiang clan, a carpenter by trade, had once joined the rebels. He told us many stories of pillage and atrocities committed by the Taipings,* of which he himself had been guilty. To listen to these horrors often made a chill run all over my body. Yet of the international wars of recent years people talked only casually, utterly unconcerned. There were fabulous stories of victory—simply amusing, in a sense tragic, as one thinks of them in afteryears. For the fact was that while Chinese troops made a good showing in some engagements, the conclusion was complete defeat.

The spearhead of modern invention had not yet penetrated to the villages and they lay there, secret, primitive, and calm, as our ancestors had founded them some five hundred years before. Yet the people were not idle. The farmers had to plow, sow, and reap; the fishermen to cast their nets in the canals; the women to spin, weave, sew; the traders to buy and sell; the craftsmen to make their beautiful articles; the scholars to read aloud, memorize the Confucian classics, and take civil examinations.

There were hundreds of thousands of such villages in China, varying only in size and mode of life according to topographical and climatic differences. The traditions, family ties, and trades which held them together were more or less the same. A common written language, common ideals of life, a common culture and system of civil examinations bound the whole country into a single nation known as the Chinese Empire.

Together with the large cities and centers of trade, these hundreds of thousands of villages in China kept the country supplied with food, goods, scholars, soldiers, and the rank and file of officials of the government. So long as they remained untouched by modernization, China would remain the same; if she could have built fences round the treaty ports they might have remained the same for centuries to come. But the tide of westernization refused to be contained within the treaty ports. It made itself felt in the immediate surroundings, extending gradually along waterways and highways. Villages and towns near the five invaded cities or along communication lines were the first to succumb.

---

* An uprising which started in the south in 1851, capitalizing peasant discontent, and swept over most of the country until crushed with foreign help several years later.

Like transplanted trees feeding on China's rich soil, branching off and multiplying fast, the modern influence extended in the course of some fifty years far into the interior.

The village of the Chiangs was one among many spread—with intervening spaces of one or two miles of luxuriant rice fields— over the alluvial plain formed by the Chien-tang River. This is well known for its scenery, both in the upper part and in the lower section near the mouth where the famous bores of Chien-tang make their impressive seasonal sweep in from the sea. The high, abrupt front of the tidal bore is of a grandeur to over-shadow Niagara Falls. Down the valley, through the centuries, the river slowly laid its rich earth, building its shores farther and farther into Hangchow Bay. On the newly formed shores people erected temporary enclosures to hold the brine from which common salt is made. A large quantity of salt was produced every year, supplying the needs of many millions.

After a number of years, as the shores were further extended, the salt would begin to exhaust itself and dikes would be built along the drying land at some distance from the water. The embanked land was now ready for pasturing. After a long period it was capable of growing cotton to feed the domestic looms, or mulberry trees to nourish silkworms. It was probably still another half century before it could be turned into rice fields. For plenty of water is needed for growing rice, and it takes time to build reservoirs and a network of canals for irrigation. And the land takes time to mature.

The village of the Chiangs, by the time I came to it, was situated about twenty miles from Hangchow Bay. Around it were endless chains of villages, large and small, running in all directions—southward to the mountains, northward to the sea, and east and west to towns and cities all connected by miles of footways or canals. The genealogy of the Chiangs tells us that our first ancestors immigrated to the Yuyao district from Hueichow, a mountainous region where the famous river finds its source. They came presumably to reclaim the then newly formed land. In my own time an ancient embankment was still visible in front of our clan temple, the Temple of the Four No's, popularly known as the "Temple Facing the Embankment."

Perhaps the reader would like to know what is meant by the

"Four No's." They mean to see no evil, hear no evil, speak no evil, do no evil. The sets of three monkeys with hands covering their eyes, ears, and mouth, respectively, that one finds in Oriental bazaars exemplify them—the fourth being left out for obvious reasons. These moral precepts came from the Confucian classics. Moral ideas were driven into the people by every possible means —temples, theatres, homes, toys, proverbs, schools, history, and stories—until they became habits in daily life. This was one of the ways by which China attained social stability: governing the life of the people by moral bonds.

During the long centuries of history the population of China had expanded from its northern beginnings to the south, first to the Yangtze Valley, then to the Pearl River Valley, and finally to the mountainous regions of the southwest. The fertile soil of the south and the devastation caused by flood from the incorrigible Yellow River, as well as by invasions of warlike tribes from outside the Great Wall, together with the natural expansion of the race, all contributed to cause repeated southward movements of the Chinese people. It was following in the wake of such a movement that my ancestors came to stay here on the shores of Hangchow Bay.

Our family tree owes its existence to a sprout of a royal family planted in consequence of a feud somewhere in the lower Yellow River Valley some three thousand years ago. That tract of land was called "Chiang," the ancient name for a species of aquatic grass (*Hydropyrum Latifolium*). The modern name of this plant is *Chiao-pei;* used as a vegetable it tastes somewhat like bamboo shoots. The country was probably so called because of the luxuriant growth of the plant in those regions. My first ancestor in the Chiang line was made the first feudal lord to rule over that land toward the end of the twelfth century B.C. He was Pei-ling, third son of Prince Regent Chow-kung of the Chow Dynasty, and his descendants took Chiang as their family name.

In the third century A.D., during the period of the Three Kingdoms, one of our ancestors appears in history. His name was Chiang Wen and he lived in the Yangtze Valley. This shows that the Chiangs living south of the Yangtze had already migrated from the Yellow River region by the third century. From our first ancestor down to the present day all the names in the direct line have been recorded in our genealogy. How authentic they are I cannot tell, for their lives were so obscure that verification is not easy, but this much we can say: all the Chiangs settled in the areas south of the Yangtze are of the same origin. How far we can trace back accurately to this origin we don't know, but it is certain that all the Chiangs living in the province of Chekiang find their common ancestral tree in Hueichow.

I am of the seventeenth generation in the ancestral line. The first settlement of our village by the Chiangs, more than five hundred years ago, came toward the end of the Yuan or Mongol Dynasty. During these five centuries, under two foreign dynasties and one Chinese, the Chiangs saw the fall of the Mongols, the rise and fall of the Mings and the Manchus, and the Taiping Rebellion which almost overthrew the latter. During these changes they lived, worked, and retired to their graves in the same manner and in the same village. Dynasties came and went, but the village of the Chiangs remained the same.

During the Taiping Rebellion a few houses were burned by the rebels. The people ran into the mountains, but as soon as peace was restored they all came home like bees to the hive. In my childhood some of the ruins still stood to tell the story of the war.

When the Ming Dynasty fell at the hands of the Manchus, I was told by the villagers, people were not aware of it until the edicts of the new regime reached the villages. There was a play going on in one of the near-by village theatres when they were informed that they lived under a new dynasty. Perhaps the only forcible change in the life of my clansmen was the edict ordering the people to wear a queue and forbidding the male population to dress in the Ming style. Resentment was so great that men wore the Ming costume to their graves; it was a common saying of our clan that "men surrendered but women did not; the living did, but the dead did not." The practice persisted in some cases until the downfall of the Manchu Dynasty in 1911, when the Republic was established—a period of two centuries and a half.

Our village consisted of only some sixty households, with a population of about three hundred. It was one of the smallest among many villages, surrounded by a canal on three sides. On the south side a footway paved with granite slabs ran along it, leading across bridges to neighboring villages and towns. The canal was but part of a network connecting with large rivers which in turn led to such far-flung cities as Hangchow, Soochow, and Shanghai.

Although the village was small, it commanded easy communication by both land and water. Bridges spanned the canals and weeping willows grew luxuriantly on the banks. Fish, shrimps, eels, and turtles were abundant. Here and there one would find anglers taking their ease in the shade of the willows. Oxen could be seen walking in leisurely fashion round the water wheels to propel the chain of paddles which brought fresh water through a long trough to the fields. Miles of wheat fields in the spring and rice fields in summer gave one the feeling of living in a land of perpetual verdure. Swallows shuttled back and forth in the blue sky above a sea of rippling green, while eagles floated high above, circling around the village in search of little chicks.

Such was the background of my childhood and the environment of my clansmen. They lived there for more than five centuries with little change in life. Nature was kind to them. The land was fertile. Floods and droughts were not frequent. Rebellions or wars in the country at large did not disturb them more than once or twice during those long centuries; they lived in peace and contentment in a world by themselves, with little distinction between the very rich and the very poor. Sufficient rice, cotton, silk, fish, meat, bamboo shoots, and vegetables kept the people warm and well fed.

Morals, beliefs, and customs remained unchanged in Chinese villages through centuries of dynastic changes, in peace or war. For the villagers the world was good enough and no improvement was needed. Life alone was unstable, but consolation could be found in the transmigration of the soul. At death the soul was said to leave the body and enter that of a baby then being born. Indeed, in my own time I have seen convicts on the way to execution who shouted to the spectators that after eighteen years they would be young men again. What a consolation!

Our villagers said that a bad or sinful man's soul would be degraded to become a poor man, a horse, or a pig, or even split into minute parts to be insects or worms, according to the degrees of sins he had committed. The soul of a good or virtuous man would be promoted to a higher station in the next life.

What was sinful or virtuous had of course its accepted standards. The highest of all virtues was filial piety; the greatest of all sins was adultery. Filial piety kept the Chinese family intact and chastity kept the Chinese race pure. Respect for the elders, faithfulness to friends, loyalty to the sovereign, honesty in word and deed; kindliness and sympathy to the poor, the infirm or sick, all were regarded as virtuous behavior. Usury, treachery, lying, cheating, and the like were among sinful acts. Denunciation of a person whose conduct one disapproved often took the form of telling him that he would become a dog or a pig in his next life.

In business dealings verbal promises were as good as gold. On the whole, people were honest and trustworthy. Any person found to cheat would be surely tabooed by the whole community.

Marriages were not the business of the parties concerned; the parents of both parties made the match. As a rule, men married at twenty and women at eighteen. The men usually remarried if their wives died, while women of well-to-do families generally remained widows if they survived their husbands. These unfortunates were regarded as most virtuous—Imperial posthumous honors were conferred upon them.

The local government of the village was a fully self-governing body without outside interference. It was a government by elders of the clan with the Ancestral Hall as its seat. "Elders" does not mean elderly men. They might be young but represented the oldest living generations in the ancestral line. They were obligated to see that the ceremonies of ancestral worship were properly performed and were entrusted with the duties of arbitration in case of dispute among the clansmen. No one was allowed to go to law without first going through arbitration. To "open the gate of the Ancestral Hall" meant to summon an arbitration court of the elders. Anyone in the village could go there to observe the proceedings. Candles and incense burned before the tablets of the ancestors and everyone felt that their spirits watched invisibly from the ethereal realm. Before these ancestral spirits the parties concerned must speak the truth, nothing but the truth. Generally they did.

For the arbitrators, fairness was the motto. Public opinion in the village was also a very important factor, of which all parties concerned were conscious, and there was also the public opinion of neighboring villages. No elders would dare to defame the Ancestral Hall with unfair judgments. Thus disputes were usually fairly settled in this way. No lawsuit was necessary.

There were, in fact, few cases of dispute which needed arbitration by "opening the gate of the Ancestral Hall," for people regarded this as a matter of weight, to be resorted to only in a case of grave importance. Disputes were usually settled by informal arbitration before the gate of the hall.

Scholars and the gentry had a strong voice in the local government. They also participated in cases of arbitration and the making of rules and regulations for the village. They formed intervillage committees to settle disputes and look after the common welfare of neighboring villages.

Land taxes were brought by owners of land to the district or hsien treasury, about twenty miles from the village. No tax collectors ever visited us. People never felt the influence of the state —it was a common saying that "Heaven is high above and the Emperor is far away."

Public worship other than ancestral, such as worship in Buddhist temples or temples of deified persons, national heroes, or local gods that had grown out of legends, was a matter of individual concern. Anyone might worship in any or all of these places; there was no religious restriction or persecution. Your gods are as good as mine. If the Christians had allowed their Christ to sit beside Chinese gods in Chinese temples, I am sure that the villagers would have worshiped Him just as reverently as they did other gods.

Superstition grows out of the credulity of simple folk—it rolls like a snowball, growing as it rolls along. Thus it is that superstitions gather through centuries of accumulation.

As I have said, the villagers believed in the transmigration of the soul. This does not seem to reconcile with the idea that there are spirits traveling about with lightning speed in the ethereal realm. Soul and spirit, however, were two different things: the soul transmigrated, but the spirit remained in space. The spirit of a great man lives eternally in the invisible realm, while that of

a common man evaporates and dwindles, disappearing entirely
with the course of time, or rather when it is entirely forgotten.
The spirit moves with instant speed anywhere it wills. It may
live in the Ancestral Hall or in its grave as it chooses. This is perhaps one reason why the Chinese are always willing to spend
large sums on elaborate tombs and palatial ancestral halls.

My people always see things in relation to man. If spirits and
gods wandered about in an unseen world without relation to, or
contact with, living man, people would not see any use for them
and would hardly believe they existed. Yes, they have images
and tablets sitting in the shrines. But these sacred things, however awe-inspiring, do not step down and talk to them except in
dreams. There must be something more active or lively. This was
found in mediums, in automatic writing, or in the interpreting
of dreams.

If someone was thinking of a departed friend or a dead relative,
he could invoke the spirit to come to him through a medium, who
was always a woman from some far-distant place. When the spirit
called for approached, she would contract her ears three times
as the signal of arrival of the invisible guest. This contraction of
the involuntary muscles of the ear was something ordinary people
could not do and this made them believe in the medium much
more. She usually spoke through her throat like a cat's purr, so
that the words uttered could be interpreted to suit the wishes of
the listeners. When she had traced out something more definite
in the course of conversation, she would purr more distinctly, to
the amazement of the audience.

False or true, it served as a comfort to the hearts of living
relatives. I still remember how thrilling it was when my dead
mother conversed with me through a medium half a century ago.

Automatic writing is of a higher order. It was generally practised by the educated class. Two persons were needed to hold
the ends of a horizontal bar with a long wooden pin attached at
the middle, which wrote on a tray of sand. A god or the spirit of
some famous personage, it was believed, could be invoked to
write. The device—not unlike a Ouija board—could be asked
to predict future events. It might foretell a bumper crop in the
coming year, or an impending famine, or peace, or war. One
could ask almost any question. Poems were written by operators

who did not know how to compose a poem; names of persons present unknown to the writers might be written out on the sand. It was all done through the subconscious as any person who knows about psychology can explain.

Mediums invoked only spirits of departed relatives or friends; automatic writing might invoke the gods as well. In dreams both might come voluntarily, uninvited. I heard numerous interpretations of dreams which I do not remember now, except for one instance. One of my great-granduncles went to Hangchow to take the civil examinations for the second degree. In his examination cell (where candidates remained for many hours) he saw in a dream a hand of enormous size stretch into the room through the window. This was interpreted to mean that, since it was the greatest hand he had ever seen, he was to head the list of successful candidates. And the good omen came true when the results of the examination were made known.

Gods, dead friends, relatives, or spirits might enter one's dreams to convey their wishes, requests, or warnings. A dead mother might request her son to repair her tomb. A dead father might demand paper money from his son. A good imitation of paper money was always burned at funerals; it was supposed to accompany the dead for use in the world to which they go.

A tragic coincidence happened in our village about which people talked for years after. Ah Yi, a young farmer, was to take his rice by boat to a neighboring town. Early in the morning he was found sitting on a bench in a somber mood, very rare for a farmer. To inquiry he replied that in his dreams the previous night his dead mother had warned him not to go near water. What could it mean? He was a good swimmer.

At dusk he brought his junk home and shoved the boat toward the landing with his bamboo pole. He joked with his friends on the bank that his danger was over, and laughed heartily. Suddenly his feet slipped and he plunged into the canal, where he struggled for a moment but went under. Friends dived for him but could not find him. After half an hour he was pulled out, cold and stiff, from the entangling roots of an aged willow tree that grew by the water.

People said it was the water ghost that hid him there. Perhaps it was a water monkey that nested in the roots. Several good swimmers drowned near that spot. Often the villagers saw the "water ghost" sitting on the bridge near by in the moonlight, staring at the moon. It plunged into the water as soon as it saw people approaching.

Illusions, hallucinations, dreams, nightmares, imaginings, wishful thinking, coincidence, rumors—every kind of inexplicable phenomenon of mind or nature, all contributed to swell the snowball. And time kept it rolling.

Medicine in the village was, of course, primitive. We had to go miles to see herb doctors in the bigger towns. For ordinary illness or certain more serious cases Chinese medicine is very effective. But in many serious ailments the old medicine is useless or even dangerous.

I myself have been twice at the point of death and was in each case saved by herb medicine, without which I would not be here writing these chapters. On one occasion I had been ill for many months and was reduced to emaciation. A famous herb doctor specializing in children's diseases saved me. On another occasion I contracted diphtheria and was treated by a Chinese throat specialist. He pricked my throat with a needle all over the affected part and then sprayed it with some kind of white powder. I do not know what it was, but my throat felt cool and soothed as after smoking a mentholated cigarette.

That part of my throat was relieved, but the case developed other complications. My tonsils swelled to the size of goose eggs, my cheeks puffed up like a balloon, and I could hardly swallow even liquid food. My nose kept bleeding as if I should bleed to death. Finally I could barely breathe and only a faint hope was left. While my life hung by a thread my father said that he would try to "treat a dead horse like a live one." This was a Chinese proverb meaning that if the horse is ready to die anyway, it is worth trying the most extreme methods to save it. He dug into old medicine books, in which he found a prescription for a case showing similar symptoms. Several heavy doses were taken. The first brought immediate relief; in an hour or two I felt much better. By the next morning my tonsils had dwindled, and after a week or so I could take regular meals.

I have seen with my own eyes broken legs healed by ancient

methods, while colds, sore eyes, coughs, and rheumatism were effectively cured by herbs.

Chinese doctors discovered long ago an antismallpox "vaccine" taken from the human body. They used a kind of herb that had once been inserted into the nostrils of an affected child. Putting it into the nose of a normal child gave the latter what was usually a very much milder form of the disease. There were some cases of mortality among the hundreds thus "vaccinated," for I often heard of a death here and there. My father preferred modern vaccination to the old Chinese method. All the children in our family and many of our relatives were vaccinated by the modern method without a mishap.

We did not know how to cure malaria in our village. We let it run for some weeks or even months until it stopped of itself. There were no malignant cases in our locality and while it might sap the energy of the affected person it was not fatal. When quinine powder was brought in by missionaries or merchants from Shanghai, people found great relief in Western medicine.

Some of our clansmen believed in the healing power of the supernatural. They prayed in a temple and took a pinch of ashes from the incense burner as a panacea for all diseases. It was a sort of psychological treatment and did cure in some cases where psychology could play its part.

In the gardens of our house each month of the year was presided over by the chief flower of that month. Camellias were for the First Moon—first month of the year in the lunar calendar, corresponding approximately to the Western late January and early February. In the Second Moon almond blossoms took over the reins of government in the flowery kingdom. Peach blossoms were for the Third Moon, roses for the Fourth, pomegranates for the Fifth, lotus for the Sixth, *Feng-hsian* (*Impatiens balsamina*) for the Seventh, *Kwei-hua* (*Osmanthus fragrans*) for the Eighth, chrysanthemums for the Ninth, *Fu-yung* (*Hibiscus mutabilis*) for the Tenth, *Shuei-hsian* (*Narcissus tazetta*) for the Eleventh, and *La-mei* (*Chimonanthus fragrans*) for the Twelfth, the last month of the year. Each plant was represented by a particular goddess whom we all loved dearly.

The most popular seasonal flowers were the peach blossoms

of spring, lotus in the summer, and osmanthus and chrysanthemums in autumn. In season, the villagers all joined in admiring
these beauties of nature.

Festivals brought much enjoyment to both children and grownups alike. The most important was the New Year Festival which
began near the end of the old year—on the twenty-third of the
Twelfth Moon—when the Kitchen God took leave and went to
heaven to report to the Supreme God the year's happenings in
the household.

The Chinese believed in polytheism. But above all deities was
the Supreme God who controlled them all. It was an anthro-
pomorphic idea that He reigned over the ethereal realm like the
Emperor of China. Other gods were his ministers, governors, and
magistrates.

The Kitchen God was entrusted by the Supreme God with
charge of the household. Naturally he had to report to Him at the
end of the year. The Kitchen God was a vegetarian and was
therefore treated with a vegetarian dinner before leaving for
heaven. Everybody had to be very careful during the year in word
and deed, since bad as well as good things were reported. Both
the sending-off and the welcome-home ceremonies consisted of
dinners for the family, burning of paper money, and firecrackers.

New Year's Eve was celebrated by a family banquet in which
every member must participate. If some member was absent, he
or she would be assigned a seat *in absentia*. Candles burned all
night until the next morning and most of the grownups sat up
through the night to watch the coming of the New Year. Next
morning, on the first day of the year, the family worshiped
Heaven and Earth. Candles, incense, paper money, and firecrackers were necessary parts of the ceremony.

The Lantern Festival, part of the New Year celebration, began
on the thirteenth and ended on the eighteenth of the First Moon,
which was also the end of the New Year Festival. Artistic lanterns—horses, rabbits, butterflies, dragonflies, mantis, cicada, lotus, anything one could think of—adorned the houses and the
streets of the towns. We used to go to large towns to see the
lantern parade; their streets were thronged with merrymakers.

There were other important festivals, such as the Dragon Festival in the Fifth Moon, the Moon Festival in the Eighth Moon,

and the like. The Dragon Festival was celebrated by a boat race with all the boats decorated to look like dragons. The Moon Festival was enjoyed quietly and poetically—after a banquet we took a walk in the bright night and looked at the rabbit on the full, silvery autumn moon in a starless, moonlit sky.

Parades were popular, with hundreds of people participating and thousands watching. They were always religious in character: some god was to make an inspection trip around the villages. An image of the deity was carried in a carved, artistically decorated sedan chain, preceded by pennants, flags, floats, bands of music, monster dragons, men on stilts, and so forth.

Dragon dances were performed in the public squares of every village as the parade passed by. The men on stilts danced in theatrical roles in the crowded streets. Monstrous flags with fantastic designs of the dragon, tiger, or lion, each carried by dozens of people and supported by lines of rope in front and rear, were indeed a great sight. They moved up the highway among the fields like the sails of the Spanish Armada on a sea of rippling green. It was said that the idea originated during the old days when pirates from the Japan Sea wrought havoc among the people.

Traveling theatres made visits to the villages during festivals or birthday celebrations of deities, or on other important occasions. Each performance started about three o'clock in the afternoon and continued until the next morning with an intermission for supper. A frantic sounding of the gong served as a prelude to let country folk know that the play was starting. Plays were mostly based on historical episodes; the people learned history from the theatre. At the end of each play the moral lesson was invariably brought out. So it served a triple purpose: to teach history and morals as well as to entertain.

The roles of women were played by men, as in Shakespearean times in England. The actors painted their faces in fantastic designs of various colors to differentiate symbolically among virtuous and vile, honest and sneaky, the great and the mean, the stern and the kind. Thus one whose nose was painted white was either treacherous, cunning, mean, or clownish. In daily life we referred to such a person as "white-nosed." A red face suggested a character which was candid or virtuous in some way, but always kind. The black face was generally severe and stern. We often called a man who behaved sternly "black-faced," while "red-faced" meant a man who acted kindly or generously. The tradition of symbolic face painting still persists to the present day in Chinese classical dramas.

Such was the world of my childhood. It has been passing rapidly into history. The intrusion of foreign manufactures began the process; invasion from the West, whether by ideas or gunboats, hastened it; modern science, invention, and industry are to give the finishing touch.

CHAPTER 3

EARLY SCHOOLING

EDUCATION was a family affair. Boys were prepared for the Imperial civil examinations, or for business, in the family school. Girls were tutored separately. Children of poorer families which could not support a teacher were destined to be illiterate.

There was generally one teacher to a dozen pupils, taught individually. There were no blackboards or classes in the school. The teacher was usually serene, sitting the whole day at his desk from early in the morning to sunset. The pupils did likewise. As clocks were very rare then, there was none in the school. In winter, when the day was short, lessons after dark were given by the dim light of a vegetable-oil lamp. Time was measured by a sun dial. On a cloudy or rainy day you had to guess your time. Often you missed the mark by an hour or two, but it did not matter much, for the lessons were given individually.

I was sent to school at the age of six, the traditional school age. But my actual years were only five and a month or so, since with us your age is called "one"—that is, you are in your first year—when you are born. The ordinary desk was a bit too high for me, so that my chair had to be raised by a wooden stand to bring me level with the desk. My tiny feet were thus left dangling from the seat.

I was given a textbook: *San-tze-ching*, or the "Classics of Three Characters." It is so named because each sentence contains three words, and it was rhymed so as to be easier for children to remember. After fifty-odd years I am still able to recite a great part of it. It starts with the following passage—I give a literal translation:

> Man is originally
> Endowed with a nature which is all-good.
> And therefore by nature people are all alike.
> It is practice that makes the divergence.
> If they are not properly taught,
> Their nature will be thwarted.

The all-good in human nature is the starting point of the Confucian philosophy of life and education, which exercised a strong influence upon the French Encyclopedists of the eighteenth century.

I understand what it means now, but of course I didn't then.

I must tell how I hated the school! After a short time, noticing that the attention of the teacher was not on me, I climbed down quickly from the chair and ran like a dog that has broken from its chain back home to my mother's lap.

"Why do you come home, my child?" asked my mother in surprise.

"The school is no good, the teacher is no good, and the book is no good," I replied.

"Aren't you afraid of your teacher? He may come and get you," said my mother kindly.

"I'll kill the teacher! I'll burn the school!"

My mother didn't send me back to school that day, nor did the teacher come.

Early the next morning my nurse woke me, spoke many kind words to me, and persuaded me to go to school again. From childhood I responded to kind words only; no coercion ever did any good. It was the gentle reasonableness of my nurse that made me go back voluntarily.

I took to school my own rattan chair, which was very light. A servant followed me and put it on the stand to match the height of the desk. The teacher made no remark and acted as if nothing had happened, but I noticed several schoolmates making faces at me. I hated them but pretended not to see them. I climbed up on the chair and sat there without resting place for my poor feet. More lessons were given, in the same book. I read very loud, as was required in the old type of school, repeating the meaningless text again and again till every word was learned by heart. When the sun shone directly above our heads it was midday. The teacher ordered me to go home for lunch. Immediately after lunch I went back to school and kept on learning the same thing till sunset.

Day in and day out, there was no change in the curriculum. When I finished one textbook another meaningless one came in turn. It was memory and patience that we were training.

We were taught the "three P's" in reading: presence of mind, presence of eye, and the presence of lips. The first means concentration, a requisite for doing any work well. The second is important because by it one gets a clear impression of the ideographic letters, with the various arrangements of fine and intricate strokes in each letter. The third is attained by reading a passage aloud several hundred times; the words then fall from the lips fluently, thus relieving the burden of the memory. We were warned not to commit words to memory by artificial means, because then we would not retain them. If we stumbled in reciting a passage we were ordered to read it over again one or two hundred times more—if the teacher was not in a good humor you would probably receive in addition, without warning, a crack on the skull. Often when the day was over some boys left school with lumps on their scalps.

Discipline and obedience were aimed at without regard for the interest of the pupil. Sundays were unknown. We had half holidays in the afternoon on the first and fifteenth day of each lunar month. In addition, we had during the year several full holidays on festival days, such as the Dragon Festival and the Moon Festival. A comparatively long vacation came about New Year's time. It started on the twentieth day of the Twelfth Moon and lasted till the same day of the First Moon of the new year, and was called the New Year vacation.

As several years went by, I grew older and learned by heart quite a number of characters. My teacher then began to explain the meaning of the text and studying grew to be less drudgery. From the Confucian classics I began to understand a little of the way to be a righteous man. It began with the culture of the person, then went on to the fulfillment of duties to the family, to the state, and finally the world. I did not appreciate its full significance until much later.

In the earliest years school was indeed a prison to me. The difference was that in a real prison the inmates have little hope, while in school the pupils had hopes for a bright future. Had not all the famous scholars and statesmen gone through years of suffering in schools? It was through suffering that men became great, we were told to believe. The path was difficult but it was the only road to success.

"If you have tasted the bitterest of the bitter you will become the greatest of the great."

"The Son of Heaven* honors the scholar. While everything else is of a lower order, learning is the highest of all."

"Do not envy others who possess the sword; you have a pen that is mightier."

These common sayings spurred me on the road of learning as the odors of an early spring in the air spur a sluggish horse to green pastures. Otherwise I should have dropped my schooling and taken to business in Shanghai. Ideals, hopes, and will power are the most important factors in shaping one's life. If education fails in these, the emphasis in modern methods upon the interest of the pupil is but a trifling thing. Interest is an important factor in education only when it is subordinated to inculcation of ideals.

It seemed tedious and foolish in the old Chinese schools to commit the classics to memory. But there was the advantage that in later years one could go to memory to find ready references for the conduct of life. In a static society where the world moved very slowly and the rules of conduct would need little modification, it seems to me that the old Chinese method of teaching and learning was quite adequate for the needs it filled. Only, in a country school like mine it ran to the extreme, giving unnecessary hardship to the pupils. I wonder how many promising boys were scared away before they began to realize the importance of learning.

There were no sports or physical exercises in any form in my school. The boys were forbidden to run fast; they must walk slowly and be dignified. Right after lunch we were required to practise calligraphy. Young life seemed to be practically squeezed out of us.

Nevertheless, the boys found their own way to satisfy their play instincts. When the teacher was absent we would take over control of the school. Sometimes desks were taken to form a platform on which a play could be staged. Chairs and stools would be used as stage properties. Sometimes we played blindman's buff. On one occasion, while I was serving as the "blind," the teacher returned and all the others slipped away. As I caught an easy prey I felt something strange—it was the teacher. The shock

* One of the formal titles of the Emperor.

was so terrifying that as I write it reels in my senses as vividly as if it had happened yesterday.

In the spring, when school was over in the afternoon, we flew kites. We made our own. Some took the form of a monster centipede, others a gigantic butterfly. At night we would send into the sky along the kite string a chain of lanterns, numbering usually five, seven, or nine. The smaller boys played with smaller kites, generally in the shape of a dragonfly, a swallow, or an eagle. The "swallows" were the most ingenious; they usually went by pairs, tied to the two ends of a slip of bamboo balanced on the kite string, and danced up and down in the currents of air like a pair of feathered playmates. Once I saw several swallows darting around such a pair, seeking their company.

In summer we played with other boys in the village during the starry evenings. The fireflies in the air looked like moving stars. Some of us preferred to listen to the stories told by some elder of the village. With a big palm-leaf fan in his hands to chase away annoying mosquitoes, and a teapot by his side, the elder would give his account of historical personages, dynastic changes, and past happenings in the village.

About two hundred and fifty years ago [he would begin], when the Ming Dynasty was overthrown by the Manchus, the whole country was in turmoil, but our forefathers living in this village still enjoyed peace. Later on, the Imperial Edict reached our village ordering all male persons to cut their hair according to the Tartar fashion and to wear a queue.* Men were terrified and women wept. Barbers came to the village to enforce the order. They had Imperial sanction, if anyone should disobey, to punish the culprit by cutting off his head instead of his hair. No one preferred his hair to his head. Since a man could not retain both his head and his hair, he would stretch his head and let the barber do his job of haircutting and queue braiding. We have got used to it now, but my! it must have looked funny then . . .

This was a bit of history we learned outside of school.

Again, a bit of local anthropology:

Tens of thousands of years ago our far-distant ancestors had tails like the monkey. The man-monkey's tail gradually turned yellow as he grew older. When nine out of the ten segments of his tail had turned

---

* That is, the hair was trimmed across the front of the head, and the long queue worn behind.

yellow, he knew he was about to die. Then he would crawl into his cave and die there. As years went by, his tail dropped. This is why we have no tails now. But you can find at the end of your backbone where it was broken off.

Here is a story about pugilism:

In front of a rice shop a small boy was stationed to sell rice. He amused himself by picking up pinches of it and throwing them swiftly back into the basket. On one occasion a monk came to beg for rice. Instead of giving him some, the boy threw a few grains of it right in his face. To his surprise he saw that the grains had pierced the man's skin. The monk made a polite bow with his hands pressed together palm to palm, saying "Namo Amita Buddha" [Hail, Great Buddha!], and went his way.

Seven days later a pugilist came to the town. By now the boy was looking rather pale. "What's the matter with you, my boy?" asked the pugilist. When he was told the story of the monk he said, "Ah, that monk is the most famous pugilist of our time. You have insulted him. You have received from his bow the terrible internal wounds which will bring you to death in forty-nine days. I have medicine for your cure, but you must run away and not meet him again. He will come again after forty-nine days. Get a coffin, put some bricks in it, and pretend that you have died."

The monk did come, and asked for the boy. When he was told of his death, he sighed and said, "What a pity!" At his request he was led to see the coffin. Running his fingers over the top of it, he muttered, "Namo Amita Buddha." After he had gone the coffin was opened and it was found that all the bricks in it were cracked.

We boys pricked up our ears and listened attentively to these stories; they were one of the sources of my extracurricular education. I could retell many like them if space would allow.

I had several teachers, one after another, in my school. One of them was a kindly rustic scholar who had failed to pass the Imperial civil examinations for the First Degree, despite many attempts, and had to content himself with teaching in a family school. He had a round, moonlike face, was short and stout, and his bespectacled eyes looked habitually over the heavy brass rims of his glasses. His grey mustache hung bristling from his upper lip and he wore no beard. After he had taken egg soup at dinner, yellow particles would be seen adhering to the tips of his unclipped mustache. He was an encyclopedia of endless stories. But his literary style was rather poor; this is why, I presume, he failed repeatedly in the examinations, though he was an endless fountain of witticism. I think his memory in certain respects must have been bad, for he always forgot to carry with him either his umbrella or towel or fan when going back to the school after paying a visit to his friends. Necessity taught him finally to make an inventory of the articles he brought with him: pipe, umbrella, towel, and fan. When about to leave he would repeat, "Pipe, umbrella, towel, and fan." Even in winter, when no fan was needed, he would continue to mention it in his list, sometimes realizing that he had brought no fan with him, but at other times trying to find it, to the great amusement of both friends and pupils.

My mental scope was thus limited to what I learned from the Confucian classics and what the teachers and elders told me. I memorized quite a few of the classics and also had a rich store of stories. My early education, therefore, consisted chiefly of memory work. Yet I was fortunate to have been born and to live in the country, where nature offered plenty of instruction. Once I noticed that some beetles which lived on a large soap tree—so named because we used its nuts for soap—had on their heads horns like those of a deer. These looked exactly like the thorns that grew at the tips of the twigs of the tree. The beetles, I was told, were born of the tree and therefore looked like their mother. Somehow I felt suspicious. I reasoned that if a tree was capable of giving birth to beetles, they would in turn be capable of laying eggs that would be the seeds for the tree. That not being the case, I felt there must be some other reason for the remarkable likeness. I found it when I saw a bird feeding on insects in the tree without noticing the deer-horned beetles near by. The horns were therefore imitations of the thorns of the tree, for protection from the birds.

On the banks of the canal there grew candle trees, so called because the oil from the nuts is good for making candles. In the winter months the farmer would tie a few straws around the trunk of the tree, which he took off in the spring and burned. It was a common belief that by virtue of this act a magic force would kill the parasites. The fact was that if you tied enough straw around the trunk the parasites laid their eggs in the straw, and by burning it you destroyed the eggs, thus preventing them from propagating. It was no magic.

There were many such instances of naïve nature study in my childhood. The two above mentioned are, I think, enough for illustration.

Thus there were three sources of the education I received in my childhood. The first was the study in school of the Confucian classics, which served as guidance to moral conduct as well as a foundation to the future study of modern social sciences. The second was the storytelling which was to prepare the way for an appreciation of modern literature. The last was the innocent nature study which later served as a stem on which the buds of modern science could be grafted. Had I been born in a crowded city, resembling—on a smaller scale, minus electricity and wide streets—the East Side of New York or London, I would have missed the all-important training of nature. The whole course of my life might have been different. For the natural endowment of sense perception, observation, curiosity, and reasoning that are in every child and indispensable to life in a modern world might have been altogether smothered by the all-memory traditional training of my early youth.

I must confess that I did not apply myself to study as earnestly as some of my schoolmates, for I did not like to memorize but to see, touch, and reason. My teachers took this as a misfortune or curse of my disposition.

I loved to play and listen to storytelling. I liked to inquire into things to a degree disgusting to the elders. I took delight in watching frogs catch locusts in the rice fields and geese and ducks swimming in the canal. I enjoyed seeing the bamboos grow and flowers blooming, and loved to make kites and fly them. All these propensities were regarded by my teachers as a curse and I myself believed it must be so. But it is an irony of fate that the curse happened to turn out a blessing to me in later years, and the blessings my teachers bestowed upon some of my schoolmates have turned out to be curses. For some have died of consumption and others became bookish scholars, incapable of adjusting themselves to a changing environment when the tides of westernization swept over China.

CHAPTER 4

FAMILY INFLUENCE

DURING the plastic years of childhood and adolescence, family influence upon youth is indeed formative. Bad as well as good habits acquired during this period are difficult to eradicate in later years. On the whole the influence exercised upon me by my family was good and wholesome.

My father was a small landowner and a shareholder in some native banks in Shanghai. My grandfather had left him fairly well off and his mode of living was always simple so that the family never had uneasiness about financial matters. Father was an honest and generous man, respected by the people of the village in particular and surrounding districts generally. He was frugal in private life but very generous toward public affairs, contributing liberally to benevolent organizations.

He would not say anything with intent to deceive and his words were accordingly trusted by those who came in contact with him. He believed in *feng-shui*, the spirits of wind and water, and in fortunetelling and therefore—with a sort of fatalism—that a man's life was predetermined by supernatural forces. However, he also believed that by virtuous conduct and clean thinking one could make these forces respond by bestowing blessings upon oneself as well as one's family; thus the predetermined course of life would gradually shift its ground to a better course. His moral influence upon me was really great. The only regret I have is that I have fallen far short of his good example.

My mother was a cultured and beautiful woman. My childhood memories of her have become somewhat vague. I recall that she could play the harp and sing to it—one of the songs she loved most still lives in my memory. It was about a buried harp whose owner had deserted her. Clink, clink, clink, the harp sang to herself that her lover had not yet kept his promises to come back to her. She waited and waited in vain. She remembered how happy they had been when they sang together. Now she was buried on the shady side of crumbling walls. The autumn wind was blowing, the grass fading, and the white clouds deepening. A near-by stream flowed under a broken bridge and no one ever passed by that place. Only gloom and loneliness reigned.

Someone remarked that it was an ill omen that such a beautiful young lady as my mother should like to sing such a sad song.

The drawing room where she played her harp looked out under a giant camphor tree. A canal wound its way around the other side of the bamboo grove which served as a fence. A crêpe myrtle, an osmanthus, and an orange tree struggled for such sunlight as the wide spread of the aged camphor could spare. There she could hear birds singing and fish splashing. At sunset the level beams pierced through the grove and cast the shadows of bamboo leaves dancing on the window screens. The walls were hung with landscape paintings and works of well-known calligraphers. Her lacquered harp, inlaid with jade, lay on a long redwood stand with legs carved in the phoenix motif.

The drawing room was kept as it was for many years after her death. A painted likeness of her hung in the middle of the wall. But Mother was no more! The harp, veiled in dark satin velvet, lay alone on the same stand in the same room. How could I help feeling that I was like that buried harp whose song she used to teach me to sing?

My mother died young. I saw her in her coffin in a beautiful embroidered jacket and skirt, wrapped in a long scarlet satin cape down to her feet. There was a hood attached to the cape. Her face alone was exposed. A large pearl shone on her forehead against the red background of the hood.

My stepmother was a very able woman and she was kind to people, but my relation with her was rather unhappy. She did not live long, and Father never married again.

My grandfather had been the manager of a Shanghai bank. During the time of the Taiping Rebellion (1851–1864) he put up a money stand in the native city of Shanghai. This grew later into a small money exchange shop which in turn developed into a native bank—a concern with unlimited liability, making loans on credit. When Mexican silver dollars were introduced into China as auxiliary currency to taels, the foreign money gained popularity among the people. Counterfeit pesos increased in proportion to the widening circulation of the money. By clinking two dollars on their fingers the bankers could tell the bad from the good. But Grandfather beat them all; he could tell by merely glancing at them.

Unfortunately in the prime of life he suffered a leg injury; the leg had to be amputated and he died of blood poisoning. To my father, at the age of twelve or thereabouts, he left some seven thousand taels, at that time considered a big fortune. This helpless orphan was looked after by his future father-in-law, who was a local scholar. By sound investment and careful economy the property grew, in the course of some thirty years, to the value of seventy thousand taels.

This bit of family history will show the reader that some Western influence must in early days have crept into the family.

Father had an inventive mind. He loved to make plans or designs and direct carpenters, blacksmiths, coppersmiths, farmers, and basket makers to carry them out according to specifications. He built houses, made experiments in raising silkworms and planting mulberry trees, manufactured guns (of a type already obsolete in the West), and made many other things according to his fancy. Finally he conceived the bright idea of building a "steamboat" without steam. Father occasionally went to Shanghai to look over his business. He took a rowboat from the village to Ningpo, where he boarded a paddle-wheeled steamer for Shanghai. "It took us three days and two nights to Ningpo in a rowboat," he would say, "and only one night from there to Shanghai by the steamer, while the distance is ten times farther." So he made a sketch of how a miniature paddle-wheel boat might be made.

Carpenters and boatbuilders came. The carpenters were instructed to make paddle wheels, the boatbuilders to build a boat according to my father's plan. A month passed and the boat began to take shape. On the day when the tiny "steamer" was to be launched many visitors came and their mouths gaped in admiration for the wonderful invention. Now the boat was on the canal near our house. Two husky fellows were employed to turn the wheels by a wooden handle. The watching crowd stirred with excitement as the boat started to plow slowly through the water. Presently it began to gather momentum and went faster. When it reached approximately the speed of a rowboat, it refused to accelerate further despite the efforts of the crew. The passengers gesticulated as if helping the boat to go faster. Some even lent their arms to the handle and helped to turn the wheels. But the boat was very stubborn and held to the same speed.

Father made several modifications in the paddle wheels, hoping to increase the speed. All attempts failed. The worst of it was that when the boat went for some distance, weeds and water plants gathered on the wheels and at length even the handle refused to pump. "We have to give all credit to the foreigners who made steamboats," said Father with a sigh.

The "steamer" finally reverted to a rowboat. But it was too heavy to row. Years after, we found it rotting on the banks of the canal, the green moss growing thick on its hull. Even when it failed, however, Father never gave up the idea of making a further attempt until he was told the story of Watt and his boiling kettle. Then he began to see that there was something deeper than appeared in the thing itself. From that time on he was heart and soul for giving his boys a modern education which would someday enable them to learn the foreigners' "tricks" in making wonderful things.

This is an example of how China began to venture on the road to westernization. However, in human relations Father never seriously advocated the foreigners' ways. "The foreigners are as honest, reasonable, and hard working as we Chinese," he would say. He never saw anything beyond that. Neither did he see any objection to his boys learning their ways and manners.

My teacher, on the other hand, was opposed to Father's ideas. "The artifice in making clever things," he would say, "would have a degrading influence on morals. Haven't our sages told us so?" He believed that good morals could only be kept on a high level by living a simple life. Uncle King, my mother's brother, held the same view. He wrote his ideals of life on a piece of red paper which he posted on the wall near his desk: "Burn a stick of incense early in the morning. Be thankful to Heaven, Earth, the Sun, the Moon, and Stars. There shall be no traitors to usurp the power of the ruling dynasty, nor disobedient sons to worry their parents. Everywhere there shall be bumper crops of rice. Then why shall I worry even if I am poor?"

Uncle King was an old scholar. He had passed the civil examinations for the First Degree in his early years. He always carried a long pipe, longer than a walking stick, and one heard him constantly knocking its brass bowl on the brick floor. There were no wrinkles on his forehead in his old age, an indication of peace, health, and contentment. He was so gentle that I never saw him in a temper. He spoke slowly but distinctly and never let unkind words cross his lips.

CHAPTER 5

TROUBLE BREWING

IT WAS customary during the New Year days for vendors to come to the village to sell pictures, some depicting important or thrilling happenings in the country, others showing theatrical performances. During one New Year vacation the attention of the children was drawn to a set of pictures which were rather novel to them. The multicolored scenes showed the Sino-Japanese War of 1894. One was of a naval battle in the north China Sea. One of the Japanese battleships had struck several large pottery jugs filled with gunpowder, which exploded and set the ship on fire, and it was sinking. There were in the picture hundreds of such jugs floating on the sea. In another picture Japanese prisoners of war were seen locked in chains, and some kept in cages. A great victory for China! It existed only on paper, but we children believed it. As I grew older I began to understand that China had been defeated, that we had lost Formosa, that our navy had been destroyed by the Japanese, and Korea torn away. Within a short span of nine years China had lost three dependencies: first Indo-China, then Burma, and now Korea.

One summer day as the sun was setting a farm helper was seen running breathlessly out of my father's study. He had heard a bell ring there without seeing anyone to cause the sound. To him it must be a ghost. But it was the clock striking seven in the evening.

From time immemorial the villagers had been getting their fire by striking a steel blade on flint. Someone brought a few boxes of matches from Shanghai. The grownups were delighted with this easy method. The children loved the firefly glow obtained by scratching a match on the palm in dark corners. It was called "self-coming light" or "ocean light" because it came from across the sea.

Clocks were unnecessary—for what is the use of keeping exact time in a village? What difference would it make to be two or three hours too late or too early? The country folk counted their time in days and months, not in minutes or hours. Matches were a luxury—had we not got along nicely with our steel blades and flints? But when we came to kerosene it was a different proposition. This made night as brilliant as day. There was a world of difference between this and the dim light of a vegetable-oil lamp.

The Standard Oil Company, known as Meifoo, was the torchbearer that was leading China out of the "dark ages" to modernization. People kept matches and clocks as curiosities but kerosene as a necessity. But if kerosene was a necessity, wasn't the telegraph a necessity to take the place of a foot messenger, and steamboats to take the place of rowboats or sailboats? And so it went.

Few could grasp the significance of one tiny segment of the vast circle. While we played innocently with clocks and matches and enjoyed our kerosene lamps, we never realized that we were toying with a fire that would some day set all China aflame. These were the signs of an impending volcanic eruption which destroyed peace and order first in my village and others like it and eventually in the whole country.

Christian missionaries played their part in introducing foreign manufactures into the interior. Braving hardship, disease, and personal danger, they went to almost every hamlet in the land to save the souls of the heathen Chinese. As a matter of course they took kerosene, cloth, clocks, soap, etc., with them into the interior. People in general were more interested in these things than in the gospel; they opened up a new horizon of wants for the Chinese people. A market for foreign goods was thus created unintentionally by missionaries whose real purpose was to preach the gospel of Christ.

I do not mean that the missionaries were chiefly responsible for the growth of modern commercialism in China. But they played their part—a considerable part, for they penetrated the vast country to every corner. The major role, of course, was played by the merchant ships and gunboats of the Western Powers. It was the Christian missions coupled with gunboats that forced the old literary and agricultural China on the road to modern industrial and commercial life.

With my own eyes I saw the growth of a new class of compra-

dors—middlemen between the Chinese and foreign merchants—
and their satellites, and the dying of the old class of literati which
I was about to join and from which I eventually sneaked away.
The foreign merchants brought their goods to seaports such as
Shanghai, Tientsin, and others. Through Chinese compradors
they were distributed to cities in the interior and from there to
the towns and villages. People were attracted by the easier and
larger sums of money they could make. The more enterprising
and fortunate entered the new business of dealing directly or in-
directly in foreign goods. Some became very rich and many others
well to do. The less fortunate were left behind, to go on tilling
their land or to remain in their old trades. As the land was less
remunerative and the old trades fast deteriorating in the face of
foreign competition, the old economic structure began rapidly to
break down. Naturally a number of people were thrown out of
economic gear. These unfortunates, jealous of the newly rich and
either dissatisfied with their old occupations or deprived of them,
became desperate. The flood was surging against the water gate
—the autumn flood, symbolic of the turmoil that was to banish
peace from my village.

One autumn afternoon as I was running in the fields I heard
the frantic sounding of a gong. As the crier approached our village, I heard his cry that the dike had broken through and the
flood was coming. I ran back home as fast as I could and told
everyone I met on the way.

Everyone got busy at once. We got ready boats, wooden bathtubs, or anything that would float, waiting for the calamity to ar-
rive. Some even chose tall trees for their future abode. None of
us slept well that night. The next morning the flood entered our
gate and the spearhead of water glided like a giant serpent into
our courtyard. By noon, children had begun to row in bathtubs
in the hall.

The dike was repaired with sandbags and the Tsao-ao River
ceased to overflow. The flood stayed in our village and surrounding districts for about a week, then gradually emptied into the
lower lands and disappeared through the rivers into the sea, and
all the crops with it.

After a week or so, late in the afternoon a large boat was seen
plying toward our village with many people aboard. It docked

near our house and they began to disembark. As a precaution we closed our gates. They stormed the main gate with heavy granite slabs and finally it crashed down like an avalanche. The crowd forced their way in. The leader, muscular and heavy built, with his queue round the top of his head, came into the courtyard with his followers after him. He shouted, "We are hungry and want to borrow rice." The crowd joined in chorus. They searched the barn but did not touch it; they wanted to "borrow." Finally, through the mediation of a neighboring farmer, several bushels of rice were "loaned" to them and they embarked with it and sailed away. This was the first intimation of troubles to come.

One incident after another of the same kind but of more serious nature happened in neighboring villages. It started with "borrowing" but ended in robbing. It spread like fire and the scant government forces in the country could not stop it. Moreover, robbery of foodstuffs was not liable to capital punishment and only capital punishment could have checked it, at least temporarily.

The thing dragged on till winter and then the first robbery of a felonious nature took place in the village of the Suns. The victim was a Mr. Sun who owned a prosperous lumber business in Shanghai. His father had amassed a fortune in that port by doing construction work for foreign "hongs" or companies.

It was a cold winter night and everybody had gone to bed early to keep warm. Someone noticed through the window against the background of darkness a column of torchlights moving along the highway toward the village of the Suns. As the lights came near the village a volley of shots was heard. It was bandits. They forced open the gates of Mr. Sun's house and seized all the treasure they could carry—valuable fur coats, silver pieces, jewels, etc. They took Mr. Sun, tied him to the end of a long bamboo pole, and thrust him into the canal. People found him the next morning by pulling up the pole.

Waves of robbery spread through the villages. Overnight the peace and tranquility that the villagers had been enjoying for centuries vanished. Night after night we could not sleep in peace. My father bought revolvers and outmoded guns from Shanghai. All of us, including children, began to practise shooting. Even the birds had no peace, for we took them as our living targets.

We went to bed by turns, some keeping a night watch. When we heard dogs barking we fired a few shots in the air as a warning to bandits, real or imaginary; to save ammunition we often mixed firecrackers with gunshots.

This sort of thing could not go on indefinitely. Reluctantly my father gathered together the members of his family and moved to Shanghai.

Meanwhile, during the two years previous to our move I had continued my education at a neighboring provincial city. When I was still studying at the family school, my father asked me one day whether I would like to enter business as a career or prepare for government service. My two elder brothers had both decided for the latter. Father said he would like me to think it over carefully before coming to a decision.

The honor of service to the state had attracted young people for generations. It was only natural that I should be strongly inclined to it. On the other hand, the life of the newly rich, who could enjoy the luxury of the many new and ingenious imported manufactures, was also a temptation. The choice between honor and wealth was more or less contingent upon the ideas and ideals already instilled into one's mind.

I had been told that the people of China fell into four classes. The highest and governing class was the scholars. Next in order came the farmers, who supplied the people with food. The artisans—the third class—manufactured goods for the use of the people. The last were the traders, who transported goods from where there was plenty to where there was a scarcity. Each class had its function to perform in society, but the scholars were the governors of all. So, theoretically speaking, if philosophers were not to be kings, they were at least to be ministers of the state. As there was no hereditary aristocracy in China, the scholars were aristocrats not by birth but by personal endeavor. It was proverbial that a *Hsiu-tsai*, or person possessing the First Degree by having passed the Imperial civil examinations for that initial degree, was an embryo prime minister to the Imperial Court. Then why should I go into business, which later in life would exclude me from the class of the learned aristocracy?

Thus my mind was set to learning. Of course I understood only vaguely what it meant; to me it was only a steppingstone to something higher up. There were many farmers in our village. There were also a number of businessmen who traded in Shanghai and brought back many interesting things: penknives, whistles, rubber balls, dolls, popguns, watches, and the like. As regarded the artisans, an elder of our clan was a carpenter, as also were his sons. A distant uncle was a silversmith who made rings, bracelets, and trinkets to adorn the ladies of the villages. Of the scholars, another uncle—my mother's brother—was one. He had passed the First Degree but stopped short of the other two. There were carved panels with golden inscriptions hanging high in our Ancestral Hall and tall flagpoles standing before it in honor of clansmen who had been successful in the examinations. I remember that one day the magistrate of our hsien came to a neighboring village to probe a murder case. Did I not see the golden button at the top of his red-tasseled hat, and the string of beads round his neck? Did I not see how his sedan chair was lined with green felt and borne by four persons—each wearing a tall black cone-shaped hat, like a gigantic ice-cream cone, with a feather tilting from the pointed top; and how, as he proceeded in his chair, a pair of gongs kept sounding to announce the presence of His Excellency and that the people must show respect? He was the governor of our district and had, as it were, power over our lives and fortunes. What stuff was he made of? A scholar.

Yes, I knew what a scholar was and the advantage of being one. He might climb up, rung by rung, to the top of the ladder and some day become a very high official, sipping Imperial tea in the majestic palace at Peking. Can the reader blame a village boy like me, whose steps had never carried him more than a few miles from his own village, for aspiring to be a scholar? My childish mind pondered the Imperial honors which were the scholar's due. I imagined myself growing larger and larger in importance year by year, passing one examination after another from the lowest to the highest, till one day I should be made a high official— much higher than the magistrate—attired in an embroidered gown with a red button on my hat, a long string of beads, and all the other Imperial honors imaginable, coming back home before the eyes of the awe-inspired folk of the village. How wonderful! All these pictures unrolled enticingly. What a bright future lay before me—but only if I applied myself to the study of the classics.

Again, my early schooling, although distasteful to me, had instilled into my mind somewhat vaguely the importance of learning above everything else. Officials of the state were selected through civil examinations and only people who possessed learning could expect to pass them. Officials were honored because learning itself was honored in China.

My own decision was finally to acquire more learning in preparation for the civil examination, to which my father readily agreed. As our family school was inadequate for my further education, I was sent to an advanced school in Shaoshing, the prefectural capital, about forty miles from the village. My two elder brothers had gone there the year before. We went in a small, slender boat, propelled by a long oar pushed by foot power on one side and a short one held by hand as a helm on the other. Along the way I saw on the river banks many pailous standing in rows—pillared arches erected in memory of virtuous widows. River towns appeared at almost regular intervals with their busy traffic on both land and water. We started early in the morning and arrived at the prefectural capital next day in the afternoon after stopping for the night at a large town.

The Sino-Occidental School, as its name implied, offered not only Chinese studies but also courses in Occidental subjects. This was a new departure in Chinese education. Here my mind began to come into contact with Western knowledge, however poorly explained and superficial. My acquaintance with the West had been limited to imported manufactured articles. A mind filled with gods, goddesses, ghosts, fairies, and timeworn traditions was now setting forth to meet some mental imports from the West.

The first and most surprising thing I learned in this school was that the earth is round like a ball. To me it was decidedly flat. I was dumfounded on being further told that lightning is created by electricity and is not the reflection from the mirror of a goddess; that thunder is a by-product of the same electricity and not the beating of a drum by the god of thunder. In elementary physics I learned how rain is formed. It made me give up the idea that a gigantic dragon showers it from his mouth like a fountain high above in the clouds. To understand the meaning of combustion was to banish the idea of fire gods from my mind. One after another, the gods worshiped by my people melted away in my mind like snowmen under the sun. It was the beginning of what little science I know and the end of animism in me. The habit I had formed in my simple nature study in the village, of observing and reasoning without knowing the significance of it, was carried over into the school. As before, I was quite good in reasoning but deficient in memory, and therefore always ready to give up what I had in memory for new ideas that seemed reasonable.

The major part of the curriculum, however, still consisted of literary studies: Chinese literature, classics, and history. There was a considerable amount of memory work to do. As I was not good at it, my name always appeared in the lower middle of the school examination list. I was mediocre in the school, falling far short of brilliance; this was the opinion of my teachers and so it was my own opinion of myself.

Foreign languages were divided into three sections: English, French, and Japanese. I took English and later also Japanese. My Japanese teacher was a Mr. Nakagawa, from whom I learned a correct pronunciation. English was taught us by a Chinese teacher, and his pronunciation of the language was so incorrect that in later years I had to spend much painful time unlearning it. He started us off wrong at the very beginning, even mispronouncing the alphabet. An extreme example is the letter Z, which he called "ütsai."

In the school, in 1898, I heard that Kang Yu-wei and Liang Chi-chao, two liberals from south China who had become unofficial advisers to Emperor Kwang-hsü, had succeeded in persuading the Emperor to abolish the civil examinations and establish instead schools along Western lines throughout China. The old scholars were shocked by the news. But the reform was short lived. The Empress Dowager came back into power; Kang Yu-wei and Liang Chi-chao fled to Japan. China was to go on along the old line. When I came home for the vacation I saw the Imperial Edict, printed in bold letters in both the Chinese and Manchu languages on a large yellow paper, posted on the walls in a busy street, ordering the arrest of the two scholar-statesmen. It looked as if the reform were buried forever.

Shaoshing is a city full of historical interest. It was the capital of the ancient kingdom of Yueh (2068–334 B.C.). In 494 B.C., during the reign of King Kou-chien, Yueh was defeated by the kingdom of Wu with its capital at Soochow. The king of Yueh adopted a "twenty-year plan" by which, within ten years, he made his country prosperous and populous and in another ten succeeded in training his people in the arts of war. Meantime he discarded all the comforts that belong to a king, taking very coarse food and sleeping on a rough bed while the king of Wu reveled in luxuries. At the end of twenty years, in 473 B.C., King Kou-chien delivered a deathblow at Wu.

This historical episode has been proverbial ever since, serving as an example for all who hope to rise again after a defeat, whether in private enterprise or national affairs. It illustrates patience, courage, endurance, self-denial, and careful planning. I absorbed this lesson in history right on the spot, and no one could help being impressed by it.

Here also the South Sung emperors (1127–1276 A.D.) made their sojourn when the Tartars had overrun north China and the capital had to be moved to Hangchow. Their Imperial mausoleums could be seen not far from the prefectural capital.

This district, with Shaoshing as its center, supplied lawyers for the whole country. In every yamen or government office throughout the country, large or small, no business could be carried on without a Shaoshing lawyer. And Shaoshing wines were the best in China. Famous scholars, philosophers, poets, and calligraphers who made history in their respective fields were born and lived in the prefecture of Shaoshing. It contained six districts, of which my own, Yuyao, was one.

Shaoshing was also famous for its beautiful scenery. Winding creeks, bridge-spanned canals, rivers, mirrored lakes, and gentle hills together formed a landscape which scholars and philosophers found congenial.

I studied in Shaoshing for two years. My mental horizon rapidly widened. I was made to understand the significance of the Sino-Japanese War of 1894: Japan's victory over China was due to the former's adoption of Western learning. Emperor Kwang-hsü's reforms were inspired by Japan's success in the war.

China was to make her erstwhile enemy her teacher. This was why the school offered a course in the Japanese language.

At the end of two years, when bandits made life in the village untenable, my father took me to Shanghai with the rest of the family. My eldest brother had died a year earlier. Here I was put temporarily in a Catholic school to continue my English study. The instruction was given by a French Brother. The pupils were told to call him "Bladda." As he was a foreigner his pronunciation of the language, I imagined, must be good; it was obviously different from that of the Chinese teacher. For instance, he taught us to say "dat" instead of "zat" and "bladda" instead of "bloder." The reader can imagine what curious English we acquired. But I did not stay long in the school. As there was no suitable school in Shanghai for me to go to, Father sent my brother to learn English from an American lady and made me study under him. He thus acted as a comprador of English teaching. I was much dissatisfied with the arrangement, but my father thought it a very clever scheme because it would save money.

Shanghai by 1899 was a small city with a few thousand arrogant foreigners. But the city was well governed, with clean, wide streets and electric or gas lights. I thought the foreigners were wonderful. They knew the secret of electricity. They had invented the steam engine and built steamboats. They took the place of my old gods, who had melted away in the face of my instruction in science, and occupied my mind as new ones. At the same time they served as new devils, too, for their arrogance, coupled with the clubs of the policemen, frightened me. In the list of regulations displayed at the entrance of a park on the banks of the Huang-pu River, Chinese as well as dogs were forbidden admission. This said much. The foreigner appeared to my mind half divine and half devilish, double-faced and many-handed like Vishnu, holding an electric light, a steamboat, and a pretty doll in one set of hands, and a policeman's club, revolver, and handful of opium in the other. When one looked at his bright side he was an angel; on the dark side he was a demon.

Western civilization, as viewed by the Chinese in China's recent history, has been either one way or the other at different periods or among different groups of individuals. Li Hung-chang saw the importance of the dark and devilish side and built a navy to beat the devil by his own weapons. Emperor Kwang-hsü saw the importance of the bright and godly side and tried to establish a new school system. The Empress Dowager and the Boxers saw the curse of the devilish side and tried to oust the devils with China's own obsolete arms. The trouble was that the god was strong for the very reason that at times he could be devilish; the devil was powerful because at times he could be godly. He was one and indivisible—you had either to take him as a whole or not at all. Was not Japan the example? Make your erstwhile enemy your teacher!

We lived in Shanghai for about two years, and this home, too, we left hurriedly one night when we were informed that the Empress Dowager had sent instructions to viceroys throughout the country to put all foreigners to death. It was 1900 and the beginning of the Boxer War in North China. The "Boxers" were a fanatical cult claiming magical powers; gymnastics formed a part of their program—hence the name by which they became known. They meant to destroy all foreign manufactured goods and kill every person found in possession of them. They wanted to kill all the foreigners who brought in these terrible things and destroyed their trade. Churches, schools, missionaries, and Christians were all guilty of introducing these poisonous manufactures into China. Get rid of these people by killing them, with swords, knives, magic! Destroy foreign properties by setting them on fire.

The Imperial Court for its own part wanted to destroy all the crazy ideas of foreign origin introduced by Kang Yu-wei and Liang Chi-chao, so that nothing like the reforms of 1898 could happen again. Thus the Boxers wanted to get rid of the manufactured goods and the Empress Dowager and her court wanted to get rid of foreign mental goods; both came from one source— the foreigners. Kill them all! In the beginning of the industrial revolution in England people smashed the machines which destroyed their livelihood. The Boxers went a bit too far. They destroyed the human "machinery" too.

In the south people looked at the foreigner in a different light. They welcomed foreign manufactures but did not understand that it was this very thing that caused the banditry. They put the blame on the obnoxious taxes of the Imperial government and the corruption and incompetence of its officials. So they wanted a revolution.

The people and the Imperial Court in the north were right in holding the foreigners responsible for destroying their trades, but found a wrong solution in smashing the "human machinery." The people of the south had a wrong reason in holding the Imperial government responsible for their plight, but did the right thing in starting a revolution. History seems to consist of a series of accidents, illogical reasoning, and unexpected results, in which the great men appearing on the scene are but the instruments of Fate.

Foreigners cursed banditry in China, but did not know that their own manufactures had caused it in the beginning. In my childhood days we all feared tigers, ghosts, and bandits, but all were imaginary; we only saw them in picture books. Then suddenly the bandit appeared in real life—as if a tiger should dash into your house or a ghost chase you. Finally we dreaded the bandits and forgot about tigers and ghosts.

CHAPTER 6

FURTHER EDUCATION

Thus at the age of fifteen I was brought back home by my father. We were afraid that the Boxer War might extend to Shanghai and so returned to the village; but after a short stay, as the bandits became worse, we moved to Yuyao, the district capital, to live. There I was sent to a local school to study English and arithmetic, and studied Chinese under a private tutor.

After a year or so I went to Hangchow, capital of the province of Chekiang. This was the center of the silk industry in China and also one center of the tea trade. Hangchow silk and tea were famous all over the country.

Hangchow is well known for its scenic beauty. To one side of the city the Chien-tang tides rush up from Hangchow Bay. On the other is the West Lake, mirrored against a blue sky with reflections of temples and villas perched on the surrounding hills. The city was known as a paradise on earth. This was the city that Marco Polo adored in his travels, and it was the ancient capital of King Chien-liao, who kept his domain in peace through long years of incessant invasions and wars in China. Here the South Sungs made their capital for a hundred and fifty years, and here famous poets and men of letters lived. It is a city rich in historical records and monuments. The Imperial Library was filled with valuable books. It was the right place for young scholars to nurse themselves to grow.

In this city of learning I stumbled accidentally into a backward school, a local Christian academy run by an American missionary. Here I hoped that at least I might learn English well. The atmosphere was far from congenial. The principal was a carpenter by trade; this pious American had been carried to China by his religious zeal. He had done some missionary work in my prefecture before being given charge of the academy. As he taught nothing except the Bible, I did not know how much he knew, and since learning was honored in China the carpenter-teacher evoked secret contempt in the hearts of his pupils. My English teacher was a man of vulgar manners, a new convert whose soul may have been saved but whose tongue remained distinctly heathen. I had tramped from this school to that trying to find a really good English teacher, but to my great disappointment I was still simply chasing after shadows.

It was compulsory in the academy to attend exercises in the chapel every morning. We sang hymns in Chinese. Sometimes the clever pupils saw fit to render them in paraphrases which gained more popularity among us than the hymns. In spite of Sunday schools and morning exercises my mind was closed tight as a clam against any spiritual foreign elements. Having got rid of its spirits, ghosts, and gods, it was reluctant to admit any new elements of similar nature. And indeed, ever since that time I have remained an agnostic, trying to find immortality rather in this world than in the next. This conforms with the basic teachings of Confucius.

The only respectable buildings on the campus of the academy were the chapel and the residence of the principal. The students lived in cell-like mud sheds, and classes were held there or in the shabby dining hall.

Out of curiosity some pupils liked to loiter around the principal's house. These unwelcome guests were often told to keep away. Usually they obeyed and walked off, but on one occasion a student rebelled and got into a quarrel with a teacher who happened by.

A crowd began to gather. The student accused the teacher of slapping his face and wept to draw the ready sympathy of the mob. The commotion spread like fire and within a few minutes the majority of the student body had joined in demanding the immediate dismissal of the teacher. The demand being refused by the principal, the crowd became enraged and emotions soared to the highest pitch. The principal told them bluntly that if they did not like the school they could leave. In about two hours the whole school walked out.

This marked the end of my education in a missionary school and I had no regret. The sooner I left, the better.

One may ask why such a thing should happen, all of a sudden. It was not a mere outburst of ugliness on the part of unruly students. The slap was only a trigger pulled on a loaded gun; the explosive charge is not to be identified with a little missionary academy. This was part of a country-wide student rebellion against school authority. Even a backward missionary school in Hangchow was not exempt.

The rebellion had started in Nanyang College in Shanghai during the previous year. A student had left an inkstand on his professor's chair and the professor had sat on it. His clothes being stained, he got very angry; it was reported to the president and a few suspects were dismissed. There followed a clash between the college authorities and the student body, the latter supported by a number of faculty members. Eventually all the students walked out.

The younger generation was changing, and it was a change from submission to rebellion. Dismayed at the encroachment of foreign powers upon China, people blamed the Imperial Court for it. The students, inflamed and aroused by Dr. Sun Yat-sen's revolutionary propaganda, were ready to strike whenever there might be opportunity and at anything they could get hold of. They delivered their first blows at the school authorities who were handiest to them.

The Provincial College of Chekiang followed suit. A minor fracas between a student and a sedan chair bearer of the Imperial governor who was visiting the college set off the incident. All the students went on strike in consequence and left the college in a body. Many incidents of like nature occurred in other schools, with eventual disruption of a number of institutions of new learning. It spread throughout the country.

The new elements in the country sympathized with the strikes and blamed the authorities for their despotism; the old elements condemned the students in no uncertain terms and sympathized with the school authorities. Whatever one's opinion, few realized that this was the eve of a revolution. From the time of these early student rebellions to the Revolution of 1911 which marked the birth of the Republic of China was only eight short years.

It was the rebellion of the coming intelligentsia against the class of old literati who controlled China, intellectually and socially as well as politically. With the introduction of the theory of evolution—with special reference to the struggle for existence and the survival of the fittest—and other scientific ideas, the mental attitude of the young generation was undergoing a radical change in social and political philosophy. Eighteenth-century concepts of individual freedom encountered the nineteenth-century industrial revolution: freedom in the form of rebellion against established authority and industrial revolution in the form of imported products which doomed the old trades to decay. China's old structure was crumbling and the new one was yet to be built.

There was a general unrest throughout the country. Poverty, bandits, famine, plague, official corruption, ignorance of world affairs, and the pinch of foreign aggressions—all were contributing factors. The students, the young blood, merely took the lead. It was not an insignificant inkstand, nor the slapped face of a pupil in a missionary school, nor any altercation between a student and a chair bearer that set educational institutions ablaze throughout China.

After leaving the academy our youthful student body organized a school for themselves—the "School of Reforms and Progress." The name was suggested by Chang Pin-ling, one of the famous revolutionary scholars of our time. Our ambition was to make the school as great one day as Oxford or Cambridge. Pretty soon, as was natural, we found ourselves disillusioned. The student body dwindled in the course of half a year to a few elected officers. When these few found no one to re-elect them, they also departed to seek educations elsewhere.

For my part, I registered at Chekiang College, under a new name lest the college authorities find me *persona non grata*. I took the entrance examination, passed it, and was admitted. The college had just been reorganized after the strike and was the highest institution of learning in the Province of Scholars, as our province was known. Its forerunner had been Chiou Shih Shu-yuan, or the "School for Seeking What Is Right." It is the proper frame of mind for a scholar to seek what is right, and this was the attitude of Chinese scholars of former generations. This had been a school similar to the Sino-Occidental School of Shaoshing, an old-style Chinese school whose curriculum included some foreign languages and science teaching. As the new subjects grew in importance and were allotted more time it developed into a new type of school and was renamed Chekiang College.

Situated in the provincial capital and maintained by the government, the college served as a center of cultural movements in the province. The curriculum was very similar to that of the Sino-Occidental school, but the courses were more advanced, more various, and better taught, with less sheer memory work. It was a modern school in the making.

I had been trotting along in the dark since entering the school in Shaoshing. My mind always rushed for the place where I caught a glimpse of bewitching light and groped in some other direction when it elusively disappeared. By this time, however, I saw things in much clearer perspective. I had begun to study world history in English. At first it seemed as difficult to understand the doings of other peoples as when one tries to understand the behavior of the masses, but gradually I began to see, albeit dimly, the development of Western civilization. This was of course only in a very general and vague way. But my interest in Western history was aroused and a foundation laid for further study.

Here I was in the midst of intellectual activities. Through reading, lectures, and conversation, my information about China and the world was accumulating. I grew familiar with some forty centuries of China's history, with a fair understanding of the causes, as given by the great historians, of the rise and fall of many dynasties. This served as the basis for a comparative study of Western history later on.

In the field of contemporary history there was plenty of material. The Sino-Japanese War of 1894, of which I had learned from the misleading colored pictures in my childhood; the short-lived reforms of Kang Yu-wei and Liang Chi-chao in 1898, which had taken place during my stay in the Sino-Occidental School; the Boxer War of 1900, news of which I learned at such close range in Shanghai; and the Russo-Japanese War of 1904 which was even then raging (with China's overwhelming sympathy for Japan)—each and all furnished rich materials for thought and study.

One might study history backward, too: there was the Sino-French War in 1885 in which China lost Indo-China; the Taiping

Rebellion (1851–64) and the ever-victorious army of Generals Gordon and Ward; the Opium War of 1840, as a result of which China lost Hongkong; and if one went farther back there was the coming of the Jesuits during the later Ming and early Ching periods, and the travels of Marco Polo during the Yuan or Mongol Dynasty; still farther back China had relations with the Roman Empire.

Liang Chi-chao's *Young China,* an encyclopedic monthly published in Tokyo, furnished a great variety of materials ranging from short stories to metaphysics and including elementary science, history, politics, biographies, literature, etc. His lucid pen was capable of making people understand almost any subject new or difficult to the reader. This was very important at a time when there was a need to introduce Western ideas into China. His style was clear, persuasive, and easy to follow and therefore very profitable reading for students. I was one among thousands who came under his influence. I think this great scholar did more than anyone else in his time to popularize modern knowledge among the rising generation. His was the fountain of wisdom from which every young man drew to quench his thirst for the new learning.

Politically he stood for constitutional reforms under the reigning dynasty. Meanwhile the revolutionaries were publishing a number of periodicals to sponsor Dr. Sun Yat-sen's radical idea that for China a republican form of government was better than a monarchy and that China must be governed by the Chinese and not by the corrupt and degenerate Manchus. That published by the Chekiang students in Tokyo was a monthly: *Tides of Chien-tang.* This magazine attacked the reigning dynasty so fiercely that it was barred from the mails, among other like periodicals, by the postal authorities. But the movement had the sympathy of the Tokyo government and the tabooed periodicals therefore flowed continuously from Japan, where they were published, into the International Settlement of Shanghai where Chinese jurisdiction reached only partially. So Shanghai became a clearinghouse for revolutionary ideas, and from there the literature was smuggled into other cities by sympathizers as well as profit makers.

Chekiang College itself was deluged with pamphlets, magazines, and books of revolutionary propaganda, some depicting the atrocities committed by the Manchus during their invasion of China, others describing their misrule and the unequal treatment of Manchus and Chinese under the existing regime. The students devoured them voluptuously. No power on earth could stop them.

Moreover, concrete examples of Manchu misrule and incompetence could be found just outside the college gate. Within the city walls of Hangchow was a walled city for the Manchus who were stationed there as a garrison to watch over the Chinese. I was warned not to enter it; anyone did so at his own risk. More than two hundred years earlier this city within a city had been set aside exclusively as barracks for the Manchu soldiers in Hangchow. After them their children's children had lived there, nominally as soldiers, for generations until they were killed by the Taipings during the siege of the capital. Intermarriage between Chinese and Manchus was in general forbidden, but Manchus were allowed to marry Chinese women if they preferred, although such marriages were rare. When the civil war was over, a part of the garrison stationed at Chingchow in Hupeh Province was moved to Hangchow to fill the vacancy. Some of these were still living and spoke Hupeh dialect; most of them had died, but their children lived there and still clung to the dialect of their fathers. Thus they were easily detected by the natives of Hangchow. But the third generation had begun to speak the local Hangchow tongue.

They sent ten of their boys to study at the college. These youths behaved wisely toward the revolutionary movement in the college by pretending not to know of it. One of them, of Mongol origin, actually told me he was in favor of a revolution against the Manchu Dynasty as he was a non-Manchu in spite of being a Manchu "soldier."

These so-called Manchu soldiers were no soldiers at all; they were just the same as civilians. They had families and reared children in the so-called barracks and knew nothing of the arts of war. The only difference was that they lived on government rations and had no occupation. Theirs was a sort of parasitic life, and they degenerated physically, mentally, and morally. They haunted the teahouses on the West Lake, some of them in the fashionable manner carrying a bird in its cage, and people generally kept away from them. They would slap anyone who offended them. These living examples of degeneration, corruption, and arrogance woke hatred and contempt in the hearts of the young students. It was just as effective as revolutionary propaganda, if not more so.

While we got our mental food from Liang Chi-chao, we drew our emotional nourishment from Dr. Sun Yat-sen and his sympathizers. Generally speaking, it is emotion that leads to action when a decisive hour comes; when that hour came in China Dr. Sun, both dreamer and man of action, won a decisive victory over the new literati who stood for constitutionalism.

Such was the general atmosphere of Chekiang College. Similar conditions also prevailed in other institutions. I was interested in all these activities. I liked to get hold of information and to think with the materials thus secured, and also to feel and to act. But nothing carried me away entirely. To play safe I still planned to take the Imperial civil examination, still the only road to a government position except by way of revolution, which seemed long and difficult to me. I was at times timid and shy, at others bold and reckless, and therefore did not trust my own temperament. So I often acted cautiously, feeling my way before making a definite move. Especially at any crossroads, I would consider again and again before coming to a decision. In case of doubt I was apt instead to sit by the roadside and indulge in daydreams. But once a decision was made I would stick to the end. I made mistakes in life, but never so fatally as to be swept away by the advancing tides.

CHAPTER 7

IMPERIAL CIVIL EXAMINATION

EARLY one morning, as the time for the civil examination drew near, I started for Shaoshing where the examination was to be held for our district. The luggage man slung his bamboo pole over his shoulder with my suitcase and bamboo basket roped to one end and bedding outfits balancing the other. I followed on his heels. As my luggage swung out of the college gate a teacher who happened to see me smiled and wished me good luck.

After passing through many granite-paved streets and zigzag narrow Hangchow alleys, we came to the banks of the Chientang River. I measured my steps along a gangway of narrow, frail planks a quarter of a mile long, with the tides flowing underneath, leading to the waiting ferryboat. The boat was plied by several heavy oars, with the occasional help of sails. It glided along in leisurely fashion. As it could only be controlled by heading against the tide, the slow speed was further reduced and it took us two hours to cross. None of us imagined then that within some thirty years a long steel bridge would span the river, with trains and cars passing over it.

I then took a sedan chair through miles of mulberry groves to a busy trading city, where I embarked for Shaoshing, arriving next morning after a night on the boat, which was packed with passengers like sardines. One had to lie flat and straight; if you tried to move your legs you found your allotted space gone; if you tried to turn on your side there was no space left to lie flat again.

In Shaoshing I got a room with board in a fan maker's family. The place was small and dark and filled with strange odors from certain vegetable oils used to make fans. In the evening I studied by a vegetable-oil lamp which did not give enough light to read small letters without straining one's eyes. We refrained from using kerosene because of the inflammable materials that filled the place. In the dark we could not walk without stumbling over some sort of stuff for making fans.

The examination began with roll call at the entrance of the Examination Hall at about four o'clock in the morning. The early autumn morning was chilly. A large crowd of literati, several thousand strong and each wearing a red-tasseled hat—without a button—and carrying a lantern, gathered around the spacious courtyard. At the entrance to the hall the Prefect sat in stately dignity at a long desk. He wore a red-tasseled hat with a blue crystal button at the top, a black jacket over a deep blue gown, and a chain of beads around his neck. This was his full official attire. With a vermilion pen in his hand he began to call the roll. As he went down the list a man standing by him called out in long-drawn tones the name of each candidate, who promptly sang out at the top of his voice, "Here! So-and-so, the guarantor." Immediately the guarantor sang his own name in acknowledgment of the sponsorship. The Prefect then glanced about quickly to see if anything was wrong and made a red dot above the name with his vermilion pen.

The candidate was then let in. His hat and clothes were searched to see that he carried no notes with him. Anything found written on paper would be confiscated.

The candidates moved on in files to their respective seats, which were numbered, each finding his place accordingly. The names on the examination papers were written on detachable slips to be torn off before the papers were handed in. Each paper was also numbered in a sealed corner, which was not opened until the papers were marked and the successful candidates selected, so as to prevent any possible favoritism. Toward the end of the Manchu Dynasty, when corruption ran rampant in many branches of government office, the Imperial examination system remained independent and free alike of external interference and internal corruption. This was one reason why the degrees conferred were so much honored in China.

Questions were limited to the Confucian classics and this was why a candidate must commit to memory all the texts in the classics. This I had done through years of laborious conning in my country school and the Sino-Occidental School in Shaoshing. Questions were shown to the candidates by means of cubic lanterns, on the screens of which the questions were written; they were lighted with candles so that the black letters on the white screens could be seen distinctly at a distance. Bearers raised the lanterns high above their heads and carried them up and down the aisles several times, so that none could miss them.

About noon officials went around to check on how far the candidates had gone with their essays and set on each paper a seal at the spot to which the lines had run. At about four in the afternoon cannon began to roar, marking the first call for the collection of papers. The gates were flung open and the band began to play. Candidates who were able to answer the first call handed in their papers and made their way out slowly through the gates with music playing and an anxious crowd waiting. After everyone had made his exit the gates were closed again. The second call was made about an hour later with the same ceremony. The third or final call was made about six, with both cannon and band remaining silent.

We had about a week or ten days to wait for the results of the examination. In the interim there was plenty of time for amusement. Bookstores, large and small, were found everywhere near the Examination Hall. There were chess stands, temporary restaurants with famous Shaoshing wines and delicious dishes at moderate prices, and traveling theatres where we could go and enjoy ourselves.

On the day when the results were to be made public a large crowd waited anxiously in front of a high, spacious wall opposite the entrance of the Examination Hall. Cannon and band announced the moment when the list of names, or rather numbers, of the successful candidates was issued. The numbers were set down in a circular formation instead of in a column, so as to avoid having a top and bottom to the list.

I was pleasantly surprised to find my own number in big black letters among the others in the circle on the enormous oblong paper posted on the wall. To make sure I rubbed my eyes and looked at it several times. When I was sure they had not deceived me, I elbowed through the packed crowd and hastened back to my lodginghouse. As I made my way out I noticed a man with an open umbrella which caught on a railing. When he jerked it off the umbrella went upward, looking like a giant artichoke, but in his excitement he kept on running and paid no attention to it.

The second session of the examination came within a few days. Everyone who had passed the first had reason to worry, since some would be eliminated. I was lucky in the second trial. In the list of names which was posted on the wall I found mine somewhere in the middle rows.

The third and final session was merely perfunctory. In addition to an essay we were supposed to write down from memory a section of the "Imperial Instructions in Morals"; in reality each of us had with us a copy of the text, which we were allowed to carry into the Examination Hall and which we copied outright. The Imperial Examiner appeared in person to supervise the final examination. His official title I learned from the inscription on two identical pennants about fifteen feet long which streamed in the air from flagpoles standing symmetrically at either side of the entrance. It read: "The Imperial Vice-Minister of Rites and Concurrently Imperial Examiner of Public Instruction for the Province of Chekiang, etc."

Early in the morning, some days later, I was awakened from slumber by the rapid beating of a tom-tom outside my window. It was an official reporter coming to announce the award of the First Degree—*Wu-shen*, popularly known as *Hsiu-tsai*. The official announcement, which was printed in bold block prints on a piece of red paper about six feet by four, read as follows:

His Majesty's Imperial Vice-Minister of Rites and Concurrently Imperial Examiner of Public Instruction for the Province of Chekiang, etc., wishes to announce that your honorable person, Chiang Monlin, is awarded the Degree of Wu-shen and entitled to enjoy the privilege of entering the District Government School as a government scholar.

The "district school" was an empty Confucian temple with one official in charge who acted as the "government teacher" but in fact never taught anyone or anything. One found, actually, neither school nor teacher; what was called a school was only symbolic. Yet I had to pay the traditional entrance fee of $100 —which I paid only partially, through bargaining.

After the examination the pendulum of life swung back once again to my new education. In a few days I went back to Chekiang College. In leaving, I learned from my landlord that one of my fellow lodgers had complained to him in a rage that the Imperial Examiner was so blind as to pass a man almost illiterate, like me, and neglect him, who possessed great literary merits. Such are the hazards of examinations!

Back at the college I plunged at once into studies again and found myself in the midst of algebra, physics, zoölogy, history, and so on. By way of extracurricular activity I indulged in reading revolutionary literature and discussed contemporary politics with my fellow students. Imperial examination days and Chekiang College were worlds apart! It seemed a transformation overnight from misty, immutable medievalism to the whirlpool of a new revolutionary world. I felt as if what had happened had been a dream.

After two months it was time for the winter vacation. I was called back home by my father to receive congratulations from relatives and friends upon my success. I was now nineteen. My close relatives saw a bright future for me; if the feng-shui of my ancestral tombs were favorable I would go right along, passing the two remaining examinations to receive the highest degree, to the glory of family, relatives, and above all, our ancestors whose spirits were in heaven. My second brother had passed his civil examination a few years before me; he was now a student at the Imperial University of Peking, of which I was to be Chancellor after some fifteen years—unpredictable chance.

An announcement printed on a big piece of red paper like the one I had received in Shaoshing was presented by official reporters, to the beating of a tom-tom, to my relatives and family friends. On the day of celebration I dressed in a blue satin gown and wore a red-tasseled hat with a silver button on top. Several hundred relatives and friends, including women and children, came to feast for two days. The spacious guesthall was decorated with artistic red lanterns and an orchestra played Chinese tunes. The happiest man there was my father, who cherished the hope that some day his son might become a grand minister at His Majesty's Imperial Court. For my part, I was puzzled. I was torn between two opposing forces, one pulling toward the old and the other toward the new. "What shall I do? What shall I do?" a voice cried out within me.

After three weeks the college reopened for the new session. Once more I swung back again to my studies in the new learning. I stayed for about half a year, leaving before the summer vacation.

All the conflicting ideas, as between new and old, constitutional reforms and revolution, buzzing around in this topsy-turvy world of mine, were more than an immature mind could endure. I became restless and often had a fantasy in which, by a sort of somersault, I rocketed high into the air and then whirled down rapidly to the ground, where I burst to bits and was gone forever.

Being born in a family which had a few cases of insanity among my close relatives, I wondered sometimes whether I, too, had inherited a faint streak of instability which might occasional tip the scale a little in my otherwise well-balanced temperament. I had been told, moreover, by my father and my grand-uncle that my ideas and actions during childhood had been quite different from those of the rest of the children. I still remember how my grand-uncle scolded me one day, remarking that when I grew up I would become either a wise man or a rascal; to which, not knowing the meaning quite clearly, I secretly replied to myself that I wanted to be a wise man.

Was I crazy in this crazy world? At least one problem always remained clear in my mind: how to save China from dismemberment by the foreign Powers. Revolutionary ideas were now fast gaining ground in the minds of students throughout the country. As more and more of them joined the movement, the influence of Dr. Sun Yat-sen grew wider and wider. The days of the reigning dynasty were numbered.

On my part, I longed for a better and more westernized school. For by this time I could see that the wind blew in the direction of westernization, irrespective of whether China had constitutional reforms or revolution. One morning as I passed unintentionally by a passageway where students were forbidden, I met the proctor, who asked me what I was doing there. On the spur of the moment I improvised the story that my mother was ill and had written me to come home.

"That's too bad," he said. "You had better go right away."

I went back to my dormitory, packed up everything, and left the college that same morning. I took a small steamboat, chugging along the Grand Canal, down to Shanghai. There I took the entrance examination for Nanyang College and passed it. This was the year 1904, when the Russo-Japanese War was raging in all intensity for the control of Manchuria.

CHAPTER 8

WESTERNIZATION

CHINA was now definitely on the track of westernization, whatever her struggles between old and new, between constitutionalism and revolution. The victory of Japan over Tsarist Russia gave further impetus to her reforms along new or Western lines. By this time about fifty thousand Chinese students had gathered about Tokyo, a center of the new knowledge. In the meantime the government had begun a series of reforms; new educational, military, and police systems were adopted, all copied after the Japanese models. Many believed that the Western systems and institutions which had been assimilated by the Japanese and adapted to Japanese life were more suitable to Chinese conditions than purely foreign forms. That is to say, China was to receive Western civilization via Japan. There were others, however, who held that if she must introduce Western civilization for her rejuvenation, why should she not go direct to the West for it?

I was one of those who believed in the direct route. In spite of the persuasions of friends studying in Japan, I stuck stubbornly to my belief. I entered Nanyang College with a view to preparing myself for American universities. As all the textbooks on Western subjects were in English, it suited me splendidly.

The college had been organized with the advice of Dr. John C. Ferguson, a former American missionary who only recently died in New York, and its preparatory department was run along the lines of an American high school. So it was most convenient as the final step to an American college. There were several American teachers who taught us modern subjects. After two years there I could read English fairly well, although I was still quite deficient in speaking. The language was not taught by phonetic methods and I found my tongue too stiff to follow.

The curriculum was divided into two groups, one of Chinese and the other of Western subjects. I always stood high in both, once winning honors in the two examinations simultaneously.

The principal summoned me and paid me high compliments, to my great satisfaction.

The college was laid out and built according to Western plan; the main building had in its center a clock tower which could be seen several miles away. In front of a row of buildings was a vast football field, green and well kept. Football and baseball were encouraged by the college authorities and games and sports generally indulged in by the students. Intercollegiate track and field games were held twice a year, with thousands of spectators.

Born physically frail, I began to realize that a healthy body was necessary for a healthy mind. Besides daily exercise and some sports of the lighter kind, I adopted a course of physical culture for myself. Every morning at about six I practised with dumbbells for half an hour, and again for fifteen minutes in the evening before going to bed. I kept this up for three years without interruption and after that time found myself in good health and always in a cheerful mood.

Spencer's principles of education—consisting of three elements: the intellectual, moral, and physical—had by now been introduced into China. So to make up my moral education I reviewed some of the Confucian classics and studied the Sung and Ming philosophers and biographies of great men in history, both Chinese and Western, with a view to imitating their conduct. I entered selected parts of their sayings and doings in my diary as I came across those that struck me. Then I did some careful thinking about them, tried to act on them, and watched the results, which were also entered into the diary for further examination.

It was exciting whenever I discovered that Chinese and Western ideas regarding certain matters were similar or almost identical. When they were I knew that in acting in accordance with them I would be guided by a universal truth. When discrepancies occurred I studied them and tried to find out the reasons for them. In this way I unconsciously made a comparative study of morals, or rules of conduct, of East and West. The most important result was that I learned to differentiate essentials from nonessentials and the fundamental from the superficial in moral ideas.

Henceforth I began to be more positive, more definite, more self-confident in steering my life on troubled waters. For moral ideas are the charts by means of which a life of action is directed.

I began to see the oneness of East and West and appreciate the dictum of Lu Hsiang-shan, a Sung philosopher, that "the sages born of the Eastern sea will have the same mind and therefore the same reason as the sages of the Western sea." I also began to see unity in chaos, for I came to realize that essentials are but few, while to know the similarities, differences, or contrasts among them is to clarify each and all of them. It was the buzzing of trifling things that made you dizzy. So I followed the teachings of Mencius and Lu Hsiang-shan that in learning we must grasp the essentials and neglect the trifles and make our own reasoning power the sole arbiter. Thus I began to establish myself on the solid rock of reasoning instead of traditional beliefs. I felt as if I had stripped off clothes that were altogether too tight and stepped forth naked and free.

However, reason does not exist in a vacuum. I indulged in too much thinking, which led to nothing but disappointment. But the way to right thinking had to start from thinking itself, and learning to think by experience. You cannot teach a person how to think if he does not think at all. My belief here was reinforced in later years in America by reading John Dewey's *How We Think*, to which I owed much.

It is the teaching of the Confucian school that mental culture is the starting point of personal culture, which in turn will serve as the foundation for statecraft. Therefore, in order to save China, save yourself first. So I devoted myself to study and thinking, to physical exercise and to proper conduct. This was, as I understood it, the way to personal culture which would some day serve as the foundation for rendering service to the state.

While I was still at Nanyang College the Imperial Court took a definite step in educational reform by abolishing—in 1905—the agelong system of civil examinations; by this act the door to the past was closed to the younger generation once and for all. The decree was prompted by the victory of Japan over Russia. To replace the old, a new educational system was inaugurated, modeled after the Japanese, which in turn had been introduced to Japan from the West. China was now surely on the road to westernization.

For some time past Shanghai had been the center of a fugitive cultural movement in China. Harbored in the International Settlement and the French Concession, where Chinese jurisdiction reached to only a very limited extent or so far as international or French authorities might agree, Chinese intellectual and revolutionary leaders made their homes and enjoyed freedom of speech and publication. Here political fugitives and men of radical thought, or those so considered at the time, gathered to discuss, elucidate, and publish their ideas. Life here was comparable to that in one of the old Greek city-states—thinking was free and active.

For my own part, in addition to my training at Nanyang I joined in various activities as a junior member, more by way of learning than active participation. On Saturdays and Sundays I frequented especially Chi-fang, a teashop on Foochow Road where all the students of Shanghai sipped their tea and indulged in lively discussions. No student of those days can forget the unique figure of the king of rogues, or "King Hsu," who was an inseparable part of the teahouse, selling revolutionary literature to the students. He was dressed in shabby Western clothes with a grey greasy cap on his head, his queue being cut. Among his revolutionary wares he included a pamphlet, *A New Treatise on Sex Problems*, which he explained was to catch the attention of the reading public. Nobody ever knew his name or where he lived. Any book on revolution nominally tabooed by the municipal authorities by request of the Chinese government could be secured through him.

In the same year that civil examinations were abolished the Tung Men Huei—the "Revolutionary Union," predecessor of the Kuomintang—was organized by Dr. Sun Yat-sen in Tokyo with several hundred students joining, and Dr. Sun was elected president. This was the year of the Portsmouth Treaty, signed by Japan and Russia to end the Russo-Japanese War. After this victory over one of the Western Powers Japan was now ready to launch aggression on China. This was a bare ten years before she delivered her famous Twenty-One Demands, and only sixteen years before the Mukden Incident which led to full-fledged war in 1937.

In Shanghai a boycott movement against American goods was proceeding in all intensity as a protest against the passing of the Chinese Exclusion Act by the American Congress. Students and merchants joined in calling from door to door on Chinese shopkeepers, urging them not to sell American merchandise. The shopkeepers tried to get rid of their boycotted goods as fast as possible at very moderate prices and a number of people were happy to buy them at the back door. Mass meetings were held in which fierce speeches against the exclusion act were made. At one of them the speaker stamped on the platform so hard that the sole of his shoe fell off and was flung into the audience while waves of laughter rang through the hall.

Another important incident, in the following year, was the agitation by the gentry of Chekiang and Kiangsu Provinces and the students and merchants of Shanghai against construction of the Soochow-Hangchow-Ningpo Railway by British capital. There were public demonstrations in the form of mass meetings, circular telegrams, and soapbox orations, and subscriptions were opened for shares in the railway with a view to building it with Chinese capital. The line was changed to run via Shanghai, Hangchow, and Ningpo; Shanghai being substituted for Soochow by the curious reasoning that the latter, an inland city, would thus be spared foreign influence, which was bound to increase with a railway. The British gave in as to the route, though the agitation was unsuccessful in obtaining Chinese capital ownership, and the railway was begun the next year.

Students all over China remained quiet in the schools during those years, partly because of their wider interests in activities outside school and partly because they themselves had wearied of the meaningless troubles they gave the school authorities. Nevertheless, they now turned their attention to the school cooks who prepared food for them. Each student paid six dollars a month for his food in Shanghai; in the interior, three dollars. One could not, therefore, expect very much from the cook, but the students were dissatisfied with what they got. They complained of the coarse rice and the poor quality of meat and vegetables, often demanding additional dishes—generally fried eggs, which were easy to prepare. Eggs were cheap in China then, about fifty or sixty for a dollar. Sometimes the students smashed the plates or bowls or beat up the cooks. No school was free from "strikes in the dining hall" as they were called.

In 1907 a short-lived revolution broke out in Anking, provincial capital of Anhwei. The leader was Hsu Shih-ling, police taotai (chief of police) of that province. He had been a teacher in the Sino-Occidental School in Shaoshing, where I received my early education in Western learning—where I first learned that the earth is round. He was a Chu-jen, the Second Degree awarded through the Imperial civil examinations; had taught in the school for a few years and then gone to Japan to study. Returning to China, he bought the office of taotai with fifty thousand dollars borrowed from friends and was appointed for the province of Anking. With the police under his control, he shot the governor with his own hand and started a coup d'état in the provincial capital. With two personal followers and the police force he occupied the arsenal, training its several cannon on the entrance. Not being adepts in military art, they were unable to make the guns work and soldiers rushed in and arrested him. One of his followers, Chen, was killed in action while the other, Ma, was arrested later.

Ma had been a schoolmate of mine at Chekiang College in Hang-chow, and on their way from Japan to Anking he and Chen had stopped in Shanghai, where they came to see me almost every day. They talked at length about the revolutionary movement, which they believed was the only course for China's salvation, and asked me to go to Anking with them; but a cousin of mine, the manager of a native bank, advised me rather to take a trip to Japan. During summer vacation I took the opportunity of going with a friend to Tokyo, where an exposition was being held. Ma and Chen and I dined in farewell at the I-tse-hsiang Restaurant the evening before my departure, and they also left the next day for Anking, aboard a Yangtze steamer which took them up the river to their fatal destination.

My first experience on an ocean-going steamer was rather thrilling. Everything was novel to me. The flush toilet was a wonder. The Japanese *boysans* (cabin boys) were courteous. We reached Nagasaki the next morning and were impressed with the beautiful scenery in that port. In the afternoon we passed Shimonoseki, well known in China for Li Hung-chang's visit to it and for the peace treaty concluded in 1895 and known by that name. We landed at Kobe and from there took a train to Tokyo, getting off at Shimbashi Station. A friend of mine who was studying in Tokyo took me to a small hotel, the Kimigayokan in the Koishikawa district. The street was unpaved and muddy on that rainy day.

I visited the exposition in Ueno Park dozens of times and was impressed with the industrial development of Japan. In a war museum where prizes of war were shown I was very much ashamed to see the Chinese flags, uniforms, and weapons seized in the Sino-Japanese War and I tried vainly to dodge the eyes that stared at me. In the evening the park was illuminated with thousands of electric lights and the happy populace of Tokyo paraded on the grounds with myriad lanterns in their hands, shouting *Banzai!* They were intoxicated with the victory over Russia two years earlier and still went wild about it. On my part, I stood alone at the top of an imitation hill and watched the parade passing. I was so much moved that tears rolled down my cheeks.

Early one morning, within a week or so of my arrival, the *neisan* or chambermaid brought me a Japanese paper from which I learned of Hsu Shih-ling's revolution in Anking and its failure. I would have been killed if I had gone there with my two friends.

The general impression I had of Japan was very favorable. The whole country was a garden. The people were well dressed, their cities clean. They were perhaps inwardly conceited, but courteous to strangers. Compulsory education made the general level of the people much higher than in China, and this was perhaps the secret of Japan's becoming a world Power. These were the impressions I carried home after a month's stay.

Pretty soon I began to work hard again at the college. The following year, during the summer vacation, I went to Hangchow to take the Chekiang provincial examination for scholarships to study in America. Having failed, I got a few thousand dollars from my father and prepared to go to California for further study.

Part II

AMERICAN YEARS

CHAPTER 9

FURTHER "WEST"

WITH part of the money my father gave me I bought hats, shoes, clothes, and other necessary things, and a first-class ticket to San Francisco. The rest I converted into American gold dollars at the rate of two Mexican to one. My queue I got rid of at a barbershop. When the barber applied a pair of long scissors to my hair I felt as if I were on the guillotine—a chill stole all over me. With two quick, heavy cuts my queue fell off and I felt as if my head had gone with it. It was given back to me wrapped in paper and I threw it into the ocean on my way to America.

I acquired a doctor's certificate and a passport, based on Section 6 of the immigration law admitting students, and went to the American Consulate General in Shanghai for a visa. This done, I secured my ticket and boarded an American Mail liner for San Francisco. It was late August, 1908. There were about a dozen Chinese students on the same boat. Leaving the shores of my country seemed to cut away the last link that connected me with my earlier life. I was lucky in being a good sailor and was never sick during the twenty-four long days aboard ship. Perhaps this was due to the practice I had had in swinging for several weeks before embarking. I was good at it, for swinging is a Chinese garden pastime.

The liner was much larger and more luxurious than the Japanese steamer I had taken to Kobe the previous year. The most striking thing to me on board was the dancing. Brought up in a society where men and women did not mix freely, I could not at once reconcile myself to it. But after watching it several times I began to appreciate the beauty of it.

On the day of our arrival at San Francisco a port doctor came on board and carefully examined the eyes of Chinese students to see whether any of us had any trace of trachoma.

The first thing I had felt on landing was the power of the state through the instrumentality of the immigration officials and police. I began to wonder why the people of a republic enjoyed less individual freedom than did the people of China, which was an absolute monarchy. In China we scarcely felt the influence of the state. "Heaven is high above and the Emperor is far away."

We stopped over in San Francisco for a few hours to visit Chinatown. Then two of us who were bound for the University of California were taken to Berkeley by the president of the Chinese Students' Alliance there. In the evening we dined at a restaurant in Berkeley, the Sky Light, on Shattuck Avenue, each paying twenty-five cents for a dinner which consisted of soup, beef stew, and a piece of pie, with bread and butter and a cup of coffee. I took a room at Mrs. Coole's house on Bancroft Way. She was a talkative, elderly lady, very kind to the Chinese students. She told me that I must turn off the light before going out and shut off the water after washing; that I must not throw peanuts into the flush toilet or leave my money on the table; that in leaving the room I needn't lock the door, but if I preferred I might leave the key under the mat. "If you want anything," she said, "you just tell me. I know how a stranger must feel in a foreign country. Make yourself at home." Then she bade me good night and left the room.

As I had arrived in San Francisco too late to enter the fall session of the university, I had to wait for the next term. Meantime I got a coed of the university to coach me in English at fifty cents an hour. I spent all my time studying English; I read the *San Francisco Chronicle* regularly every morning and subscribed to a weekly magazine, *The Outlook,* for more serious study. By the aid of Webster's *Collegiate Dictionary,* which was always at hand and to which every doubtful word was referred, my vocabulary increased day by day and at the end of four months I could read papers and magazines quite freely.

In the beginning I found myself partially blind, deaf, and dumb so far as the English language was concerned. These difficulties had to be surmounted before I could hope to get along well in the university. By concentration and perseverance the first obstacle was largely overcome in the first four months and it was only a matter of time to reduce it completely. The second had to be removed gradually by listening to conversations and lectures. It was easier to understand lectures because they were in the form of organized thought and were slower and more distinct in delivery. Conversations were generally wider in range and carried on in a rapid succession of varied or disconnected groups of ideas in which one had difficulty in following the thread of thought. To listen to a play at the theatre was midway between the two.

It was most difficult, however, to overcome the dumbness. First of all, I had been started off wrong from the very beginning in China. The wrong habits were deeply rooted and it took time to dislodge them. In the second place, as I was ignorant of phonetic methods the mere effort to imitate a word did not necessarily lead to a correct pronunciation. For there are wide gaps between the tone uttered and the ear that hears it, and between ear and tongue— the ear does not necessarily catch the right tone, nor does the tongue always follow the ear in reproducing it. Moreover, California was not so hospitable a land socially for the Chinese as to make one feel congenial or at ease; I was always overconscious of this, slow to mingle with others and shy when others tried to approach me. Thus many available social connections were cut off, and as language improves only with intercourse, the improvement in the spoken language was indeed very, very slow. This hampered my participation in discussions, both in the classroom and out of it, when I later entered the university. As a rule I remained mute in class and when a question was put to me responded only by a blush. My professors were very considerate and on no occasion tried to exact an answer. Perhaps they realized my social plight, or excused me simply because I was a foreigner. At any rate, from my examination papers—in most cases above "B" grade—they knew I did my classwork conscientiously in spite of muteness.

Time flew—it was soon Christmas. On Christmas Eve I dined alone at a restaurant with better food than on the first occasion, and a larger bill. After dinner I strolled about the streets watching the happy family gatherings through the windows where curtains were not drawn. Christmas trees, some lighted with tiny electric lights and some with candles, were everywhere.

With a few Chinese friends on New Year's Eve I went across the bay to San Francisco. From the ferry we could see at a distance, on the other side of the bay, the Clock Tower bejeweled with hundreds of lights. Moving through the crowd to the exit on landing, one heard the player pianos going full tilt for their nickel's worth. As I followed the packed crowd streaming slowly along the main street, flooded with lights, my ears were deafened by toy bugles and rattles. People took particular pleasure in blowing and rattling at the ears of pretty ladies, who returned the compliment good-naturedly with smiles at the merrymakers. Paper streamers floated in the air and were strung around people's necks. Confetti showered on the crowd like many-colored snow. I branched off to Chinatown, where I found throngs admiring the window decorations with their Oriental touch. Firecrackers made you feel that you were celebrating New Year's Eve in China.

When the clock struck midnight people began to shout "Happy New Year!" at the tops of their voices, and to blow horns and shake rattles. More confetti and more streamers. This was my first New Year in America and I was impressed with the good-naturedness of the American crowd and the spontaneous play spirit of the grown-ups. They were a young race in their merrymaking.

I got back home quite late and pleasantly tired, went to bed, and slept soundly until late in the morning. After breakfast I took a walk in the residential section of Berkeley. The houses on the gentle slopes of the Berkeley hills were surrounded with flower beds and green lawns. Roses were in full bloom in the mild California winter, for Berkeley, like Kunming in China, is blessed with perennial spring.

After the New Year I looked forward to the beginning of the second term of the university in February. With new hopes and vigor I worked hard at my language study. When the term drew near I applied for admission on credits from Nanyang College in Shanghai and was entered in the College of Agriculture, with Chinese as a substitute for Latin.

Here I must explain why I turned to agriculture when my preparation was along literary lines. This was not a happy-go-lucky move as it might have been with many a young student; it had been carefully considered and decided upon in all seriousness. Since China was mainly agricultural, the improvement of agriculture, as I saw it, would bring happiness and prosperity to the largest number of people in China; moreover, I had always taken delight in plants and animals since my early years in the village, where farming was the main current of life. For national as well as personal reasons, therefore, agriculture seemed the most appropriate study to pursue. Another minor consideration was that as I was born a delicate child my health could be improved by having plenty of fresh air in the country.

I took botany, zoölogy, hygiene, English, German, and physical culture for the term—a period of three hours a week for each course except the last, which took six hours. We were told to buy textbooks at a bookstore on College Avenue, so I went to the store and asked, among other things, for so-and-so's *Botan'y,* with the accent on the second syllable.

"What is it you want?" the sales clerk demanded. I repeated the word with the same accent. He shook his head. "Sorry, haven't got it."

I pointed to the book on the shelf. He smiled and said, "Oh, excuse me, you mean bo'tany."

I was glad to have the book and also to learn the right pronunciation of the word. Again, we were told to observe certain plants in the botanical garden. Failing to locate the place, I asked a janitor where the bótanical garden was—with the accent on the first syllable.

"What?" he said. I repeated.

"Oh, oh—you mean the botan'ical garden," he responded after a moment, enlightened.

I would have liked to swear in good American slang if I had learned any. Years after, when I related the incident to an American friend in Peking, he told me the story of a Frenchman who was asked what difficulties he found in speaking English. The Frenchman replied with characteristic gesture, "Oh, English is easy— but the *abominable accent!*" pronouncing the last words in French. Indeed, the *abominable accent* has discouraged many a student who has tried to learn English and found himself caught in an intricate maze. Of course there are rules by which one can somewhat steer his way. But there are too many exceptions; often the exceptions are the rule, so that one has to consider each case and acquire them all gradually and with great pains.

I studied botany and zoölogy with great interest. I still remember the jocular remarks of the professor of botany as we were being taught to use the microscope, "Don't think you're going to see through the microscope a fly as big as an elephant. No—you can't see even a section of the fly's leg."

My interest in the observation of nature had its roots in the naïve nature study which, during my school days in China, I carried on outside of school as a sort of diversion after the day's tiresome classical study. My improvised observations years before and my interest in botany and zoölogy now all proceeded from a common source—curiosity. The one great difference lay in the tool used. The microscope is an extension of the eye and enables you to see minute particles which the naked eye can never hope to reach. Use of this tool has led to the discovery of microbes, whose limitless numbers are comparable to the stars—which in turn are studied by another extension of the eye, the telescope. I longed to make a pilgrimage to Lick Observatory to see the world's largest telescope, but for some reason or other did not go. Instead I paid twenty-five cents to look into a telescope on the streets to see the planets and was thrilled to behold silvery Saturn in its shining ring, sailing in the blue sky as I had seen it on a celestial map in school.

I stayed in the College of Agriculture for half a year. One of my friends had meanwhile been urging me to take up some branch of social science instead of a practical science like agriculture. He argued that though agriculture was very important, there were other studies more vital for China; unless we could solve our political and social problems in the light of modern developments in the West we could not very well solve the agricultural ones. Moreover, my world outlook would be limited, in agriculture, to a practical science and would not embrace anything beyond the narrow scope of that special field.

As I had studied Chinese history as well as the general outlines of Western history, and was familiar with the general development of national strength in various countries at various times, I could very well appreciate my friend's advice. It set me thinking, for I was again at the crossroads and must sooner or later make a final decision. As I have mentioned, I was always careful in making any decision as to a new field which would determine my future course of life.

Early one morning, on my way to a barn to watch the milking, I met a number of fresh-looking youngsters—pretty girls and lively boys—on their way to school. Suddenly an idea struck me: I am here to study how to raise animals and plants; why not study how to raise men? Instead of going to the barn I went up into the Berkeley hills and sat under an old oak tree overlooking beautiful sunlit San Francisco Bay and the Golden Gate. As I gazed into the bay, thoughts on the rise and decline of the successive dynasties in China presented themselves one after another. All of a sudden I saw as if in a vision children emerging like water nymphs from the waters of the bay and asking me to give them schools. I decided to take education as my major, in the College of Social Science.

It was already late in the morning when I rushed down from the hills, went directly to the Recorder's Office to see Mr. Sutton, and asked to be transferred from the College of Agriculture to that of Social Science. After some argument the transfer was granted. In the fall of 1909 I began to take courses in logic, ethics, psychology, and English history, and was thus launched on what became my real college career.

My student life moved along in an atmosphere of intellectual activity. Days and months rolled on smoothly and pleasantly. As the sands of time gathered, so grew my knowledge.

In logic I learned that thinking has its method—that is to say, we must think logically. There is a difference between inductive and deductive thinking. Observation is very important in inductive thinking, so I wanted to practice it. I began to observe the many things I came across on campus or near the university. Why were cows belled? Why do the leaves of the eucalyptus hang vertical? Why are all California poppies yellow?

One morning as I was walking along the slopes of the Berkeley hills I noticed a pipe from which water was flowing. Where did the water come from? I followed up the pipe line, which led me to the source, and rejoiced over the discovery. Quite high on the hills I began to wonder what was on the other side of them. I climbed over one hill after another and found that there were endless hills, higher and higher as I went farther and farther. Finally I gave up and took a path which led down to a number of farmhouses, finding by the way creeks and woods which I enjoyed immensely.

Of course the endless chain of observation running merely from one thing to another could lead only to disappointment. Finally I learned that observation must have a definite object and a definite purpose, not ramble aimlessly. The astronomer observes the stars, the botanist the growth of plants. Later I came to know that there is another kind of observation, a sort of controlled observation called experiment, by means of which scientific discoveries are made.

In the field of ethics I learned that there is a difference between ethical principles and rules of conduct. The principles tell you why certain accepted rules are desirable at certain stages of civilization, while the rules themselves merely exact observance without inquiry into the underlying principles and their relation to modern society.

As life in China was governed by accepted rules of conduct, the inquiry into their underlying principles created storms in my mind. The old moral foundations which we had taken as final truths began to rock as in an earthquake. Moreover my professor, Harry Overstreet, was not the kind of traditional teacher who simply believed in accepted truths and expected his students to do likewise; his searching mind led me to peer into every crevice in the foundation stones of moral principle. In class there were lively discussions, which I refrained from joining partly because of my deficiency in the spoken language and partly owing to shyness, which grew in me out of a sense of inferiority. For around the year 1909 China was in the darkest period of her recent history and we had very little self-confidence about her future. But I pricked up my ears and listened like an intelligent dog to its master, understanding the meaning but unable to talk.

We were required to read Plato, Aristotle, the Gospel of St. John, and Marcus Aurelius, among other sources. I was impressed with the all-searching mind of the Greeks as revealed through the two Greek philosophers; I felt that while the Confucian classics were richly tinged with moral sense, the Greek philosophers were permeated by all-piercing intellect. This led me later on to a study of Greek history and a comparative study of ancient Greek and Chinese thought. It also led me to understand what an important part Greek thought has played in modern European civilization, and why Greek has been regarded as an indispensable part of a liberal education.

With St. John I began to appreciate the meaning of love as preached by Jesus, stripped of creed and church. It is indeed the highest ideal to "love your enemy." If one could really love one's enemy there would be no enemy.

"Can you love your enemy?" the professor asked the class. There was no answer.

"I can't," the attentive dog yelped.

"You can't?" he smiled.

I quoted Confucius, "Love those who love you, but be fair to your enemy." Upon this he commented, "It's quite sensible, isn't it?" The class made no response. As we dispersed a young American boy came up to me and patted me on the shoulder. "Love your enemy! Tommyrot, eh?"

Marcus Aurelius talked like a Sung philosopher. He meditated and discovered reason as the measure of all conduct. Translated and put among the Sung philosophers, he could easily have passed for one of them.

Things European or American I always measured with a Chinese yardstick. This is the way that leads from the known to the unknown. To gain new experience based upon and constructed out of past experiences the way to new knowledge. For example, a child who has not seen an airplane can be made to understand it by reference to the flying bird and a "boat with wings." A child who has not seen a bird or a boat cannot easily be made to understand an airplane. A Chinese student learns to understand Western civilization only in the light of what he knows of his own. The more he knows of his own culture, the better able he will be to understand that of the West. Thus arguing in my mind, I felt that my midnight lucubrations on the Chinese classics, history, and philosophy in school in China were not labor lost. Only because of those studies was I now in a position to absorb and digest Western ideas. My work hereafter, I thought, is to find out what China lacks and take what she needs from the West. And in the course of time we will catch up with the West. With these views I grew more self-confident, less self-conscious, and more hopeful for the future.

My interests among the fields of knowledge were indeed rather broad. I took ancient history, English history, the history of philosophy, political science, and even Russian literature in English translation. Tolstoy absorbed me, especially his *Anna Karenina* and *War and Peace*. I attended many public lectures given by prominent scholars and statesmen and thus heard Santayana, Tagore, David

Starr Jordan, Woodrow Wilson—then president of Princeton—and many other scholars. Science, literature, the arts, politics, and philosophy all interested me equally. I heard Taft and Roosevelt. "I took the Panama Canal and let Congress debate about it," said the latter in one of his lectures in the Greek theatre. His emphasis and characteristic gestures still stand out clearly in my memory.

Traditional education in China seemed narrow, but within its walls one found a diversity of subjects almost encyclopedic. This apparently narrow education, it is not paradoxical to say, furnished the basis for a broad view of knowledge. My diversity of interests probably derived from my past training in that traditional body of thought. The ancient classics contain many branches of knowledge: history, philosophy, literature, political economy, government, war, diplomacy, and the like. They have never been narrow. After the classics, scholars were initiated into even such practical arts as agriculture, irrigation, astronomy, and mathematics. Thus the traditional Chinese scholar was no narrow specialist but had a broad foundation for learning. Moreover, an open-minded search for truth was the aim of Confucian scholars. Their deficiencies seemed to lie in the fact that their knowledge was rather limited to books. Book knowledge can be narrow in another sense.

In school I remember I was given a rhymed book which contained a great variety of subjects, starting with astronomy and geography and going on down to vegetables and insects, including between them such topics as cities, commerce, farming, travel, inventions, philosophy, government, and so on. Rhymes are easier to learn by heart and even at the moment of writing I am still able to recite a great part of that rhymed encyclopedia.

The Berkeley hills with their moss-green oaks and scent-laden eucalyptus, their fields of golden poppies and gardens of crimson roses bathed in smiling California sunshine, served as an ideal nursery for the native sons of the Golden West. I felt ever-grateful to share in the care and protection of my Western Alma Mater, in whose lap her foster son from the ancient Eastern empire was nursed to grow.

In this climate in which there was no very cold winter nor any very hot summer, it was indeed pleasant to live in a sort of perpetual spring for four long, enjoyable years. There was no rain to interrupt outdoor life except for winter showers which turned the grass on the hills green again and washed the roses in the gardens clear as with morning dew. Otherwise no inclement weather interrupted the performances in the Greek theatre, surrounded by its forest of eucalyptus. Shakespearean plays, Greek dramas, Sunday concerts, and public lectures were given in the open air. Not far away were the athletic fields in which intercollegiate games and track meets took place. Young Apollos strove hard for the fame of their alma mater. Beauty, health, and intellect were cultivated at the same time. *Mens sana in corpore sano*—was this ancient Greece re-enacted?

Almost in the center of the campus stood the campanile towering high above the other buildings. At the main entrance leading to College Avenue was Sather Gate with nude carvings standing out in vivid relief which invoked protests from parents who had daughters at the university. "Let girls see more of these nude figures of boys and they will be cured of their false decency," remarked my professor of ethics. We had Venus and other goddesses of the ancient Greeks in our reading rooms in the old library (later torn down when the new Doe Library was built), but there was no criticism from the parents of boys. When I saw these Greek figures for the first time I wondered why the authorities should put such "indecent" things at the fountain of wisdom. But later I assumed that they were meant to teach the idea of *mens sana*—sometimes translated as "a beautiful mind in a beautiful body." For with the Greeks beauty, health, and wisdom are one and indivisible.

The performance of *A Midsummer Night's Dream* among the oak groves on campus was really a masterpiece of beauty. Youth, love, beauty, and joy of life are all vividly portrayed in the pleasant masquerade.

Greek-letter fraternity and sorority houses were numerous on the campus. I was told what a wonderful life the members enjoyed together, but I had not visited any until on one occasion I was invited on a bargain—I was to vote for members of that fraternity for class president and other officers. They canvassed the whole class from a list; when they came to a classmate who was likely to vote for their opponents they would say "No good!" and mark the name "NG."

I was received with such cordiality as one would remember a lifetime. The vote was cast next day and I kept faithfully to my promise, for a "Chinaman's" word is as good as gold. I was glad to have made friends with quite a few fellow students during the campaign.

A few days after the election, for some occasion which I don't remember now, a bonfire was made. The glow of the flames lit up the happy faces of the young people. Boys and girls sang, ending each song with college yells. The crackling of the burning logs, the giggles of the girls and the shouts of the boys still echo in my ears. There in the light I came across a fellow student for whom I had cast my vote. To my great surprise his cordiality toward me had already turned to indifference. This is how things go in the world! His kindness to me had been paid for by my vote; the bills being paid, the account was squared—neither owed anything to the other. Thereafter I exchanged no more votes for cordialities and never again voted in college elections.

In the basement of North Hall was a student "co-op," at the entrance of which was a sign which read, "In God we trust, all others pay cash." The most prosperous business in the co-op was the sale of hot dogs at five cents apiece (cash). They tasted fine.

One memorable character on the campus—probably forgotten by my contemporaries but not by me—was the aged janitor of the philosophy building. He was tall and spare, with a very straight carriage. His eyes were deep-sunk in their sockets and his grey eyebrows grew very long, almost covering his eyes, like a Pekingese toy dog. From under his brows one could see him twinkling with friendliness and warmth of heart. We took a mutual liking to each other. After classes and sometimes on Sundays I was a frequent visitor to the basement where he had lived from the time when the university was a small college.

He had been a soldier and fought many battles under the Union flag in the Civil War. He lived in memories of the past and related to me many stories of the war and of his childhood. From him I learned that conditions in America in older days—it is almost a century now—were not very much better than in China then; in some respects worse. He told me that there had existed in his youth many kinds of money: English pounds, French francs, and Dutch guldens. I heard Lyman Abbott speak of this several years later in New York. Modern sanitation seemed to him nonsense. Once he showed me a roll of toilet paper and said, "Nowadays people die young with these sanitary things. We didn't have any sanitation or what you call modern medicine. Look at me, how healthy I am at my age!" He stood erect like a soldier at attention for me to look at him.

West Point was also a joke to him. "You think they can fight? No! They're puffed up by uniforms and sure know how to dress in a parade. But fighting—no. I can teach 'em. In one battle I killed a whole lot of rebels singlehanded. If they want to learn to fight, let 'em come to me!"

He still harbored a grudge in his heart against the Confederates after these long years. He said he once found a rebel lying wounded after a battle was over and tried to help him. "You know what that crittur did? He fired right at me." He leveled his angry eyes at me steadily as if I had been the culprit. "What did you do?" I ventured. "I shot the beast dead right on the spot," was the reply.

To me this old soldier-janitor was an inseparable part of the university. He thought himself so, too, for he had seen the place grow.

CHAPTER 10

CHINA IN AMERICA

BEFORE the end of October of my first year in America an important change had taken place in China. This was the death, in rapid succession, of the Emperor Kwang-hsü and the Empress Dowager. There were two versions to the story; one was that she died first, whereupon he was murdered by her followers in the fear that he would come back into power. The other was that, near death, she sent a eunuch to Yun Tai—the island palace in the Imperial Chung Hai Park where this strong-willed woman had kept her Imperial consort imprisoned ever since the short-lived reforms of 1898—who informed the Emperor, always in poor health, that Her Majesty the Illustrious Buddha, as she was called, wished him as a favor to take the medicine she sent. According to this version the poor imprisoned Emperor understood the message and obeyed, succumbing to the poison in a short time. The fact was made known to her before she died and she ordered the issue of an Imperial Edict by which the death of the Emperor was announced and his nephew, little Pu-yi, made successor to the throne.

Whatever the truth of it, the unanimous opinion of the Chinese students in Berkeley was that with the death of the "old woman," as the Empress Dowager was disrespectfully called, there would be plenty of trouble in China. It proved to be so. For with a baby Emperor on the throne and his inexperienced father, Tsai Hsun, as Prince Regent, the authority of the Manchu Dynasty fell into meteoric decline until its last vestige was swept away three years later by the Revolution of 1911.

In 1909 I had joined as an editorial writer the *Chinese Free Press*, Dr. Sun Yat-sen's revolutionary organ in San Francisco. One evening in the fall of that year, with my co-editor Liu Chun-yu, I called for the first time on Dr. Sun Yat-sen at a hotel on Stockton Street on the outskirts of Chinatown. My heart throbbed with excitement as we entered. Dr. Sun received us cordially in his room.

It was a small room with a couch, several chairs, and a small desk.
There was a wash basin by the window. The curtains were drawn.

Mr. Liu introduced me to the esteemed leader of China's revolutionary movement. His magnetic personality was such as to win
the confidence of any who had a chance to meet him. Dr. Sun's
ample and majestic forehead and strong dark brows gave signs of a
forceful intellect and indomitable will. His clear, inviting eyes revealed his candor of thought and warmth of heart, while his com-
pressed lips and set jaw made people readily understand that he
was a man of courage and decision. His general build was muscular
and sturdy, giving the impression of strong nerves and steady emotions. In conversation his line of argument was clear and convincing, whether you agreed with him or not; unless you wished to dis-
continue he would keep on untiringly expounding his theories to
you. He spoke slowly but distinctly and one felt behind his words
a deep sincerity. He also listened easily yet was not slow to catch essential points.

Later I found him to be an ardent reader of a variety of books,
both Chinese and English. He saved all the money he could to buy
books. He was a slow reader but had an extraordinary retentive
power. Dr. Sun's wide reading gave him a clear understanding of
the development of both Chinese and Western civilizations.

He enjoyed jokes—though he seldom jested—laughing heartily
when a good one was recounted to him.

He liked fish and vegetables for his meals, but seldom touched
meat and preferred Chinese to Western cooking. "Chinese food is
the best in the world," he would say.

Dr. Sun was a real democrat. He lectured in the streets of Chinatown in San Francisco. With banners of the Nationalist party
streaming in the air, he would stand on the sidewalk and talk to the
crowd gathering around him. He understood the psychology of the
man in the street and could reduce his own language to the simplest
terms. "What is revolution?" he would ask rhetorically. "Down with
the rule of the Manchus!" The crowd understood and joined in in
chorus. Then he would go on explaining in very simple language
why the Manchus must be done away with and what he would do
when a republican form of government was established in China—
how many benefits the people would reap from a new regime.

He would often size up an audience to which he was about to

speak, choose an appropriate subject, and improvise a suitable discourse, expressing himself with great eloquence. He usually carried the audience with him to the very end. He was always ready to speak for he possessed a remarkable ability to carry it with him.

Dr. Sun's deep understanding of human nature, his intense love of his country and people, and his insight into what China needed in building up her new nationhood gave him unquestioned leadership in the development of young China. Between travels in the southern and eastern states and in Europe he came back every so often to San Francisco, where Liu Chun-yu and I had the pleasure of seeing him whenever he came.

On October 8, 1911, at about eight o'clock in the evening, Dr. Sun came into the editorial room of the *Chinese Free Press* wearing a dark overcoat and a derby hat. He appeared happy, though not in the least excited, as he said calmly that from news he had received through certain sources things seemed to be turning out well— the group of people who had laid plans for revolution in Hankow and Wuchang were ready for action. Two days later news reached San Francisco that revolution had broken out in Wuchang. This was the revolution of October 10, 1911, which eventually overthrew the Manchu Dynasty. On that day the Republic of China was born.

Urgent cablegrams advised Dr. Sun to come back to lead the revolution. He left San Francisco and returned to China by way of Europe. On January 1, 1912, he was inaugurated at Nanking as Provisional President of the Republic, and China entered on a new life.

Under Dr. Sun's guidance, for three consecutive years Liu Chun-yu and I wrote editorials for the *Chinese Free Press*, each of us at first writing one every other day. We supplied these articles to the paper while studying at the university, often burning midnight oil to finish a piece for the next morning's issue. The university work was by no means light and we felt—especially myself—the burden of this extra labor. After the successful revolution Liu went back to China and I had to bear the brunt of the daily editorial war. Though I felt deeply for the future of my country, the constant practice of writing against my will ultimately killed in me all interest in writing. In the unremitting pressure and rush under which I labored, the quality of production deteriorated and I formed the habit of loose and hurried thinking and careless choice of words. Sometimes my thought flowed reluctantly as water through a clogged pipe, but the words still rushed from my pen like a swarm of aimless wanderers. I was rather exasperated at these unwelcome guests. I would, however, let them go since they filled up the columns.

When I first took the job I found a real pleasure in writing, fitting words to thoughts like coins into a slot machine. Only when I tried to jam all the coins into the slots at once, the machine got clogged and refused to take in the superfluous ones, which spilled all around the floor, so to speak. This is how meaningless words fill space when you are forced to write in a rush.

After my graduation in 1912 I gave up the job and felt a great release. Thereafter I feared writing as a schoolboy would Latin composition. When labor is drudgery and done in a hurry as well, no good work will come of it. The bad habits thus formed were difficult to eradicate for years after.

On the Pacific coast during my college days about fifty thousand Chinese immigrants clustered around the centers in the various cities—Sacramento, San Francisco, Oakland, San José, Los Angeles, and others—with isolated small groups or individuals dotting the smaller towns and villages. These centers were called Chinatowns. Chinatown in San Francisco was the largest of all, with a Chinese population of more than twenty thousand. The main street was originally Dupont Street, but its name was afterward changed to Grant Avenue, for what reason I do not know. Grant Avenue was a very prosperous street. Oriental bazaars, Chinese restaurants known as "chop suey houses," fortunetelling stands, gambling houses in the guise of social or literary clubs, and temples for worship of Chinese gods—called "joss houses"—attracted the attention of tourists, sight-seers, and pleasure-seekers. Once a pretty young American told me that she had seen a wonderful thing in an Oriental bazaar—a Buddha sitting in an artichoke; and had eaten bird's nest soup, sharks' fins, and chop suey in a Chinese restaurant. She was much excited over it. Her younger sisters listened with wondering eyes and gaping mouths. "I declare!" said the grand-mother, looking over her spectacles while her hands were busy with her knitting.

"How do you eat soup with chopsticks?" a younger sister asked curiously.

"As you do with your soda straws, my young lady," said I. All joined in the laughter.

In small towns my countrymen kept laundry establishments. Day in and day out they washed and washed from dawn till dusk and often late into the night. The reason many American families liked to send their laundry to the Chinese was because hand wash did not wear out the materials as easily as machines. These hard-working sons of the Celestial Empire saved every bit of their earn-ings by living a frugal life; they slung silver or gold pieces into the savings bags hidden under their beds and made liberal contribu-tions to the cause of Dr. Sun's revolutionary movement or sent money home to support their families and relatives in Canton, thus helping to enrich the villages of their province.

Kwangtung was the richest province of China, not only because the people did prosperous business in Hongkong and elsewhere but because it was the reservoir into which gold trickled from all parts of the world where there were Chinese colonies—Malaya, the Dutch East Indies, the Philippine Islands, North and South Amer-ica, etc. It was from this province that most of the émigrés from China originally came.

The Chinese working and living in foreign lands, numbering in the millions, were not there to exploit. Rather, their labor has been exploited. They had no capital other than the flesh and blood they were given in their mothers' wombs. With hard work, frugality, and endurance, they labored like bees carrying their tiny specks of sweetness from distant flowers to build up honeycombs in China. There was no political power to back them up, and they carried no guns. They helped to build railroads, open mines, raise rubber; in return for their labor they received a few dollars or shillings or rupees or guldens for a day's hard work. Some, to be sure, especially in Singapore and the Dutch East Indies, became rich and owned palatial mansions and villas, living like maharajahs. A number rose to the level of the middle class and owned property. But the rich and well to do were in the minority; the rank and file had to work hard, and only by hard work managed to make a living and put by some savings.

Among the Chinese in America there were neither very rich nor very poor. Most of them were honest, hard-working people. Almost all had some savings to contribute to that great reservoir, the province of Kwangtung. Their mode of life was mainly Chinese. Taking a boat along the Sacramento River, one would see Chinese towns or villages perched on the banks with bold Chinese signboards in front of the shops. One felt as if he were sailing on the Yangtze River or the Grand Canal in China.

I landed once at one of these Sacramento River Chinatowns and stayed with the owner of an asparagus plantation, Tin San, a friend of Dr. Sun Yat-sen. He treated me to tender asparagus, fat and juicy. Thereafter, whenever I had asparagus for dinner I thought of him. He had a cannery for this delicious vegetable, under American brand names. So I often think that some of the American canned asparagus may have been raised and canned by the Chinese. His way of making money was really good and ingenious. He kept places of amusement for his men, arguing that they must have some diversion after the day's work and if he had not established these houses they would go to other places run by his neighbors. He wanted the water to flow into his own gardens, so to speak, to feed his own plants. His plants—or rather dollars— did indeed grow from the voluntary contributions of his men to these amusement places.

The Chinese immigrants in America as well as elsewhere were truly loyal sons and daughters of that Flowery Kingdom. The men wore queues and some of the women even practised foot-binding. In the streets of Chinatown in San Francisco one could find fortunetellers. One such man who was telling a white man's fortune said to him, "Good luck. By and by, plenty of money." A Negro standing by wanted to have his fortune told and was very much pleased to hear the same words repeated to him. Everything would have been all right if the prophet had stopped there. But he went on to say, "By and by, no more black. Like him—" pointing with his index finger at the white man. The Negro instead of being pleased got mad and kicked over the fortuneteller's stand. This was a case where compliments, overdone, become insults.

There were grocery stores selling salt fish, eels, edible snakes, bean sauce, sharks' fins, birds' nests, dried abalones, and other Cantonese stuff brought to America from Canton or Hongkong. Once I went to one of the groceries and tried to buy something. Failing to make the man understand my poor Cantonese dialect, I wrote on paper what I wanted. An old woman standing by saw my writing and being ignorant of the fact that China has only one written language for the whole country, despite her many dialects, was surprised and asked, if this Chinese cannot speak Chinese (meaning Cantonese), how can he write it? A group of curious people gathered around me. One who could speak enough mandarin to make me understand asked, "Have you ever been in the provincial capital of Canton?" "No," I replied. "Then where did you do your shopping?" "Shanghai," I laughed, and went away with a bottle of bean sauce and a package under my arm.

Schools in Chinatown still stuck to the old curriculum. Pupils were taught to read aloud the old books just as I had been taught in China. The American schools not far away had no influence on them.

These were the times before the revolution. After that date Chinatown began to change, for China herself was changing— changing rapidly. In the course of a few years the fortunetellers disappeared. The number of queues fast decreased until they were gone. The young girls stopped their foot-binding. The schools were reformed and adopted a modern curriculum; more children were sent to near-by American schools. Chinatown resisted the in- fluence of its American neighbors but followed in the footsteps of the mother country in reforms and mode of living. These loyal sons and daughters of China!

CHAPTER 11

NEW YORK

As THE years went on my mental horizon extended and I became more and more self-confident. In 1912 I was graduated with honors in education and went to Columbia University in New York City for my postgraduate work.

Here I learned the method and acquired the spirit of scientific research as applied to social phenomena. Among the professors who taught me untiringly, from whom I drew my inspiration and to whom I am greatly indebted, there is one I wish to mention particularly because of his connection with Peking University. He is Professor John Dewey, who taught Dr. Hu Shih and myself at Columbia, and later through his writings, lectures, and personal contacts with contemporary thinkers in China, during his two-year sojourn as visiting professor at the National University of Peking, influenced Chinese educational theories and practice to a great extent. His pragmatism finds its counterpart in the practical Chinese mentality. But he warned us that "if a thing is too practical it becomes impractical."

Of the years at Columbia I shall not speak in detail. They were most enriching. I was now acclimated to America and to the language and could absorb what came within my orbit with less overwhelming effort of adaptation.

In New York I was impressed by the skyscrapers, the rapid circulation of subways and elevated trains, the dazzling lights of moving advertisements on the tops of tall buildings; the theatres, night clubs, hotels, and restaurants; fashionable Fifth Avenue, Greenwich Village, the East Side slums, and so on.

On the social side one found Yankees, Irish, Poles, Italians, Greeks, Jews, all living side by side in a neighborly way, and a few thousand of my own countrymen clustered around Chinatown. In my time there were in the great metropolis five hundred Chinese restaurants catering to the public. The agglomerated cosmopolitan mass of the city population, with its politicians, gangsters, scholars, artists, financiers, industrialists, multimillionaires, slum-dwellers, and many others, was fundamentally an American product. There is nothing further from the truth than to say, "When you get into New York, you get out of America." America alone is capable of producing such a great, highly industrialized city and vast melting pot. There was little racial friction. For in New York anyone can do anything he likes if he knows how to stay inside the law. Everyone is permitted to go his own way if he observes a certain degree of public decency. Anyone can expound his theories of society and government if he can find an audience.

Liberty within the orbit of the law and freedom of thought and speech within the domain of reason had free play. Great industries, international banking and big business, and the utilization of invention, engineering, and material resources to the fullest extent, all showed the spirit and application of Americanism. In New York one found it in concentrated form. In the midst of this concentration the eye of the observer is easily dazzled by the glaring lights, thus losing sight of Americanism in its normal state as one would see it elsewhere in America.

During the summer vacations I would go to the Adirondacks. One summer, with a few Chinese friends, I went to Rainbow Lake and camped on one of its hilly islets. In the daytime we went boating and fishing on near-by lakes. Our catches were quite rich—pike weighing over ten pounds were among our prizes for a day's work and pleasure. Big fat frogs were found a-plenty around the island on which we camped. I had learned to catch frogs in my village childhood in China and carried the art over to America. A rod, a string, and a hook rounded out of a good-sized needle with a piece of red cloth attached to it were sufficient for frog fishing; the improvised outfit worked wonders. Usually we could catch two dozen of them in an hour. This was more than enough for two delicious meals a day. The people living around the lake had never eaten frogs—they admired our art of frog fishing but at the bottom of their hearts must have thought, "The heathen Chinee is peculiar."

In the evenings we often joined their barn dances to the tune of the fiddle played by the host. One of the songs they all sang, a part of which still lurks in my recollection, runs something like this:

All the hinges are rusty
And the doors are falling down,
The roof lets in sunshine and rain—
And the only friend I have
Is the little yellow dog
On the trail behind the bush.

This reflects the loneliness of a solitary hermitage in the mountain region, but to the city-dwellers it depicted a charming, quiet life.

Sometimes we penetrated into virgin forests where the luxuriant leaves veiled the sky like thick clouds. The junipers growing along the trail gave out their aromatic scent, and we picked fragrant evergreen branches to make pillows which would bring nature to our beds and send out floating odors to sweeten our gentle sleep.

Sometimes we lost our way back in the dense woods. We would listen then for the whistle of a train to lead us to the railroad tracks. Experience taught me later to take a compass when going into the woods.

To go back to city life after staying in the country for some time is really a pleasure. The city looks refreshed when you come back to it; the country seems doubly enchanting if you go there from the city. It is all because of the change, the contrast. When foreigners go to China they are often charmed with the complacent Chinese life and with the scenery. A Chinese in a foreign land is often delighted with its city life. So you frequently find a Westerner more enthusiastic about things Chinese than the Chinese themselves, and vice versa. It is a change, a contrast, which breaks monotony and refreshes the mind. But the intrinsic values of things are not altered by these changes of mental approach.

During my student days in New York Sino-Japanese relations took a turn which left the two countries at loggerheads later on. After some fifty years of reforms, Japan showed her strength in 1894 by delivering a blow at China. Instead of resentment and enmity, China returned good for evil. The unfriendly act, contrary to expectations, invoked rather the admiration and gratitude of the Chinese people—admiration for Japan's great reforms, accomplished in the short span of fifty years, and gratitude for thus awakening China to her future possibilities. It rekindled the dying flame of hope in China's heart. For some time thereafter she lived under inspiration drawn from Japanese example.

Students went to Japan by thousands every year to study. China's new military, police, and school systems were developed and headed by students returned from Japan. Through Japan, China began to see the significance of Western civilization. The Russo-Japanese War gave further impetus to China's reforms—Japan was held in the hearts of the Chinese as an idol.

China absorbed Western civilization gradually through her neighbor, but soon realized that the currents flowing in Japan, from which she drank the waters of modern wisdom, had their source in Europe or America. It was a happy coincidence that America returned the Boxer indemnity; China used it to send more students to the United States than she had done before. Students had previously been sent to Europe and America on government scholarships or by private means, but the number was small. Those who returned direct from the West now grew in numbers and began to occupy some of the key positions in government, industry, commercial enterprise, and educational fields. Missionaries, especially American, helped to educate the youth of the country through mission schools.

Thus, culturally speaking, China began to drift away from Japan. The Japanese idol dwindled in Chinese hearts. And the Japanese were not aware of it.

Taking advantage of the first World War, in 1915 Japan suddenly delivered to Yuan Shih-kai's government the famous Twenty-One Demands, enforcement of which would have reduced China to a Japanese protectorate. This rash act grew out of the upset of the balance of power in the Far East, owing to the preoccupation of the Western Powers with the war and the rapid decline of the military might of Tsarist Russia. It turned China's face once and for all toward the West, and the consequent parting of the ways of the two countries was to change the course of international politics in the years to come. Had Japan been farsighted enough to lend a helping hand to her neighbor in her period of distress, China would have remained a friend. What would have been the effect of this union upon World War II?

While I was in New York the substance of the Twenty-One Demands was allowed to leak out by the Chinese Legation at Washington. It created consternation in all the capitals of the Western Powers. A boycott of Japanese goods spread like wildfire throughout China as a feeble protest, but the Japanese navy was concentrated at important Chinese ports and her armed forces mobilized in south Manchuria and Shantung. On May 7, 1915, four months after the presentation of the demands, Japan sent an ultimatum to Yuan Shih-kai and two days later it was accepted.

By force of circumstances the demands in the course of time dwindled to virtually nothing. But the admiration and gratitude of China were thus turned into fear and suspicion which were to grow in the hearts of her millions. Thereafter, whatever Japan had to say China received with suspicion; whatever she did China watched with fear. The more she professed sincerity, the more China suspected a sinister design behind it.

"Why don't you love us as we love you?" our neighbor would ask. "How can we love you when you make love with the bayonet?" we would reply.

"Why should China play off the Western Powers against Japan?" a Japanese general asked me one day, a few years before the Mukden Incident.

"To maintain the balance of power and thus save China from being swallowed up by you," I replied frankly.

"Japan swallow up China! How could we? It's silly."

"It is not silly, General. Didn't Japan deliver us her Twenty-One Demands during the last war, when the Powers were preoccupied? If those demands had been carried into effect, Japan would be in a position to gobble up all China."

"So, so—?" said the general, as if in surprise.

"Yes, yes," I replied briefly.

Part III

THE NEW CHINA

CHAPTER 12

RAPID CHANGES

IN THE midst of American mobilization for a European war for the first time in her history, in June, 1917, I left for home with mixed feelings. The last night I spent in Hartley Hall at Columbia my mind was too much occupied to sleep and I lay the whole night in meditation. The hours ebbed away until the early summer dawn came in at the window through the creeping vines. The morning air was mild and the petals of the roses were dew-laden. Near by, on the granite steps of the library, the Alma Mater was smiling her grave smile as if wishing her foster son Godspeed. As I stood at the window looking out on the familiar scene that had meant so much to me those five years, tears began to well up in my eyes. Was I to be torn away once and for all from the fountain of wisdom, leaving my friends behind? But it was my duty to go home, just as it had been my privilege to come.

In the afternoon I boarded a train at Grand Central for a city in Ohio. As the train crawled out of the station I kept looking back at the waving hands of my American friends, boys and girls, until they were lost to sight.

One friend accompanied me to Ohio to visit with friends of his there, and we were welcomed to the family by its charming hostess. The host had some sort of business in that city. There was no son in the family; the girl was the sunshine in the house. She was an attractive brunette with an oval face, and the warmth that poured from her young heart would endear her to anyone who met her.

We stayed for about two weeks. It was in the midst of registration and draft; the first groups gathered, marched on the streets, and were sent off for training. The sidewalks were thronged with people. Mothers, sweethearts, and friends bade good-by to their soldiers with kisses, tears, and throbbing hearts.

We formed rowing parties on moonlit ponds dotted with islets of gold and silvery lilies. Fireflies twinkled like moving stars. Fish splashed. The girls sang together—I still remember one of the songs they loved to sing:

> The June air is warm and tender.
> Why do you hold your petals to display?
> Are you afraid someone will
> Come and steal your heart away?

The frogs echoed with their ungainly chorus. The girls sang and sang until the breezes of late evening brought a chilly warning. Then we would all go ashore and walk home over the dew-laden grass under the slanting moon.

Time flew and soon the two enjoyable weeks came to an end. I said good-by to my friends and took a train for San Francisco. When the ocean liner steamed gently out of the Golden Gate I stood on the deck facing east thinking of my friends in New York. Good-by, my friends! Good-by, America!

It was still summer in Shanghai. The city had changed much during my absence of nine years. Many streets were wider and better paved. New roads had been built beyond the limits of the Foreign Settlement. Department stores, fashionable hotels, roof gardens, amusement parks, and cabarets had multiplied. Shanghai had caught up with the spirit of New York.

The number of schools had increased manyfold in the city during the years of my absence; all but a few, however, were supported by private or Chinese government sources—these few had been established years before by the international municipal government. I suppose the revenues of the Settlement must have increased a hundred times since these few outmoded schools had been founded decades earlier. But let the Chinese remain ignorant —they would be easier to control and exploit.

The young girls had bobbed their hair and wore short skirts up to their knees in the fashion of the day. No—excuse me—I mean they wore gowns down to their knees. For the dress of the modern Chinese girl was very sensible. It consisted of a straight piece of silk hanging from the shoulders, longer or shorter according to fashion. This had been originally the Manchu gown, and Chinese girls had adopted it after the downfall of the dynasty some six years earlier.

Here, there, and everywhere on the streets high-heeled shoes adorned the dainty feet of young women. When one heard quick heels tapping the sidewalks one felt at once that the rising generation were radically different from their mother. The old modesty had disappeared. They were also better-developed physically, however, thanks to the modern shoes. In the old days women had practiced foot-binding. The movement to free women's feet, as a part of China's reform program, began around the time of the Russo-Japanese War and went on rather slowly until after the Revolution of 1911. I think the high heels helped to accelerate it, for women were surely more ready to give up the practice of squeezing their little daughters' feet into tiny slippers when they saw others wearing dainty high heels.

Men had dropped their queues but still clung to the long gown. It was funny to see a long gown without a queue. But before long I found myself one of the multitude, for Chinese clothing is more convenient and comfortable. No one can resist the temptation of being comfortable and convenient at the same time—it is a matter of practical common sense.

There were still a few individuals who wore queues, especially among the old men. They did not see any sense in getting rid of it; the queue had grown on Chinese heads for more than two centuries and it would do no harm to have it for a few centuries more. There are always die-hards in any movement.

In America I had measured things American by the Chinese yardstick. Now I reversed the process, measuring things Chinese with the American yardstick, or most likely with a sort of hybrid stick, neither Chinese nor American but something of both, or vacillating between the two.

I pitied the rickshaw coolies who ran for a few coppers, out of breath, their sweating tanned backs turned toward you in the hot summer sun. It was something inhuman, my American yardstick would say. Once in a while I came across some of the beastly foreigners who kicked them like dogs—but no, in America I never saw a man kick a dog. Blood rushed to my head and I often wanted to kick back at the human beasts, but refrained from venting my noble sentiments when I saw extraterritoriality looming large behind them. Then I reverted to my ancestral patience. "Coward!" the American yardstick would say. "Patience," returned the Chinese stick of my forefathers. Stop using these rickshaws and have more busses and tramways. But what were the poor coolies to do to eke out their meager subsistence? Return to the farms? No, they were surplus farmers. Three ways were open to them: to turn bandit with the strong, petty thieves with the weak, or beggars with the still weaker. Well then, let them pull the rickshaws. Here you are in a vicious circle.

Build up industry, it will give them employment. But industry is impossible without a stable government. A stable government is hardly possible when there are so many surplus farmers in the country, always ready to join mercenary armies and fight for the warlords who pay them or who let them loose to plunder the people. Here is another vicious circle, difficult to break.

There was an improvement in the notice boards of the Settlement public parks. The list of regulations forbidding the entrance of Chinese as well as dogs now displayed the modified clause: "Respectable Chinese only are admitted." At last even the arrogant foreigners had begun to be aware that there was something to be respected rising in China.

So much for Shanghai.

The great eastern seaport and trading center was now connected by rail with Soochow to the west and Hangchow to the south, cities both regarded as paradises on earth. The line ran from Soochow farther west to Nanking, connected by a ferry across the Yangtze River; and north through Tientsin to Peking, then capital of the Republic. The southern branch stopped at Hangchow and remained as yet to be connected with Ningpo.

My home was not very far from Ningpo, native city of Generalissimo Chiang Kai-shek. It is one of the five treaty ports but has never come into any considerable importance as a port, for the rapid growth of Shanghai as one of the great ports of the world overshadowed it. Three lines had ships running between Shanghai and Ningpo nightly, both incoming and outgoing; two of these were British companies and the third the China Merchants Navigation Company. These ships were the models for the steamless paddlewheel "steamboat" my father had built so many years earlier and failed to make go. My brother and I took a second-class cabin on one of these boats.

There was not much change in the life of the passengers in twenty years. The gangways and decks were packed with human sardines and one could hardly set foot on the floor without stepping on somebody. We went on board about five in the afternoon to occupy our berths. Hawkers came by in great numbers, selling every kind of goods that a household might need, mostly imported manufactures. Fruit sellers brought bananas, apples, and pears on board. My brother and I had an argument. He wanted to buy the partly rotten fruit because it was much cheaper. "No," I argued, "you will pay much more for the doctor's bill."

"Ha, ha! I have been eating rotten pears and apples for years," he said. "They taste better. I have no trouble from them." He picked up a big, partly decayed red apple, bit off the bad parts and ate the rest. I shuddered. He laughed.

Before dawn we passed the fortresses of Ningpo Harbor, which fired a cannon ball that hit and killed a French admiral in the Sino-French War of 1885.

Day dawned. Clamorous voices from the dock rose to my ears. Streams of porters rushed up, fighting for luggage. The slightest negligence would find your possessions removed without permission. My brother and I elbowed down through the packed crowd, closely following our porters lest they walk off with our belongings.

Ningpo was practically the same as it had been nine years earlier. The air was laden with the smell of salt fish. I felt at home with this smell, for salt fish had been a staple food since childhood. Ningpo is a fishing town and large quantities of salt are produced not far away. We followed our porters to the station and found a train waiting to depart for Yuyao, our home city. Along the railroad I saw miles of well-cultivated fields cushioned with rippling rice that flowered in the autumn morning sun, unfolding like a never-ending scroll of landscape painting before the windows of the moving train. The morning air was stimulating and laden with the scent of flowering rice. Oh—this is my homeland!

As the train pulled into the Yuyao station my heart throbbed with excitement. We crossed the river by a long stone bridge built centuries ago. The ebb tide was racing down the river; through the arches of the bridge anglers could be seen casting their lines in the flowing water. The bridge was called Wu-shen, meaning "brave and victorious," because at the bridgeheads some four centuries ago people fought from time to time to defend the city against the invasions of pirates of uncertain origin from the Japan Sea. The Chinese believed they were Japanese, but Japanese historians deny it.

It was late in the morning when we hurried into the court-yard steeped in brilliant autumn sun. My father stood on the granite steps leading to the spacious hall. He was somewhat aged, his hair turning grey; otherwise in good health and splendid spirits. His kind eyes and smiling lips glowed with the tender emotions that flow from the heart of a loving parent. Before him my brother and I bowed three times in respect; the old way of kowtowing on one's knees had, among certain sections of the people, passed into history with the vanished dynasty.

Father had given up his queue but still wore Chinese slippers. He did not say much: silence conveyed much more than words on such an occasion. Then we all entered the hall. Stiff-backed chairs arranged symmetrically along the walls showed little sign of change in his way of living. The couplet panels inlaid with mother-of-pearl shone on the back walls. On the right side one read: "Fishes have greater freedom in the vastness of the sea," and on the left: "Birds take broader liberty in the wide span of the sky." Between the two panels was a painting of bamboo shadows which seemed to bend in an autumn breeze, all the leaves pointing with the wind. These things all speak of a contented, quiet, and unchanging life.

Behind the hall was a narrow strip of back yard. Miniature mountain scenes set in large rectangular pots brought landscape within the high walls. Tiny temples and pagodas perched on the miniature mountains, and dwarf trees that looked centuries old grew around them. Little monkeys with still smaller babies sitting innocently by their side sat here and there in the quiet recesses of the mountains. They all looked so cute that I wished some of them could grow life sized and jump into my lap. There was a tiny bamboo grove flourishing around a toy pavilion. Goldfish snapping at the air and shrimps stretching out their claws for food all enjoyed undisturbed life in the imitation ponds. All of this led one's mind to nature.

On hearing of my return old Mr. Liu came to call in the afternoon. He had told me stories in my childhood. How we children loved him! That day he recounted many amusing things. He described how the people acted on learning of the successful revolution. All the queues in the city vanished overnight. Young people bought foreign clothes and looked like monkeys in them. And how the short skirts and bobbed hair invaded the city later on! But for him the cutting of the queue that had grown on his head for more than seventy years was sufficient support of the revolution and the Republic. At first he wondered how the world could go on without an emperor sitting upon the dragon throne in Peking, but after some time he was sure that a republic with a president had the same power of maintaining peace and order in the country. At any rate, he said, "Heaven is high above and the Emperor is far away." It was up to the local authorities to do their job of maintaining peace, and they did it well.

When the Taipings had invaded the city some half century before, he said, heads went off shoulders with the queues. Now we lost only our queues and retained our heads. Talking thus, he touched his grey head with his bony fingers in such a comical way that it made everybody laugh. At dusk, after an early supper, in taking his leave he happened to slip on the steps leading to the courtyard. Someone rescued him, holding him up by the arms. He shook his head and joked, "Three thousand years ago Grandfather Chiang at the age of eighty met King Wen and helped him to build a new kingdom. Now Grandfather Liu at the same age may meet King Nian of the other world and help him to govern his invisible realm." He laughed heartily and went away in good spirits.

Several days later word came that "Grandfather" Liu had passed into the invisible realm. For me, I lost my childhood friend and old companion, and there were no more stories from his endless fountain of wit.

A school which my sister and I had established some fifteen years earlier had been turned into a district government school for girls. A hundred girls or so were studying there. They ran and laughed in the playgrounds and rode high in the air on the swing. A new generation of womanhood was in the making. They played Western tunes on a portable organ; "Swanee River" and "Tipperary" and popular Chinese tunes were wafted through the doors and over the walls.

I stayed at home about a week and then went to the country to pay a visit to the village of the Chiangs. There the children of my childhood had grown to maturity. The grownups of older days had come to old age, their hair turning grey. The old people of days gone by had retired to their graves, except for a few who were still alert, witnessing the turns of fortune in the village.

The village did not look as bad as I anticipated. The banditry of early days had subsided, for people had now adjusted themselves to new trades and many had gone to Shanghai, which was able to accommodate larger numbers as commerce and industry expanded. Change, like birth, gives pain, but after the delivery the mother comes back to her normal state and feels happy with the newly born. Change that China had once hated had come to stay, ever deepening and widening, until she was constantly on the onward march—whither and for what purpose her teeming millions knew not.

My aunt whom I called the Great Mother had been bedridden for months. She was very happy on seeing me, made me sit by her side and stretched out her feeble hands to touch mine. She told me all about the births, marriages, and deaths which had occurred in the village in the last sixteen years. The world was not the same as before, she said. So many changes and so many new things had come in. Women did not weave and spin any more because foreign cloth was much cheaper, and better too. They had not much to do now; some spent their time in quarrels with their neighbors and others devoted themselves to Buddha. The younger ones went to school. Girls made hair nets and crocheted napkins to be exported to America. There was good money in it, she said. The boys were sent as apprentices to factories and machine shops in Shanghai. They took to new trades and made more money. There was now a dearth of farm hands in the village, but there were no more bandits. Tranquility and peace had come to stay. When dogs barked at night people did not have to be anxious for their safety as they had ten years before.

But something very bad she noticed in the girls and boys who had been in schools. They called the worship of gods a superstition. They said that the burning of paper money before our ancestors was silly. To them there were no kitchen gods. All the images of gods in the temples were only blocks of wood and lumps of clay. They thought these images ought to be flung into the river, so as to banish superstition along with them. They said girls had the same rights as boys. The girls said they had the right to marry by their own choice, and to remarry after a divorce or the death of their husbands. The foot-binding of old days was a cruel and inhuman practice, they said. Foreign pills were much better than Chinese herbs. They said there was no such thing as ghosts or transmigration of the soul. Nothing would be left after death but a heap of chemical compounds. They said the only immortality was to render services to the people and the country.

She shook her head and sighed. "Do they teach these things in America?" she asked. I smiled. Apparently she did not like my smile. Perhaps she suspected that the crazy Americans were responsible for teaching Chinese boys and girls these silly notions, for she told me that an American missionary lady had come some time earlier to tell her not to worship idols.

A fat black cat leapt up on her bed and began purring around her pillows. "Are there cats in America?" she asked feebly. I said yes, and saw that she was already asleep. I left her with the purring cat whose soft paws rested upon her pillows and touched her cheek.

My niece, who had been listening all the time, ran out after me. She put her tongue between her teeth for a moment and said mischievously, "Grandma is too old for the change." After a month or so the old lady left this crazy, changing world.

I went to visit with another aunt of mine, whom I called Third Mother. She was a strong elderly lady. Her husband, my "Third Father," owned large farms. There were chickens, ducks, geese, and pigs in abundance. My aunt told me the tragedy of a childhood friend of mine who had speculated in gold in Shanghai and incurred heavy losses. He had lost his job and retired to his home village. The year before, he had committed suicide by taking a big dose of opium. His widow and children were destitute and one of the children had drowned in the canal while fishing for shrimp under the big soap tree.

My aunt snatched a big fat capon which struggled and screamed in her hands and dressed it herself. Later a delicious chicken dinner was served, with fish and shrimp in addition.

My uncle told me that people had used chemical fertilizers for cabbages the year before, and these grew to such enormous size that they thought the abnormal growth must contain poison. So they pulled them up and threw them away. But he kept his, bought them cheap from others, and salted them. They were tender and delicious. A wise old man he was.

An old woman who had held me in her arms when I was a baby came to the village to see me. She must have been over ninety and was partially deaf, yet had walked from her own village some four miles away. She examined me from top to toe and was satisfied to find nothing strange about me. This big boy was once a small, skinny child, she said, and very naughty. He bit his own brother on the knee and left purple marks on it. Then he cried and blamed his brother's knee for having hurt his teeth.

"Do you remember the two brothers who divided their father's property into equal parts when he died?" she asked. They had each got a wing of their father's house and had set a bamboo partition in the middle of the hall, which was thus evenly divided so that each could get an exactly equal portion. One kept a cow in his part and the other retaliated by making his a piggery. They even sawed the boat in two equal halves. The wicked brothers—may the gods curse them! Then there came a fire and turned their house into ashes. Heaven must have eyes.

They sold the lot and a big house of foreign style was later built on it. It belonged to a rich merchant who was in business in Shanghai. When the house was completed she paid a visit to it and got into such a labyrinth of passageways and stairs and doors that she was confused and could not find her way out. She tried the soft chairs and spring beds and was frightened when she sank deep into them. The most curious thing to her was the machine which the owner of the house had brought from Shanghai. When the wheels turned swiftly it lit up bulbs all over the house. The night was as brilliant as day.

The boy who took charge of the machine was the son of her neighbors. He had learned to operate it in Shanghai. She would never have thought that stupid boy could manipulate such an intricate piece of machinery. She stood far away from the swiftly turning wheels lest she be caught and turned into sausage or tough meat balls.

Another curious thing she noticed was that there was no Kitchen God in the kitchen. And the family worshiped no ancestors. The kitchen gods she did not mind so much, but how could a family have no ancestors? The master of the house believed a sort of religion which precluded the worship of other gods. She would not like to belong to that religion, because she wanted to go to any temple she chose and worship any gods she wanted to. She wondered how a god could be so jealous as to forbid people to worship other gods. She was willing to worship that god, for the man in his temple gave her quinine pills which cured her malaria last summer; but she wanted to bend her stiff knees to other gods also to ask for blessings.

She said she had scarcely enough to eat and often went hungry. My father gave her a monthly allowance in rice as a charity, but since her orphaned granddaughter had come to live with her the small girl ate a portion of it. I pulled out a twenty dollar bill and squeezed it into her hands. She scurried away happily, muttering, "From his childhood I know he is a kindhearted boy, a kindhearted boy."

Late one afternoon I made a visit to my mother's tomb. A pair of candles and a bunch of incense sticks were displayed before it. The air was still and streaks of smoke from the incense went straight up in the air. Instinctively I bent my knees to the ground and kowtowed. My childhood memories revived. Everything seemed to have happened only yesterday. I felt as if I were still a child paying respects to my mother. I wished her spirit could welcome me with open arms and caress me. I wished I could curl up on her lap and listen to her soothing lullabies. All my thoughts and feelings reverted to childhood days. My mother had died when I was only seven, so I had not much experience in mother love. Perhaps an imaginary mother was even tenderer and sweeter than a real one. A dead mother could not spank you and would not get cross with you when you were naughty.

From the village I walked some three miles through the rice fields to the railway station, on the banks of a placid lake, the reservoir that irrigated thousands of acres of land. It is surrounded on three sides by mountains famous for berries and bamboo shoots. Here I took a train to the bank of the Tsao-ao River. The railway bridge was uncompleted, for the materials ordered from Germany had been held up by the war. Construction of the railroad to Hangchow had also been suspended. A steamship line supplied the missing link. Most travelers took steamships and left the small boats struggling for existence.

I arrived at the Chien-tang River late in the afternoon and crossed it in twenty minutes by a steam ferry. The rowed ferryboats of my high-school days had disappeared.

By sunset I found myself in Hangchow, comfortably settled in a hotel overlooking the West Lake. The sun was sinking behind the thunder peaks, casting red, golden, and purple beams up into the sky. On one side the needle-sharp Pao Su Pagoda stood clear on the mountaintop in the evening light, while directly opposite, in the valley across the lake, the squat Thunder Peak Pagoda was silhouetted against the distant shady blue mountains. Tiny pleasure boats dotted the rippling lake. Fish splashed in the water. Birds flew homeward. Villas and temples perched on the mountainside were gradually enveloped by a thin veil of evening mist, leaving only the streams of smoke from their chimneys standing motionless in the still air. An utter peacefulness stole over me. Despite all modernism, the West Lake retained its enchantment as of old.

But things had changed. My reverie was soon broken by the tapping of the high heels which adorned the short-skirted, bobbed-haired young women of fashion parading the lake boulevard. This new section of the city had been during my school days the seat of the Tartar or Manchu garrison. The Revolution of 1911 had razed it to the ground and upon its ruins a new town had been built, with wide streets and ugly-looking buildings in semi-foreign style. In place of medieval barracks, restaurants, theatres, wine-shops, and tea pavilions had sprung up, and an amusement park, all catering to week-end tourists who came by railway from Shanghai. Hangchow had become a tourist center.

Chekiang College, which I had attended years before, was closed and the buildings had been turned into offices for the new governor. The once-palatial yamen of the Imperial governor had burned during the revolution, leaving a vast rectangular space in the heart of the city overgrown with wild plants and grass.

Revolution had come to Hangchow without shedding a drop of

blood. The commanders of the new army met and sent a few pieces of light artillery into the streets in the dark of night. Without firing a shot they forced the Imperial governor of the province to surrender. The army then set his yamen on fire as a symbol of the revolution and the city was lit up with its flames. The Manchu garrison entrenched itself in its own walled city but surrendered after negotiations in which it was promised that no one would be molested. Mr. Kwei Han-hsiang, a Manchu leader, accepted the terms on behalf of the garrison. He was, however, seized by his personal enemies and shot, on the false charge that he was plotting a revolt. It was a case of sheer murder. The newly elected governor, Tang Shuo-chien, a famous old litterateur, was indignant over this cowardly act and threatened to resign, but the matter was patched up until he was called to Nanking to take up the portfolio of Minister of Communications under the presidency of Dr. Sun Yat-sen.

Northeast of the modern town which had replaced the Manchu city, rows of shacks, totaling five hundred rooms, had been erected to house the families of the former garrison. Some had already melted away into the vast ocean of China's multitudes and left their houses vacant. In the course of a few years all the remnants of the once-conquering race had vanished into the common stream of life of the once-conquered. The Manchus were gone forever. Pictures of their lives still linger in my memory, but the stories about them have sunk into folklore. It is left to history alone to tell the rise, decline, and fall of the Manchu Dynasty.

The quaint old teahouses at which I used to sip my tea quietly with the lake view filling the windows had disappeared in the face of the diabolic modernization; only one or two lingered to recall the memories of the good old days. This was the kind of time-mellowed teahouse I still loved to frequent. I would go there and read Tang poems over a cup of Hangchow tea. It took one back to the dear old days.

I have said that the city was the center of the silk industry. Some factories had introduced textile machines, but many of the smaller establishments still retained the hand looms. A college of engineering had been established in which practical courses in textiles were given. Graduates who had taken courses in mechanical engineering set up small machine shops in the city, with machines run by electricity. The city now had electric light and a telephone system. Hangchow seemed on the eve of industrialization.

I stayed for about a week, visiting many historical sites to refresh my boyhood memories. As I wandered away from the center of commercial activity I found the old life less affected by modernization. The charm of old days still remained intact in the mountain regions and out-of-the-way villages. The monasteries surrounded by tall trees and bamboo groves stood as calmly as they had centuries ago. The life of the monks had undergone little change; they chanted their Buddhist hymns as before. The villagers raised their tea and mulberry leaves as their forefathers had done. A few imported articles were to be seen here and there, but the quantity was negligible. However, the spearhead of future modernization had already reached them—in the schools, where modern textbooks were in use. The mental attitude of the coming generation was changing, under the influence of modern education, in spite of unchanged ways of living. Seeds of new ideas sown in the minds of the young were bound to sprout in the course of time.

CHAPTER 13

WARLORDS

In MY youthful days I noticed that civil ranks came invariably above the military. Imperial officers wore buttons of different colors at the tops of their red-tasseled hats. The red button was highest in rank; next came the pink, then dark blue, brilliant blue, white, and finally golden, the lowest. Often my wondering eyes watched a military pink-button, though higher in rank, bowing before a blue-button civil official. It was explained to me that the Imperial system had chosen to put the military under control of the civil in order to eliminate the evils of military dictatorship in the country. Through centuries of history we had learned that when the country came under the control of warlords it was divided into spheres of influence; the authority of the Imperial Court became a mere shadow and peace and order vanished like a bubble. We learned this lesson from the later Tangs. Thus there was a popular saying that "good iron is not to be beaten into nails, and good men are not to be made into soldiers." We were taught to look down upon soldiers. I remember that a man of questionable character in one of our neighboring villages joined the army, and when he came home on leave we used to avoid him like a plague. It was borne in upon us that soldiers were a bad lot, something to be despised, feared, and detested.

On the other hand, when a country sank into military impotence it lost all power of resistance before the onslaught of powerful invaders; thus it was that the Sungs fell into the hands of the Mongols and the Mings into the hands of the Tartars. So we were between the devil and the deep sea. What should be our choice?

China must be saved—saved from powerful invaders by land on the north and by sea from the east and south. What, then, was to be done? Build up a modern army in which modern weapons of war would be employed and soldiers well trained and imbued with patriotism. How could we look down upon soldiers? They were the defenders of the land, the saviors of China from partition by the Western Powers. Despise them? By no means—we must elevate and honor them, even worship them. Or who would join the army?

Our people began to argue in their minds. As necessity is the mother of invention, we organized a modern army with imported weapons, modern uniforms, and military bands. Once I saw such an army on the march, bugles blowing, drums beating. It was inspiring. I imagined myself grown up and joining them in the march —marching to victory! Meanwhile I found my real self standing among the silent crowd and watching, overwhelmed with joy. It was my first glimpse of a modern army. Yes—we must honor the soldiers and the commanding officers. Hereafter only good men should be made into soldiers. We must depend upon them to regain the past glories of China. In the old armies of yesterday the soldiers wore jackets and carried bows and arrows, or in some cases obsolete guns discarded and sold to China by European countries. How different from the modern army of today!

While I was studying at Chekiang College in Hangchow I saw a former student who had just come back from a military academy in Tokyo on a visit to the college. He was in military uniform, spick and span, carrying a sword in its shining sheath. A future great general of the Chinese army—how our hearts rushed out to him!

There were a number of embryo generals of that kind who came back from Japan and were entrusted with the duty of organizing new armies. In the course of a few years army units had been organized and stationed at various strategic centers in the country. China was armed, armed to defend herself.

Then came the Revolution of 1911. The revolutionary armies were perhaps not so well trained as the government armies, but commanders and men were full of patriotism and ready to sacrifice their lives for their country. The new armies of the government went over, one after another, to Dr. Sun Yat-sen. Within a few months the agelong Imperial regime had vanished like a ghost at the least rustle of leaves into the dark night. Waves of enthusiasm spread far and wide over the country. China was reborn with little regret for the past and great hopes for the future. Let the Manchus lament their mistake in forming a new army, and let the people be overjoyed by the splendid actions of these modern-trained generals.

But the hour of triumph passed. The candle flickered out in dark streaks of smoke. The generals of the new army had little pity for the Manchus and less love for the revolution; they had tasted power and resolved to keep it. As appetite grows with eating, they longed for larger and higher power, and so fought among themselves for it.

Dr. Sun Yat-sen had returned to China in 1912. After negotiations between the revolutionaries and the Peking government the dynasty agreed to abdicate and the Republic was established. Little Pu-yi was allowed by agreement to retain residence in the Forbidden City, ancient palace of the emperors of China. A constitution was to be drafted, providing for a President and a National Assembly; meanwhile the Provisional Assembly elected Dr. Sun Yat-sen Provisional President of the Republic.

After a short time he resigned in favor of Yuan Shih-kai, who was later elected President by the National Assembly, more or less through coercion and intrigue. Political power again slipped into the hands of the reactionaries. Yuan was a mandarin of the monarchical regime who had begun the training of a modern army. He had fallen into disfavor with the Imperial Court but had been recalled to Peking when the revolution broke out.

Dr. Sun believed that the most important service he could render China was to build railroads; he was content to be at the head of China's national railways and let Yuan Shih-kai hold the reins of government. But he was soon to be disillusioned. When Yuan came into power he knew very well that his strength lay in the army under his control. The National Assembly he regarded as a mere necessary evil; so long as he controlled the army it could prove at worst no more than a nuisance to him. With strong armies behind him the new head of the state usurped all sorts of powers that did not properly belong to the President. He employed methods of intimidation and resorted to the dastardly means of assassination. Politically, he knew the trick of "divide and rule" and fostered dissension in Dr. Sun's Nationalist, or Kuomintang, camp. He went further and encouraged political parties to multiply, so that the influence of the Nationalist party would be further reduced.

Then he took steps to remove its military power. He first assassinated its political leader, Mr. Sung Chiao-ren, on his way to

Peking from Shanghai. Then he removed all the Nationalist military governors of the southern provinces by a stroke of the pen, thus provoking those provinces in order to crush them. Dr. Sun Yat-sen attempted a second revolution, but failed. Yuan Shih-kai had by this time almost the whole country under his military control and took steps to disqualify the Kuomintang members of the National Assembly on account of the "rebellion." With the south crushed his appetite grew; he longed for more power and glory. In 1915, as he was about to proclaim himself Emperor of a new Chinese Empire, the provinces revolted, whereupon he abandoned his monarchical scheme and soon died, broken-hearted.

In 1917 Dr. Sun Yat-sen finally entrenched himself in Canton, hoping to form a nucleus of an army in preparation for a new revolution to dethrone the warlords, only to find himself overthrown in 1922 by the warlord of Canton, Chen Chun-ming. In the next year, however, he succeeded in organizing a new Kuomintang government there, in a reinvigorated Nationalist movement to which the Russians gave some assistance after an agreement between himself and an unofficial Russian adviser. But this was only a beginning. After the death of the ambitious and unscrupulous Yuan Shih-kai the country as a whole remained divided among the warring provinces and political turmoil continued for twelve long years until Generalissimo Chiang Kai-shek unified it in 1928, after the triumph of the Nationalist movement.

For sixteen years after the founding of the Republic China was in the grip of warlords. One civil war after another, often supported by foreign interests, devastated the country, bringing innumerable hardships to the people and paving the way for Japanese aggression. The cause of revolution seemed to be doomed. Victorious generals, elated, reached for more and more power. Wounded lions and tigers fell in ignominy and with their tails between their legs limped into the foreign concessions or settlements of Tientsin or Shanghai to lick their wounds and wait for opportunities to come back. When opportunity came they sneaked out, entered the arena again, and caused more suffering to the people.

The soldier, who had been once despised and then honored, was now again despised.

CHAPTER 14

INTELLECTUAL AWAKENING

FROM Hangchow I went to Shanghai, where I entered the Commercial Press—the largest publishing company in China—as one of its editors. Board and lodging were accorded me at the headquarters of the Kiangsu Provincial Education Association, in return for which I served as a member of the executive committee. But I was not yet old enough to be pinned down to a desk and resigned at the end of a year. My financial arrangements with the publishing company were cleared within another year.

Together with friends I began to issue a monthly, *The New Education,* published under the auspices of the National University of Peking and the Kiangsu Education Association. I was editor-in-chief. Six months after its inception the magazine had reached a circulation of ten thousand. Its chief aim was to "develop individuality and attain social progress." Encouragement of liberal ideas as against purely traditional thought was what the monthly stood for.

These were the times immediately after the European war when liberalism and democracy were in vogue all over the world and Wilsonian ideals had caught the imagination of the thinking minds of China. Chinese youth was imbued with the new ideas that came in torrents from postwar Europe and America. Newspapers and magazines devoted large sections to international news and developments. China was beginning to think with the world.

La Jeunesse, a radical magazine launched by Chen Tu-hsiu some years before and then taken up by a group of professors in the university of Peking, was advocating democracy and modern science for the rejuvenation of China. In introducing new elements of thought it was quite natural that they should fiercely attack the old beliefs and traditions. Some contributors even went so far as to cry "Down with the Confucian shops!" While all this evoked strong antagonism from the reading public, the youth of the country caught the spirit of the intellectual revolt.

In 1918 Dr. Sun Yat-sen came to reside in Shanghai. As we have seen, the government of the young Republic was having its ups and downs and had come partially under the sway of independent warlords. The Kuomintang, or Nationalist, party of Dr. Sun was strongest in the south and here, in 1917, a government was set up, separate from the Peking regime, to maintain the principles for which the revolutionaries had labored and re-established them throughout the country. Now, however, the veteran leader left his southern government in Canton under the control of a Directorate. The political views of its members did not go beyond their noses, a brevity of outlook to which Dr. Sun could not subscribe. So he settled down in Shanghai to work on his plan for the industrial development of China.

His vision carried him far beyond the political squabbles of the time and his plan, if successfully carried into effect, was one which would relieve the poverty of the people, bring prosperity to the country, and put China on the level of modern industrialized nations of the world. According to Dr. Sun, China's industrial reconstruction fell into four categories: clothing, food, shelter, and transportation. All are necessary for the livelihood of the people, and with these elements in view he planned the industrial development of the country.

He worked out a system of railroads and highways to cover all important commercial and military routes in the vast territory of China. He planned ports and harbors through which China's future commerce could flow abundantly. He outlined a project for river conservation, irrigation, and reclamation which would feed millions more in the country. He worked out a scheme for the development of natural resources and for the building up of both heavy and light industries. Seeing China far on the road of deforestation, he made plans to reforest great areas of central and north China.

He laid down two principles or categories under which industry was to be developed: (1) that which could be maintained as private enterprise was to be under private ownership, while (2) that which was beyond the capacities of individual citizens to undertake, or tended to create monopoly, was to be under state ownership. The government was to encourage private enterprise and to protect it by law. Obnoxious taxes must be abolished, the currency system must be improved and unified. Official interference and obstacles must be removed and communications developed to insure an easy flow of trade.

Railroads and highways, river conservation, irrigation, and reclamation, ports and harbors and the like, were to come under state control. The government was also to develop coal and iron resources in Shansi, and establish iron and steel works on a large scale. Foreign capital was to be welcomed and foreign experts employed.

Dr. Sun Yat-sen was the first Chinese statesman to have modern scientific training. His knowledge of scientific data and his mathematical accuracy were amazing. In planning China's industrial development he himself drew up maps and charts and collected his data and checked them carefully. He was familiar with such details as the depths and gradations of the riverbeds and harbors which came under his plan. Once I gave him a map of the Huai-ho Conservancy; he at once spread it on the floor and began to study it seriously. Later it was seen hanging on the walls of his study.

After a careful investigation of the various phases of industrial reconstruction and how they might be dealt with, he wrote it all out in English. Madame Sun Yat-sen did all his typing, while David Yui and I were entrusted to go over the manuscripts carefully. Data were checked over and suggestions gladly considered. Any project that Dr. Sun worked on, political, philosophical, scientific, or whatever, was carried out with great enthusiasm. His broad-mindedness echoed every suggestion or criticism that was offered him.

Because in his views and plans he was ahead of his time he was often exasperated at the shortsightedness of his contemporaries, who frequently dismissed his projects with the proverbial saying, "It is easy to know but difficult to do." From the beginning of his revolutionary movement some forty years earlier he had met with the same stubborn obstacle. So he wrote an essay on "Psychological Reconstruction for China" in which he advanced the theory that it is difficult to know but easy to do. Here he brought out a significant difference between Chinese and Western thought. The practical-mindedness of his own people often unduly emphasized the difficulties—imaginary or real—that lay in the way of practice, at the cost of neglecting the principles underlying the practice. A mind used to handling abstractions and generalizations and familiar with the process of seeking out the basic principles involved in any problem would find it easy to understand what Dr. Sun Yat-sen had in view. For minds, on the other hand, habitually intent on short-range practical results and impatient of deeper effort it was difficult to appreciate what he stood for. In China, during the declining days of the Imperial regime, men of strong will and determination to carry out reforms were not lacking, but those who perceived underlying causes and could lay plans which would strike at the root of things were rare. Dr. Sun, who possessed a clear understanding of the development of Western civilization as well as vision for the future development of China, could not but appreciate the importance of the kind of knowledge which implies foresight, or seeing beyond immediate needs, and a clear understanding of problems.

Once knowledge of this fundamental sort is secured there is no inherent difficulty in carrying it into effect. The real difficulties lie in discovering it. Indeed, even lacking essential knowledge, if one is willing to follow the direction of those who know, as masons and carpenters follow the architect, he may have no difficulty in executing a complex plan. Thus it is very plain in the field of medicine that to diagnose a case is often more difficult than to apply the cure. A medical student knows well that he must have a grasp of biological sciences such as physiology and anatomy before he is in a position to study medical science, and he has had to learn even more general science, such as physics and chemistry, before studying biological sciences. And each science is the result of centuries of research by men who have loved knowledge. Therefore it is very clear that the process of learning medical science is more laborious than the practice of medicine.

Dr. Sun's practical-minded contemporaries wanted to get things done without taking much interest in studying the underlying causes of conditions in China in the light of knowledge gained from history, sociology, psychology, science, or the like; or making plans for the country accordingly. They branded his plans as visionary and impractical. Unaware of the problems which lay beyond their "practical" mental horizon, they did not realize that their own difficulties usually arose from lack of knowledge, or an insufficient or superficial knowledge of problems—certainly, in any case, not alone from lack of practical ability. What they thought they knew was often limited to immediate personal experience or empirical reasoning. Such knowledge is not only easy to obtain but dangerous as a basis for practice.

To the Western mind these are mere philosophical squabbles of theory and practice, or knowledge and conduct—and what have they to do with revolution and reconstruction in China? Yet Dr. Sun Yat-sen was very serious about it, considering psychological reconstruction the first step to successful reconstruction in other realms, whether political, industrial, or social. "Overpractical becomes impracticable," Professor Dewey said to him. "No one in the West would think that 'to know' is an easy matter."

Amid the revolutionary atmosphere of the intellectual world and my own inspiring contact with Dr. Sun, *The New Education* stood pedagogically for initiative, the needs of children, and much that John Dewey stands for in his *Democracy and Education*. As regarded Chinese principles of education, it stood for Mencius' ideas on human nature: that it is good. Hence education means a proper development of what there is in the child. As a matter of fact, in its main current Chinese education had followed since Confucius the principle that human nature is all-good. The trouble was that as the centuries accumulated, what is good in human nature came to mean certain moral precepts shrouded in age-worn tradition. Thus while in theory it was very modern, in practice it might lead miles away from original principles. "Development of nature" may in fact come to mean mere conformity to traditional morals, and this is what happened in China.

With the introduction into Chinese thought of Rousseau, Pestalozzi, Froebel, and later Dewey, the Mencian principles came into better perspective and shed a more living light. Children of China were to be set free of hard and fast rules of conduct and traditional moral ideas incongruous to modern society. Thus children must be led to think for themselves and helped to solve their own problems in accordance with their needs and not those of grownups. They should be led to an interest in nature and in their environment. In accordance with the principles of child psychology, a child must be treated as such; he is not a little man and must not be stuffed with knowledge only, much less with books. Education should help a child to grow—mentally, physically, and socially.

Such were the lines of thought that guided the policies of *The New Education*. As the reader will easily see, it fell in line with the current revolutionary thought of the country. The intellectual ties between *The New Education* and the professors and students of Peking University, the whirlpool of intellectual revolt, drew me the next year to that much-troubled institution as professor of education and Acting Chancellor.

CHAPTER 15

PEKING UNIVERSITY AND THE STUDENT REVOLT

IF YOU throw a stone into a body of still water, rings of waves begin to rise and travel farther and farther, ever widening and extending away from the center. In Peking, capital of China during five dynasties and more than ten centuries—the seat of conservatism where the Empress Dowager ruled the country from her dragon throne—stood the oldest modern institution of learning in the country, known as the National University of Peking. It was the only landmark left by Emperor Kwang-hsü's short-lived reforms of 1898. The brief tide of reform had ebbed and vanished into history; only a few scattered shells remained, witness to the vicissitudes of fortune in that placid ancient capital. But the university, in which were clustered the living shells that contained pearls, was destined to make valuable contributions to culture and thought within the short span of one generation.

The man who threw the stone of intellectual revolt into that placid water was Dr. Tsai Yuan-pei, who in 1916 became Chancellor of the university. Dr. Tsai was an eminent scholar of China's ancient culture, but imbued with the spirit of Western scholarship and especially the spirit of free inquiry which prevailed in the Hellenic world. His belief in "knowledge for knowledge' sake," in contrast to the "learning for its practical use" of Chinese thought, had its foundation in a thorough knowledge of ancient Greek culture. His views on knowledge were essentially the same as those of Dr. Sun, but the latter had acquired his outlook from the natural sciences, Dr. Tsai his from a study of Greek philosophy.

This renowned scholar preferred the appreciation of beauty to belief in religion. Here we find an interesting blending of Greek and Chinese culture. The traditional love of nature of the Chinese scholar and the Greek sense of beauty working together in Dr. Tsai's mind resulted in a love for Western sculpture and Chinese carvings; Chinese landscape painting and Western portraits; both Chinese and Western architecture, and Chinese and Western music. His views on religion were essentially Chinese: religion is but part of morality. He wanted to elevate the moral sense of youth to a higher level by love of beauty. It was an ancient Chinese belief that there is no greater moral force than that of music. Good morals had their foundation is well-balanced emotions, which could only be brought about by the fine arts and music or poetry, which is closely allied to music.

Dr. Tsai had great faith in natural science. He not only trusted it to yield inventions, engineering, and other benefits, but believed it would foster the mental habits of methodical thinking and research which led to the discovery of general truths, the foundation of all true knowledge.

In his younger days his brilliance was less veiled in modesty. When he was principal of the Sino-Occidental School at Shaoshing which I attended in my boyhood, one evening at a banquet, after a few cups of Shaoshing wine, he stood up and announced at the top of his voice that the reforms of Kang Yu-wei and Liang Chi-chao were too superficial, since they retained the Manchu court to lead them. "I, Tsai Yuan-pei, will not do that. Unless you overthrow the Manchus no reforms will be possible!" He shouted it out, raising his right arm over his head.

Dr. Tsai in his early years wrote essays full of brilliant and stimulating ideas contrary to the common practice of writing in the days of civil examinations. My uncle King told me of a strange essay of his which began, "In sex, food, and drinking human desires lie." He handed in his paper to the Imperial examiners after the time limit. The night was getting on to the small hours and the eyes of the examiners were heavy with sleep. His paper was accepted and he passed the examination for the Second Degree—Chu-jen, or the Promoted Scholar. In the following years he achieved the Third or highest degree—Chin-shih, or Advanced Scholar—when still under thirty. He subsequently entered Hanlin Academy, composed of the highest ranking scholars, which has since ceased to exist.

In his later years he was the personification of what is best in a Chinese scholar, with a broad mind open to Western ideas. His eyes, looking over his spectacles, were alert but calm; his speech easy, clear, fluent, and sincere, though often drowned in a monotone. He never let harsh words cross his thin lips, but when he was indignant his utterance was quick, weighty, and concise—as clearly to the point as a judge rendering judgment or a dagger popping out from under soft velvet cotton.

He was of a light build but his movements were steady. His artistic fingers would run deftly through the pages as he read, as if he read by paragraphs, even by pages, his quick sight grasping essential points and his retentive memory keeping knowledge in store. His love of nature and the arts made his emotions tranquil, thoughts lofty, tastes refined, manners sincere and modest, and ways of living simple and retired. His broad-mindedness was as responsive to every shade of opinion, criticism, or suggestion "as a hollow in the mountains that echoes with every vibration of sound."

In such a scholar the government of Li Yuan-hung, then President of the Republic, found a chancellor for the university. Under his administration the institution underwent a radical change. Science was put on an equal footing with literature, which had reigned in the realm of knowledge in China from time immemorial. History, philosophy, and the classics were studied in the light of modern scientific method. The spirit of knowledge for its own sake was encouraged. Scholars of old conservative schools, new schools, and radical schools were all given an equal chance. Old literati with queues hanging down their backs who still retained faith in a monarchical regime sat shoulder to shoulder with men of radical thought, discussing problems, joking and laughing at the same dinner table. Free inquiry into problems, of knowledge, culture, family, social relations, and political systems was found in the classrooms, seminars, and social gatherings.

It was the intellectual life of ancient China of the pre-Ching period or ancient Greece of the times of Socrates and Aristotle reenacted. Dr. Tsai was the old, wise Socrates of China, and would have suffered the same fate had he not had sympathizers on a nationwide scale, especially among the Kuomintang members who had a strong hold in Canton. Yet by conservative Chinese and foreigners alike the university was accused of advocating "A-three-ism"—no religion, no government, and no family—just as Socrates was accused by the ancient Greeks of corrupting the souls of young men. No argument could dispel these unfounded suspicions. History alone would disprove them, as it has absolved Socrates.

I have said that Dr. Tsai advocated esthetics as a substitute for religion, and free inquiry as a means of approach to truths. Mr. Chen Tu-hsiu, Dean of the College of Literature, advocated science and democracy as the twin weapons to modernize China. Free inquiry led to freedom of thought. Science sapped the old beliefs. Democracy meant the assertion of popular rights. Meanwhile Dr. Hu Shih, professor of philosophy, worked for a literary revolution by which the language in common use by the people was to replace the classical language as a medium of thought and expression. The colloquial, or common written language, is nearer to the Chinese spoken language and therefore easier to learn, to write, and to understand. It is a better and easier medium for the expression of thought. Its use was to popularize knowledge, hitherto a monopoly of classical scholars. The movement developed a host of young writers throughout the country. After a few years the Ministry of Education made compulsory the use of the vulgate as a medium of instruction in all elementary schools.

The university was an oasis in the intellectual desert of Peking. But the seeds of intellectual revolt grew in that small green spot with remarkable rapidity. Within three years the whole institution was filled with it.

In that vigorous atmosphere of intellectual activity a mental and moral unrest developed among the students. I have related earlier how, under the influence of French eighteenth-century political idealism with its catchwords of Liberty, Equality, and Fraternity, and as a revolt against established authority which the youth of the nation believed responsible for retarding China's progress and thus inviting the encroachment of foreign Powers, students had gone on strike against their school authorities upon the slightest pretext. This first happened in Shanghai in 1902. The first student revolt had spent itself in the course of a few years and degenerated into strikes against the school cooks. In the end the authorities outwitted the students by handing the management of the kitchens over to the student body. Isolated cases of strikes still persisted for some years. In one instance this ended in tragedy when a dozen students in the provincial high school at Hangchow died of arsenic poisoning which the cooks put in their rice as a revenge. I went to the school after the outrage and found a large number of youths moaning in their beds, while a dozen caskets stood in the open-air gymnasium waiting for relatives to take them for burial.

While the spirit of revolt in the form of school strikes was gradually spending itself, its force turned inward into revolutionary ideas which gained much wider ground outside the schools in the form of a political revolution, resulting ultimately in the downfall of the Manchus in 1911.

The second student revolt burst out suddenly in Peking on May 4, 1919, the eighth year of the Republic. What happened was this. From the peace conference in Paris news reached China that Tsingtao in the Shantung Peninsula, a German-leased port taken from German hands during the war by the Japanese, had been awarded to Japan by the victorious Powers. As China had declared war against Germany, the leased territory should in all justice have been returned to China. The whole nation was indignant over the news. Students in Peking, under the leadership of the National University group, demonstrated against the signing of the Versailles Treaty. Three thousand students held mass meetings and paraded in the streets demonstrating against acceptance of the terms, shouting "Return Tsingtao to China!" "Boycott Japanese goods!" "Down with the traitors!" Banners streamed in the air bearing the same slogans.

The Peking government, despite the efforts of Dr. Sun Yat-sen's Kuomintang or Nationalist party in Canton and its adherents elsewhere, was still under the thumb of military men and ruled China with a mere semblance of the democracy and parliamentary procedure which the revolution had labored so earnestly to establish. Among its influential high officials were three members of a notoriously pro-Japanese group. Their sympathies were well known. These men—Tsao Ru-lin, Minister of Communication; Chang Chung-hsiang, Chinese Minister of Tokyo; and Lu Chung-yu, another minister—now became the targets of student wrath. The crowd streamed to the residence of Tsao, where secret meetings were supposed to have been going on; they broke in, and combed the house for the three "traitors." Tsao and Lu escaped by the back door; Chang was caught by the mob and badly beaten. Leaving him for dead, the students dispersed, in their retreat smashing everything in sight and setting the place on fire.

Meanwhile, the armed police and gendarmery had thrown a cordon around the house. They arrested some sixty students and sent them to headquarters. The rest—about a thousand strong—

followed after, each claiming individually to have been responsible for the outbreak and asking to be arrested. Finally all were put under heavy military guard in the compounds of the Law College of the university.

News concerning the demonstration was strictly censored. Some students outwitted the government, however, by sending a cable through a foreign agency in one of the foreign concessions of Tientsin, and this cable was the sole source of the news that appeared in Shanghai papers on the morning of the fifth.

I was at breakfast on May 5 when the newspapers reached me. On their front pages appeared in bold letters a news item something as follows:

Students in Peking demonstrated against the signing of the Versailles Treaty. Three pro-Japanese high officials—Tsao, Lu, and Chang—were beaten by the students. The residence of Tsao Ru-lin was burned. Several thousand have been detained under heavy armed guard in the Law College of the National University of Peking. Ringleaders were arrested and their state is unknown.

There were no further details.

The whole city was excited by the news. In the afternoon public organizations such as educational associations, chambers of commerce, and provincial and local guilds sent telegrams to the Peking government demanding the dismissal of the three high officials and the release of the students arrested or detained. Through the following day all Shanghai waited anxiously for a reply from the government but there was none. Then the students of the city went on strike, making the same demands as the public organizations, and went forth lecturing on the streets.

Next morning schoolboys and girls went by hundreds from door to door on Nanking Road, the main street of Shanghai, begging the shopkeepers to go on strike. Some in sympathy and others out of fear closed their doors. Many followed suit in imitation of their neighbors. In about an hour's time all the Nanking Road shops were closed as tight as clams. Police interfered but to no avail.

The shop strike spread like fire. By noon all Shanghai was shut. Thousands of people wandered about the streets and traffic was almost blocked. Settlement police became powerless. Boy and girl scouts went out as police to keep order and direct traffic. To see order maintained in the crowded streets by bobbed-haired girl scouts was something novel in the International Settlement of Shanghai. Both Chinese and foreigners wondered why the crowd willingly obeyed the orders of young boys and girls while showing such an ugly temper toward the police.

Within a few days the student strike had grown into a nation-wide movement. Shops and commercial houses closed in all the cities near Shanghai. As Shanghai was the center of commerce in the lower Yangtze Valley, these cities were paralyzed when the heart of the great metropolis ceased to beat, and suspended their affairs, not necessarily out of sympathy for the students.

Settlement authorities were alarmed when employees of the water works and the electric company wanted to join the strike. Through the mediation of the chamber of commerce and student representatives they were persuaded to stick to their jobs. The pressure continued for more than a week and the Peking government finally gave in. The three pro-Japanese officials resigned and all the students were set free.

With country-wide sympathy behind them, students everywhere were intoxicated by their success. Thereafter there was no peace for institutions of learning, or for the government. The students of Peking, having won their victory, continued to agitate against corruption in the government and the old traditions which, they thought, enslaved the minds of young people. They had won over the government because they had national sentiment behind them. Everybody in China would have liked to join the demonstrations and parades against the signing of the Versailles Treaty. The students, who were better organized, more articulate, more impulsive and less hesitant, took the lead and thus plucked at the heartstrings of the nation.

When the pro-Japanese officials had resigned and the students had been released by the government—when the general strike had been called off in Shanghai and elsewhere—the incident was considered closed, for the time being at least. But the university itself became a problem. Chancellor Tsai Yuan-pei, apparently shocked by the violence, had resigned and quietly left Peking. He went first to Tientsin, then to Shanghai, and finally slipped into Hangchow, where he lived in a friend's house on the historic West

Lake, surrounded by gentle hills, enjoying nature as a traditional scholar of the old days. Despite repeated persuasions he declined to go back to the university. He said that he had never intended to incite the students to revolt, but that in demonstrating against acceptance of the Shantung clause of the Versailles Treaty they had acted on patriotic impulses which could hardly be condemned. As regarded the university, he thought that thenceforth it would be difficult to maintain discipline, as the students were likely to be intoxicated with the cup of success. Once they tasted power there would be no end to their appetite. This was the stand he took in regard to the student movement. The belief that he was always ready to encourage a student revolt was far from the truth.

Finally he approved my going to Peking to take charge of the university for him. I consented rather reluctantly. With the heavy responsibilities thus thrust upon me, I went to Peking in July with one of the student delegates. The student body convened in a mass meeting of welcome, and this was the gist of my first speech to them:

Your patriotic motives in the recent demonstrations are to be highly commended. But if you keep on doing this your valuable time will be wasted and the existence of the institution where you drink at the fountain of wisdom will be endangered. A new nation is not made in one day, and certainly not by demonstrations alone. The demonstrations are trifles in comparison with the work you have to do in classrooms, in the library, in laboratories, and in seminars . . .

After the storm the clouds began to disperse and a clear day emerged. Dr. Tsai returned to his office in September.

The university was again reorganized, on a sounder basis. The office of dean of administration was created to take charge of the business side of the university. Existing offices were modified and systematized into an organic whole. The dean of faculties was responsible for academic affairs. The Academic Council, members of which were elected by the professors with the deans as ex officio members, was the highest legislative body, empowered to pass on university regulations, grant degrees, and enforce discipline among the students. Various executive committees were set up to perform administrative functions. The university was put on a basis of faculty control. Academic freedom, faculty control, and a fearless spirit of searching for truth were the guiding principles in administration. Student self-government was encouraged as a step to democracy.

For seven long years, in spite of intermittent strikes and demonstrations, the university sailed along under full canvas on the rough sea of political turmoil, with men of courage and foresight at the helm. The number of volumes in the library was vastly increased, laboratory equipment much improved. Scholars of international fame such as John Dewey and Bertrand Russell were invited to join the university as visiting professors.

The two Western philosophers contributed their part to the great intellectual movement in China. Dewey directed the young minds of China to the study of educational and social problems in accordance with the needs of the individual and society. It is true that the very act of thinking of problems in this way led naturally to the creation of other problems which caused trouble in such a static society as that of China in those days. Hu Han-min, a Kuomintang leader, once told me that it was Dewey's teaching that caused unrest in the schools. But he ignored the fact that there were many student strikes under the Imperial regime during prerevolutionary days; as well as the fact that Dewey's teaching, which interested the students in social problems, thus helped the movement against the warlords later on.

It was due to Russell that young minds began to get interested in principles of social reconstruction, which roused them against both religion and imperialism. To the missionaries and members of the British Legation he was an unwelcome guest. He lived in a Chinese hotel and refused to see officials of his own legation. I heard one of them express the view that his coming to China was a matter for regret. In Peking Mr. Russell contracted a serious case of pneumonia and at one time the doctors gave up hope. On his recovery I heard a missionary lady say, "That's too bad." I repeated it to Mr. Russell, who laughed heartily.

During those days of freedom of thought in China just after the first World War, thinking about either social problems or social principles created storms in the thinking mind and waves of emotion in the feeling heart. This prepared the way for the further introduction of Western ideas from postwar Europe. All the "isms" had full play in China. While the intellectuals on the whole moved along the line of Western democracy, a section of them, inspired by the success of the Russian revolution of 1917, were attracted to the ideology of Marxism. Chen Tu-hsiu, editor of *La Jeunesse,* resigning from his deanship at the University of Peking, became the leader of a Chinese Communist movement. The anti-imperialist movement against Japan also prepared the ground for general sympathy among intellectuals for the Russian Revolution. In 1923 the Third International sent Mr. Joffe to Peking to make contact with Chinese intellectuals, and one evening at a dinner given in his honor at the Chih-ying Restaurant in Peking, Dr. Tsai made a speech of welcome in which he said, "The Russian Revolution has given great inspiration to the revolutionary movement in China."

Russia had repeatedly announced that she was ready to give back to China the Chinese Eastern Railway in north Manchuria, and wished China success in getting rid of both the warlords and the imperialistic Powers that had a grip on the country. This good will of Soviet Russia toward China was welcomed by all the intellectuals as well as by the people as a whole. Among other things, it paved the way for the growth of Communism in China.

Meanwhile, eminent scientists from European and American universities came to guide students in scientific research. A number of periodicals were issued by the faculties as well as by the students. Music and art clubs, athletic associations, library and science associations sprang up in abundance. A society for the study of Marxian theories was established under the leadership of Professor Li Ta-chao. The student army corps, organized some time earlier to give military training to the students, was growing in size. The university gates were flung open to girls—Peking University was the first institution of higher learning in the history of education in China to accept women on an equal footing with men. Faculty and students, immersed in an atmosphere of academic freedom and free inquiry, worked in unison, happy and contented.

The influence of the university was far-reaching. From every intellectual pebble thrown into the waters of ancient Peking waves traveled to every corner of the land. Even the middle schools of the country—the equivalent of American high schools—copied its organization, introducing freedom of thought and opening their doors to girls. Progressive newspapers, magazines, and political parties echoed every movement of the university. In this atmosphere the influence of the Kuomintang revolution extended far and wide, while at the same time the Communist party began to take shape.

The conflicts of the warlords meanwhile roared intermittently around the ancient capital. In one of these internecine wars the gates of Peking were all closed for almost a week. Fighting was going on some ten miles outside the city. It usually began at nightfall and lasted until dawn. Once we went to watch the artillery fire from the top of Peking Hotel. It was like watching a fire on the other side of a river; you got the entertainment of a bonfire at the expense of others without incurring the risk of being licked by the flames. A crossfire of tracers spanned the earth in the dark night like multitudes of rainbows crossing each other. The roar of cannon set the roof trembling as if in a mild earthquake. From dusk till dawn there was no pause in the fighting. When I went home to bed I could not turn my ears to the pillow, for the thundering of the cannon seemed much louder that way. So I lay flat in bed with my eyes toward the ceiling and noticed that the beautifully painted shades of the electric lights were swinging slightly. Glasses rattled. Wolfy, my German police dog, kept moaning, unable to enjoy her usual peaceful slumber on the floor. As soon as she laid her ear to the floor, she would start, get up, groan, dart for the door, and scratch it violently, thinking that these abominable sounds came from beneath the floor of my bedroom. The next morning I scolded her for being naughty the previous night. She stared at me with guilty eyes. From the breakfast table I called to her but she did not respond. I never saw her again. Presumably she wandered away in search of a land of peace where no mocking devils would pound the ground at night and she could sleep well. But I am afraid she was sorely disappointed.

On one of those days in the besieged city I took a walk with a friend along Shun-ching-men Street. People went about their business as usual, without a trace of excitement. As usual, people were pulling or being pulled in rickshaws. We turned at Hsi-tan Pailou into Hsi-ching-an-chieh and then into Central Park. The yellow enamel tiles of the imposing towers on the Wu Gate of the palace glittered in the slanting autumn sun against the cloudless blue. We chose a spot under the spreading branches of one of the ancient spruces planted there in rows and squares by early Manchu emperors centuries ago. The air was laden with their fragrance and light winds brushed our faces with the soothing odor. We sat at a table listening to the gossip at neighboring tables. People all talked about the war and wondered which side was going to win and who was going to have Peking as a spoil of war; all seemed to be utterly unconcerned. What is the use of worrying? Peking had seen many wars and vicissitudes of fortune but remained the same, as the towers of the Wu Gate bore silent witness.

"Let's order a fish for dinner and see whether we get it, with the city gates all closed," said my friend.

A waiter came with a fish wriggling in his hand. "How would you like to have it?"

"Two ways. Split it in half—one half fried with sweet-and-sour gravy spread on top; the other half cooked with bean sauce." The fish came. One of the two halves tasted stale.

"Why, one half of the fish was from a dead one," said my friend to the waiter, who bowed and smiled.

"Oh, I see. The fish sailed in over the city wall. The side that hit the ground was dead, while the other was still alive," I said. When the waiter came back again my friend snatched one of the empty wine jars on the table and showed it to him. "What! You have given us an empty jar."

"Sorry." The waiter was smiling. "The liquor has evaporated." He immediately brought us a new one. Of course both were charged to our account.

We went back home at dusk. That night the fighting ceased. I thought of Wolfy. She must have slept in peace somewhere in the city. The next morning we found the government had changed hands. The palace remained the same. The people went about as usual. The city was undisturbed. The gates were flung open, and thousands of people from the country streamed in with vegetables, meat, eggs, and fish. Donkeys, mules, and camels followed in the wake of the pedestrians. Children gathered empty cannon shells and shrapnel from the battleground and sold them in the streets for a few dollars. Out of these shells we made flower vases.

Many people outside the city lost their property, a number of them lost their lives. I lost my Wolfy.

On the whole the losses to property and life in the various war areas during those long, distressing years were negligible. It was the unsettled state of mind, the disruption of communications, the ruined finances, the disturbances of order and upset of administrative machinery of the government—above all, the obstruction of the tranquil flow of blood in the veins of national life—that reduced China to such a paralyzed state that she became an easy prey to the aggressor neighbor. The division of the country made any nationwide constructive plan for the country well-nigh impossible. Unification was what China needed.

I acted for the second time for Chancellor Tsai when he went for a visit to Europe. At this time a letter from Dr. Sun Yat-sen lauded the movements in the university and ended in the following words: "Lead the three thousand disciples to help the cause of revolution."

Dr. Sun did not live to see his hopes come true, but only a few years later his successor, General Chiang Kai-shek, led the Nationalist army sweeping down from Canton to the Yangtze Valley, then to the Yellow River Valley, and finally to Peking, treading the path psychologically prepared for the new Nationalist victory by the revolutionary movements which had started in Peking and permeated the minds of all classes of people in the country.

CHAPTER 16

YEARS OF TROUBLES

THE students after their May 4 victory were indeed intoxicated with the cup of success as Chancellor Tsai, Dr. Hu Shih, and others had predicted. It was beyond their power or any other power in the country to stop, for the root of discontent lay deep in the political, social, and intellectual soil of China. In the schools the students usurped the right of the authorities to engage or dismiss a teacher. Failing to meet their demands, the administration invariably faced a strike. The students struck against teachers who required a severe examination or stood for sterner discipline. They demanded subsidies from the schools for their traveling expenses during spring vacation, or money for student activities. They demanded free copies of the lecture notes (a kind of course syllabus). It was a matter of trying to get as much as possible out of the school in every conceivable way, never thinking of their duties toward it. They were intoxicated with power; their selfishness ran wild. The mere word "discipline" found them with rolling eyes, lips curled, and teeth bared, ready to fall upon you in packs.

Once the senate of the University of Peking passed a regulation that all students must pay for the copies of lecture notes provided by the university. This touched their private pocket. A crowd of several hundred demonstrated against the rule. Chancellor Tsai arrived on the scene and told them that they must obey the university regulations. His words fell upon deaf ears. The mob streamed into the classrooms and offices to find those responsible for the "obnoxious" rule. The Chancellor told them that he alone was responsible.

"You cowards!" he shouted indignantly, rolling his sleeves up to his elbows and shaking his fists in the air. "I'll fight a duel with any one of you who dares. If anyone dares to touch his teachers, I'll knock him down."

The crowd stood in a semicircle in front of him. As the Chancellor moved toward them they stepped back, always keeping at a safe distance. This quiet scholar, tame as a lamb in daily life, was suddenly transformed into a moral lion.

The crowd dwindled; he walked to his office. About fifty students still waited outside the door demanding the abrogation of the rule. The corridor was packed with spectators curiously looking on. The thing came to a deadlock. The Dean of Faculties, Ku Men-yu, brought about a settlement by promising to see that the assessment of lecture note fees was postponed—indefinitely, of course.

Among the worst agitators, who usually took cover behind the crowd to shout their shrill accusations, I noticed a tall young man, too tall to be hidden by the crowd. I did not know him—he was not among those whose names were later struck from the university register. But a number of years afterward, when I saw him as a puffed-up official, I recognized him at once. His countenance was unmistakable; his shouts still rang in my ears. He had developed into a skillful politician and unscrupulous grafter, and died a rich man a few years after the war.

In another demonstration several years later against myself for refusal to listen to their demands, a number of students closed the gates of the compound and thus shut me in my office. Dr. Hu Shih telephoned to ask whether I would like police to break the siege, but I replied in the negative. The gates were closed for two hours. Those who wanted to leave after their classes clamored from inside, while others who wanted to come in to attend courses echoed without. At length the ringleaders, no longer able to withstand the protests of their fellow students, opened the gates. As I came out of my office a score or two of them followed, vociferously denouncing me. Turning my head, I saw a few at close range. The university senate decided to dismiss those whose names I could remember or afterward ascertained.

Several years later as I was walking on the campus of the Central Aviation School, transferred from Hangchow to Kunming during the war, a fine-looking young officer stepped forward and after a military salute told me that he was a student dismissed from the National University of Peking. At once I recognized his honest-looking face and fine, strong physique. The ugliness I had seen in his face as he dogged my steps that day of demonstration was all transformed into shining happy eyes and smiling lips. We were happy to see each other. The president of the school told me later that he was one of the best flyers and instructors they had.

These instances are indicative of the fact that the student demonstrations contained all elements. Those who honestly believed in their cause, rightly or wrongly, and were willing to be responsible for what they had done, often turned out to be good citizens, while the sneaky fellows often proved undesirable elements in society.

The students usually took as their target some international problem which the government was not in a position to solve, or had failed to solve to the satisfaction of the people. Thus they always carried with them the sympathy of the country; herein lay their power. As "incidents" grew in number between China and Japan, their demonstrations were naturally interpreted by the Japanese as an anti-Japanese movement. The root of the trouble lay in the Twenty-One Demands and in the Shantung question created by the Versailles Treaty. After the balance of power in the Far East was upset, Japan enjoyed almost exclusive privileges in strangling China. The policy of partitioning China had given way to the Open Door policy, which was fundamentally dependent upon a balance of power; once this balance was kicked over, China had only two alternatives—to submit to the domination of Japan or fight it out alone every step of the way.

So the students fought, first with demonstrations, strikes, and boycotts against Japanese goods, then turning their attack on the government at Peking, which they believed responsible for all evils. When they found nothing internationally or nationally important to fight, they fought the school authorities. The cause lay in the psychological unrest of youth. Once they were aroused to act, it tended to express itself; to repress emotions that ran so high would have been difficult.

A number of student groups, among them the young Communists, turned their attention to the labor movement and the labor unrest which was then brewing in the treaty ports. Railway and factory workers began to show activity and agitation, which spread like patches of oil. Soon they joined the students in mass meetings and parades. The labor movement was no negligible weapon. With it the Kuomintang government in Canton once devastated Hongkong with a general strike, reducing the British island colony to a commercial and industrial desert, as it were, for eighteen months.

Nationwide anti-British feeling had been provoked in Shanghai on May 30, 1925, when International Settlement authorities gave orders to shoot into a crowd of sympathizers with the labor movement there, gathered on Nanking Road. A few were killed and many wounded. Under the leadership of both the Kuomintang and the Communists a general strike of laborers, merchants, and students followed. Once more Shanghai was a dead city. On June 23 students, workmen, merchants, and soldiers in Canton demonstrated in sympathy against the British. As the crowd passed through the outskirts of the Foreign Settlement the British garrison fired on them. As a result of the firing Hongkong went on a general strike which rendered the British colony a dead city. At the instigation of the students Chinese employees of the British Legation at Peking also went on a sympathetic strike, which left these diplomatic officials without cooks or boys for some time.

After the workers had joined the student movement, the number of demonstrators was increased by thousands. Often one would see a vast motley crowd in the mass meetings or parading on the streets of Peking, shouting slogans and waving banners. In one of these meetings a White Russian, shuddering, remarked that he had seen many such mass meetings in Russia—the sure signs of an impending revolution—and he wondered whether it was safe for him to stay in China.

The workers, like the students, when there was no more important demonstration to make, turned their hostility against their employers. There was little peace for the factories. However, it was much easier for the central or local government to deal with striking workmen than with students. In many instances they stopped the strikes by force of arms, in some cases simply firing on the strikers with machine guns.

Supposing that this would be an effective way to stop all strikes, the government under Tuan Chi-jui gave orders to train machine guns on a crowd of students gathering around the executive mansion. I had previously been informed that the government had given the order to fire if the students besieged the building, and I warned them of the danger and tried to prevent them from participating; but they formed in lines on the campus, ready to march, and refused to listen to me. No sooner had they approached the entrance of the mansion than bullets rained upon them.

About four o'clock in the afternoon news reached me of the tragedy. At once I rushed to the scene. The open space in front of the official residence of Tuan Chi-jui was literally covered with bodies of young boys and girls. It was difficult to distinguish the dead from the dying. Ambulances came and picked up all who showed any sign of life. About two dozen remained lifeless on the ground. A number died on the way to hospitals and still more lost their young lives on the operating table. We checked with the various hospitals and found that the casualties ran up over a hundred. This did not include those who left after receiving first aid.

This dastardly action of the Tuan Chi-jui government drew a wave of protest from the whole country, and its resultant unpopularity was among the reasons for its later downfall.

Besides the factors I have mentioned, the most important element in making the students so powerful and uncontrollable at this period was the fact that most of them were the sons and daughters of the ruling classes of China. A revolt of students meant, so to speak, a revolt of sons and daughters against their fathers. The most knotty problem a parent had to face was that of a rebellious son or daughter, especially when his children's actions enjoyed the popular support of his neighbors. Workmen were a different proposition; neither their parents nor relatives held any power in the government or in society. So it was their lot to submit to the whips of policemen or the bayonets of armed forces. Only when they were under the guidance of, or in co-operation with, the students was their power strongly felt.

The student movement was further fortified by the sympathy of teachers within the schools and Kuomintang members and Communists outside of them. Other political forces were also involved. So the movement grew in complexity and magnitude. There were always teachers behind it, from its beginning in 1919. Even during the first student revolt under the Imperial regime there had been teachers behind the movement.

A strike of teachers, to support their demands for payment of arrears of salary owed them by the government at Peking, caused further complications. The poor teachers in the university and in seven other government colleges were very irregularly paid. Often they received only half a month's salary in two or three months. When they demonstrated they could usually squeeze out from a half to one month's salary from the Ministry of Education.

Once several hundred teachers, supported by a still larger number of students, occupied the premises of the Ministry demanding payment of their arrears. The presidents of the eight government institutions went to act as intermediaries. Teachers and students coerced the vice-minister and all the presidents into marching to the presidential mansion to demand their pay. At the exit of the Ministry the vice-minister refused to go any farther on the pretext that it was raining. A student walking beside him opened his umbrella and handed it over, saying brusquely, "Here is an umbrella," and the vice-minister took it from him and marched on reluctantly. The presidents followed grudgingly after. As the crowd approached the entrance of the mansion the gendarmery and police closed the gates. Teachers and students clamored for admittance. Suddenly the gates were flung open and swarms of armed police and gendarmes streamed out with bayonets and rifle butts, stabbing and beating at random. Aged teachers and young girls alike fell into the ditches with hands muddy and faces bleeding, screaming and crying. The president of the College of Law lay on the ground as if dead. A professor of political science argued with the soldiers as to why they should be so unsympathetic as to insult the hungry teachers. A professor of Chinese literature with a big lump on his forehead, his nose bleeding, shouted at them, "You fight your own people. Why don't you fight the Japanese?"

This professor was taken to the French Hospital, where a former provincial governor was sent by the government to offer its apology. The professor's aged mother was sitting by.

"This boy is my only son. The government almost killed him. I demand the reason why?"

To this the former governor replied, "Never mind, Aunty, I am a good fortuneteller. By looking at my cousin's countenance I can see he has a great future before him. Don't worry, dear Aunt, the government is sorry for the misbehavior of the ignorant soldiers. Aunt, I apologize to you."

The old lady was humored into calmness, while everyone in the room repressed his laughter. The faces of the teachers in their hospital beds all lighted up at this humor in the midst of tragedy.

Thus it went. On another occasion the teachers streamed into the Ministry of Finance, demanding their arrears of salary. All the members of the Ministry sneaked out the back doors, leaving the buildings empty behind them. Once the students, in disapproval of government policy toward a certain foreign Power, forced themselves into the Ministry of Foreign Affairs and smashed the big looking glass and quite a few nice chairs. Students, teachers, and workers all joined in strikes against the government in Peking and the aggressor Powers that encroached upon the rights of China. In bad years not a month passed without strikes of some sort.

To be president of a university in those days was really more than a headache. Funds came from the government only occasionally—usually a year or two in arrears. While students demanded more freedom of action, the government desired order and discipline. For whatever happened, in or out of the school, the president was responsible. In demonstrations, parades, and riots, he was called upon either to stop one party or to help another. Every time the telephone rang his heart beat against his ribs, and he was rewarded for untiring work only by the grey hair that grew rapidly on his head.

The writer does not speak idly. After setting down the events in these pages he again spent a night of nightmare, seeing at one moment young boys and girls lying dead on the streets of Peking, at another the gendarmery besieging the university and demanding the surrender of ringleaders. Nor, when he started and woke, and lay sleepless with his head upon the pillows, could he shut out by closing his eyes the unfolding pictures of that tragic record.

Sipping tea under a scent-laden spruce in Peking's Central Park, an old scholar made a remark to me which was, I think, typical of those bad days of the strikes.

"Strikes here, there, and everywhere—strikes yesterday, today, tomorrow and every day. Mr. Chancellor, what are you going to do about them? When is the thing going to end? Someone has said that the new spirit is born, but I say the old tranquil spirit is dead!"

Part IV

UNIFICATION

CHAPTER 17

AN EXPERIMENT IN CONSTITUTIONALISM

DURING the warlord regime one evening the Soviet Ambassador at Peking gave a banquet at the Embassy to leading men of the city. About sixty people were present. When the roast suckling pigs were passed round the table some of the guests looked at the steaming roast and burst into subdued giggles, while out of the corners of their eyes they glanced at the President and Vice-President of the National Assembly, who were among the guests. The contagious giggles spread until the whole table caught them except the two officials, who pulled long faces but remained calm. Finally I saw somebody whisper in the ear of the Soviet Ambassador and he, too, succumbed to the contagion.

The story was this. In the old days when the Dutch Indies needed labor, owners of rubber plantations and mines resorted to getting laborers from China by fraudulent means. By painting a rosy picture of the prospects and offering a sum of money, labor agencies in China enticed workers to cross the sea to the islands and there sold them to the development companies with or without the knowledge of the human goods. These unfortunate people were called "pigs" because they had been sold for money like the meanest livestock.

During the early years of the Republic the irregular practices of certain members of the National Assembly became so notorious and contemptible that people reminiscently called them "pigs," since they were willing to sell themselves to the highest bidder. The great majority of members were upright men, but they were unorganized and therefore powerless to check their fellow members. They, too, were so unfortunate as to be tagged with the epithet. When bad men combine the good must associate; if they do not, it is their own fault and they have only themselves to blame.

The idea of a written constitution for China had been introduced from America. The Constitution of the United States was an embodiment of ideas and beliefs of the American people and grew out of the life of the people. The Constitution of China was a copy of imported ideas, adopted according to the fancy of those who drafted the document and alien to the habits and ideas of the Chinese.

During the Imperial regime, in the last few years before the revolution, the provincial assemblies representing the gentry class achieved creditable results because their main interests were more or less the same and there was leadership in that class. The Imperial governor of the province had enough prestige to serve as a check to the assembly. Little or no political squabbling went on in the assembly to obscure the larger issues. The bills passed were generally for the welfare of the people of the province. Little or no corruption was known.

In 1912, when Dr. Sun Yat-sen was Provisional President of the Republic at Nanking, the National Assembly showed healthy signs of becoming a modern parliament, for its members represented revolutionary interests and there were revolutionary leaders to guide it. Dr. Sun's prestige as Chief Executive was high. But when the Assembly came under Yuan Shih-kai, trouble began to brew. This autocratic and reactionary President was hated by the revolutionary leaders and the President hated them in turn. With a strong army in his hands he resorted to intimidation, thus setting a very bad precedent for future development of the legislative body. To illustrate the ludicrously bad effect of this technique on the morale of the members, I may relate here an incident which occurred during Yuan's election to the presidency. Photographers covered the event. In those days indoor picture-taking involved the use of flashlight powder, which exploded noisily with a dazzling light. On this occasion, taking it for a bomb explosion, people ran wildly for safety. One member ducked under a table, shouting, "I voted for Yuan Shih-kai!" Quite a few lost their slippers (Chinese masculine footgear is comfortably loose) and were obliged to look for them after the scare was over. The episode ended with the impeachment of the secretary-general for allowing photographers to frighten the Assembly by a "bomb."

Under Yuan's presidency the activity of the half dozen political parties degenerated into mere political squabbling. Party and

personal feelings ran high. The Assembly, discredited in the eyes
of the people, was finally washed away in the tides of Yuan's
maneuvers for a monarchy and the restoration movement of Chang
Hsun. These movements failed, however, and the National Assembly was restored. Political power was now divided among the military governors of the provinces, the shadowy central government
in Peking having neither prestige nor power to control the Assembly. Through corruption Tsao Kun, a northern warlord, got
himself elected President, and the prestige of the national legislative body sank rapidly as subsequent developments led ever downward to new lows of political integrity.

Quite a number of representatives were elected through corruption. Ku Hung-min, a well-known cynical scholar of international
fame, told me that during an election he got eight hundred dollars
from a man who bought his vote. He took the money but did not
go to the polls. Instead he went to Tientsin and spent all the
money there. Later, at an international party in the Grand Hôtel
de Pékin, Ku got hold of the man and pointing to him said to the
gathering, "This man wanted to buy me for eight hundred dollars.
Gentlemen, do you think Ku Hung-min is so cheap?"

When undesirable elements came into the Assembly in this
manner, even though the number was not large they naturally
made it look like an auction house, representation being sold to the
highest bidder.

The students of Peking now directed their attack upon the
"House of Corruptions." One afternoon several thousand boys and
girls surrounded the Assembly and demanded that a certain bill
concerning educational measures be deleted from the agenda.
There was a clash between the police on duty there and the student body. Some of the students became so incensed that a few
days later they smuggled in three bombs from Tientsin intended
for the Assembly. They were persuaded not to carry out this violence and the bombs were taken outside the city and thrown into
a river. A few weeks later a fisherman caught one of them and
shook it in his hands to find out what was inside. Bang! The bomb
went off and carried with it the hands and head of the inquisitive
fisherman. Police assumed that it had been dropped there in the
days of the revolution and no investigation was made.

Conflicts between the Assembly and the students continued.

The Assembly members tried at first to assert their right as representatives of the people. The students retorted, calling them by their now familiar contemptible name. The Assembly tried to impeach the Chancellor of the National University of Peking; the students retaliated by staging mass demonstrations in which flags bearing the likeness of a pig streamed in the air amid threats to smash the Assembly. Finally the Assembly, conscious of its weakness, declared a truce by letting the universities and students alone. Ku Hung-min, whose cynical views made him contemptuous of students and representatives alike, said to me one day, "You believe in democracy. But to me it is demo-crazy."

If an institution is hated by the public it may still have some grounds to exist; but when it is sniffed and mocked at, even though for the acts of a mere minority, the whole suffers from the inadequacy of the part and goes down together like a sinking boat. So it was with the Assembly in the early phases of constitutional government in China. At length some of the warlords snatched the opportunity to brush it aside as a scrap of paper.

The story of constitutionalism in the days of the warlords had, of course, two sides to it. On the one hand, the warlords wrecked it by intimidation through force and by corruption with money. They had no prestige, no principle, and no policy by which to guide a democratic body. After Yuan Shih-kai, the power of the central government was a political shadow, the real power being divided among the provinces by the warring rulers who set themselves above the law. What they knew was the military strength of their feudal armies. The central government was not in a position to have any principle or policy; fundamentally it was worthy neither of support nor of opposition.

On the other side, most members of the Assembly were little concerned with national interests. Their preoccupations were either provincial or local, or still worse, personal. National interests they conceived only vaguely, and they themselves were therefore not in a position to have any coherent guiding principles or policy on national issues. Consequently no leadership was possible except in matters of local or personal interest. The Chinese people love freedom but were inexperienced in organized democracy—in other words, in constitutionalism. They did not see the importance of it. For China to follow the constitutional pattern of the West without its background was to hitch China's wagon to the Western star. It was small wonder that the experiment failed miserably.

With this failure before his eyes Dr. Sun Yat-sen devised a system of tutelary government as a steppingstone to constitutional government in his plan for an organized democracy for China. According to this scheme the period of national unification was to be followed by what might be called government in a state of tutelage—i.e., government by the Kuomintang—as a transition to the full-fledged constitutional form. And when the Kuomintang came to power in 1927 the tutelary government at Nanking was indeed meant to offset the bad effects of the corrupt National Assembly, which had become a headache to the entire country. During the next ten years the Nationalist party, under the leadership of Generalissimo Chiang Kai-shek, dislodged many a local warlord from the provinces and achieved to a large extent the unification of the country. The danger to national existence brought upon China by the Japanese militarists further intensified the unification.

Unification of the country was a necessary condition to constitutionalism. With respect for the law on the part of governing and governed alike—with the principles laid down by Dr. Sun Yat-sen, and with efficient leadership both in the government and in the National Assembly—China will be on the road to successful constitutionalism and organized democracy.

CHAPTER 18

THE DEATH OF DR. SUN YAT-SEN

Death calls before Victory descends upon my country.
Patriots that come after me will forever think of the tragedy in tears.

THE above lines are from a poem by a famous general who was
sent to defend China against an invasion of the Tartars in the
twelfth century. They apply only too truly to the death of Dr. Sun
Yat-sen. The great leader had struggled in the cause of revolution
for forty long and strenuous years, and death snatched him away
when the nation needed him for its regeneration.

In the spring of 1925 he had been for some months in poor
health as a result of his untiring work for the country. Having admitted the Communists to the Kuomintang he went one step
further. Seeing China still a divided house and knowing that
strength lay in union, in response to an invitation of the northern
generals he came from Canton to Peking to discuss a plan to unify
the country. On his way north he made a trip to Japan in an effort
to convince the Japanese people that a strong and unified China
would be beneficial to that country. When he arrived at Tientsin
he fell sick. He was carried from that port to the capital, accompanied by Madam Sun Yat-sen. But he was too ill to discuss plans
and could only lie in bed. The doctors of the Peking Union Medical College were at their wits' end. Dr. Hu Shih recommended a
Chinese herb doctor. Dr. Sun declined to take the Chinese medicine. He said that as a physician himself he knew that an herb
doctor might sometimes cure a disease where scientific medicine
failed. "A ship without a compass may reach its destination," he
said, "while that which has one may not come to port. But I prefer
to sail with that scientific instrument." However, he was persistently advised to take the Chinese medicine, and to meet the wishes
of his friends he at length consented. But the ship without a compass did not reach port.

Dr. Sun was presently transferred from the Medical College to
the home of Dr. Wellington Koo. This magnificent house, built

in the seventeenth century, had once belonged to a famous beauty, Chen Yuan-yuan, wife of General Wu San-kwei of the Ming Dynasty, who surrendered to the Manchus and conducted them inside the Great Wall, so the story goes, in order to rescue the lady from the hands of the bandit leader Li Shih-chung.

On the morning of March 12, 1925, a telephone call from Ma Soo informed me that Dr. Sun was nearing his end. I hastened to his temporary residence. When I entered the chamber Dr. Sun Yat-sen was beyond speech. A moment earlier he had muttered, "Peace, struggle, save China . . ." These were his last words. We retired to the reception hall and looked at each other in silence. "Is there any chance for the Doctor to recover?" whispered an aged Kuomintang member. All shook their heads, stifling the word upon their lips.

Silence gathered and deepened until one could hear it. Minute melted insensibly into minute. Some leaned against the wall, staring blankly at the painted ceiling. Others sank into the comfortable sofas and closed their eyes. A few tiptoed to the chamber and back without a word.

Suddenly everybody in the hall was alert, listening to sobs barely audible from the bedroom. The faint sounds gave way to a chorus of loud cries—the great leader had passed into history. As we entered the death chamber I saw that Dr. Sun's countenance was serene, as if he were asleep. His son, Sun Fo, was sitting on a bench at the bedside staring into space like a man of stone. Madam Sun bent over the edge of the bed with her face buried in the soft mattress, shaking with sobs that would break one's heart. Wang Chung-huei, standing at the end of the bed, was rocking convulsively, wailing and wiping away his tears with a handkerchief. The elder statesman Wu Chi-huei stood with his hands clasped behind him and tears welling up in his eyes.

As Dr. Sun's body was carried out of the hall covered with a big national flag, Mr. Borodin, the Soviet adviser, said to me sadly that if he could have lived a few years or even a few months longer things would have been very different.

An autopsy made at the Medical College proved that cancer of the liver had caused his death.

Dr. Sun's body lay in state in one of the former palace halls in Central Park. Every day for a week at least twenty to thirty thousand people came to pay their last respects to their leader. The funeral procession, four or five miles long, was joined by all the students from elementary schools up to colleges, and by teachers, government officials, tradesmen, workers, and farmers, a hundred thousand strong.

The casket was placed temporarily in a stone pagoda in Pi-yun Ssu, the Purple Cloud Temple in the Western Hills, about fifteen miles from Peking. This picturesque pagoda was built centuries ago under Tibetan influence, of white marble with a pointed top of gilded bronze. It perches majestically on the south side of Purple Cloud Mountain, surrounded by tall pine trees, and overlooking a sea of whispering pines which sound like waves in the spring breeze and scent the air with their fragrance. The sky was serene. Streams wound their way among the moss-grown rocks. The bells in the eaves of the temple chimed melodiously in the wind.

Dr. Sun, who had lived a life of science and struggle, now rested in peace amid the beauty of art and nature.

While the leader of China's revolution lay in peace, trouble began to brew in his party. A group of leading members of the Kuomintang, who had come to Peking to take part in his funeral, gathered around his temporary tomb in the Western Hills discussing ways to circumscribe the growing influence of the Communists in the Kuomintang. The Communists and pro-Communists in the party rushed to the scene and broke up the meeting. From that moment the cleavage between the regular members of the party and the Communists grew wider and wider until two years later, in 1927, the latter were purged from the party when the Nationalist armies occupied Nanking.

CHAPTER 19

THE ANTI-WARLORD CAMPAIGN

YEARS of student demonstrations and strikes coupled with internecine wars had sapped the strength of the government in Peking.
In the provinces the warlords ruled like maharajahs. The power of
the overlord in Peking at any one time depended upon the good
will and support of the provinces which had easy access to the
city. As its roots in the provinces weakened, the tree of power in
Peking grew shaky. No sooner had one warlord entered the capital
to take over the reins of government—either himself or through a
puppet of his creation—than another would conspire to overthrow
him and come to power in turn; when public sentiment as revealed
in student demonstrations ran high against the regime in power,
some other provincial general was always ready to take advantage of it. Through intrigue, civil war, coups d'état, or reshuffled
combinations of power, the government changed hands constantly.
During my first nine years in Peking I witnessed so many changes
that the rapid shift of scene left in my memory only a jumble of
disconnected, though vivid, pictures of the tragicomedy. I could
imagine myself a pyramid sitting in the Egyptian desert, watching
utterly unconcerned the constant coming and going of caravans
and listening to the camel bells chiming their sad tunes.

Financial stringency was acute for the Peking government. National revenues were detained by the warlords in the provinces and
spent in maintaining their private armies or to enrich their own
coffers. A portion of the money that came to the central government, usually through loans from banks at exorbitant interest,
had to go to military expenditure to placate the insatiable warlords who supported the government. Salaries, not only of teachers, as we have seen, but also of government employees and of
diplomatic officials stationed in foreign lands, were left unpaid
for months at a time or even years.

"What is the future of the Peking government?" asked an American diplomat one day.

"It will dry up like a clam and only the shell will remain," I replied.

The situation grew worse year after year until the last vestige of the public respect due to a government was gone. The students helped to destroy its prestige and the warlords buried it in the Peking dust.

In the meantime the Kuomintang movement in Canton grew in strength by leaps and bounds. It had enjoyed public faith for some time, especially among intellectuals and students, and even won the sympathy of certain enlightened generals of the north— for among the warring northern generals enlightened ones were not lacking. In the basket of rotten oranges it was possible to find a few good ones.

Even after the death of Dr. Sun Yat-sen the spirit of the Nationalist party of China remained undaunted. Dr. Sun's nucleus of an army kept on growing at Huang-pu Military Academy near Canton, of which General Chiang Kai-shek was the president. In the course of a few years General Chiang's newly trained Nationalist troops were ready to deliver a deathblow to the warlords of the north. In 1927 this army of the Nationalist government of the Kuomintang swept northward at lightning speed through the heart of the country to Hankow, and another wing moved along the coast to Hangchow. In a pincer movement the two converged on Nanking, which was made capital of the Nationalist government when the victorious armies entered the city.

That same year, at about the time the Nationalist army started its northern expedition, a notorious warlord, Chang Chung-chang, entered Peking. This renowned leader had the physique of an elephant, the brain of a pig, and the temperament of a tiger. His powerful paws were always ready to snatch at any person he disliked or at any good-looking woman he coveted. I saw him several times in a peace-preserving committee of which I was a member, and felt that he was dangerous even to look at. When I was informed by Sun Pao-chi, ex-premier of the Peking government, that I was on the blacklist, and news reached me in the evening of the execution of Shao Piao-ping, editor of the newspaper *Ching Pao,* I began to see the shadows of those powerful claws. Without hesitating I got into the car of Dr. Wang Chung-huei, who happened to call on me, and went directly to the Legation Quarter, where I got a room in the Hôtel des Wagons Lits. Here I stayed for three months and passed my time in studying calligraphy.

There were several others in similar plight; Dr. Chu Chia-hua, professor of geology and now director of the Academia Sinica, was one. Quite a few friends ran in from time to time to visit us. But spending three months in even a de luxe prison was no fun at all. We plotted escape and at length, when the situation was somewhat eased, sneaked out one after another. A very able young lady, the wife of a friend of mine, planned my escape. Acting as my wife she escorted me to the East Station without our being noticed by the police. Every casual look from a stranger startled me, though I remained outwardly calm. Following a stream of passengers I boarded a train to Tientsin and from there went by British merchant liner to Shanghai.

On the boat I met Dr. Chu Chia-hua, who from Shanghai was to proceed to Canton, where he later became president of the Sun Yat-sen University. For my part, I went to Hangchow. As the railway from Shanghai had been cut I reached the city by a roundabout way. At this time, before the Nationalist army commanded by General Ho Yin-chin reached the province, the governor appointed by Peking was attempting to revolt against the northern government and go over to the southern side. I called on him, and he revealed to me his plan for joining the southern camp. He told me that he had sent about a thousand men along the railway to the Kiangsu border, where the line was already cut.

I thought privately that he must be intoxicated with the cup of other people's success, or he would not attempt to fight an enemy at least ten times stronger than himself. I left Hangchow again the next morning by the roundabout route back to Shanghai. Within a few weeks his army was utterly routed by northern forces. When they entered Hangchow he was captured and executed.

Then the tables were turned on the northern warlords and Nationalist forces entered the city. Again I went there. Hangchow welcomed the Nationalist army with open arms. Thousands of spectators lined up along the streets with smiling faces to see the victorious modern-equipped troops march through the city. I stood watching in the crowd with my heart thumping against my ribs in ecstasy. After some sixteen years the good name of a modern army in China was once more established.

In about a year's time, in 1928, General Chiang Kai-shek was ready to launch his northern expedition. The army under his command crossed the Yangtze River and moved along the Tientsin-Pukow Railway with Peking as its objective. When it reached the outskirts of Tsinanfu, capital of Shantung Province, the Japanese—fearing a unified China—moved troops from Tsingtao down along the Tsingtao-Tsinan Railway to that capital under the pretext of protecting their vested interests and the lives and properties of the Mikado's subjects. This was intended to frustrate the unification plan by provoking an "incident," i.e., an open clash between China and Japan. The Japanese army murdered the Commissioner of Foreign Affairs and his staff in Tsinanfu, hoping that China would retaliate.

With foresight and forbearance and a sound strategy, the General saved his army and his hopes of unification by turning the spearhead of his forces away from Shantung, quickly crossing the Yellow River, and marching right on to Peking. The Japanese were thus outwitted and left to fight shadows.

Peking fell when the Nationalist army arrived. The giant of hollow papier-mâché toppled over before the merest breath of wind from the south.

When the Nationalist army entered Hangchow the year before, I had been appointed a member of the provincial government and Commissioner of Education. Thus in Hangchow, capital of Chekiang Province and city of my boyhood days, my experience in government administration began. The provincial government was formed with a council in charge. Before the national government in Nanking was organized, all the members of the council, with its chairman, were appointed by the supreme commander of the Nationalist army, General Chiang Kai-shek.

Five members of the council acted concurrently as Commissioners of Civil Affairs, Finance, Military Affairs, Reconstruction, and Education. Above the provincial council was a branch council of the central political council of the Kuomintang, of which I was appointed secretary-general. This council was in charge of general

policy for the province and gave orders to the provincial government to execute. It was later abolished as conditions in the province gradually settled down.

The provincial government was imbued with the same spirit of
reform and reconstruction as the national government of Nanking, whose broader program we shall take up in the next chapter.
The provincial reconstruction plan was rather ambitious, but after
a revolution it was necessarily handicapped by lack of funds. So
it concentrated on building more roads. Within a few years many
roads were built—in the capital itself the provincial council ran
a pencil through the map of the city and ordered roads to be built
accordingly. After two years Hangchow was blessed with many
wide streets within the city and roads running along the shores
and on the dikes across the West Lake, leading to scenic spots in
the Western Hills. A highway linked the city with Shanghai, and
this brought many week-end motorists. In the short span of three
years everyone noticed how the city had changed. New buildings
shot up like mushrooms in the city, around the lake, and in the
mountains. The population increased and business prospered.

Many electric plants were set up in local areas. In some rural
districts gas pumps were installed to irrigate the rice fields. As
Chekiang was the center of silk production, scientific sericulture
was started by the government: silkworm eggs were raised scientifically and distributed to the silk producers at cost. The first year
strong objections were raised to the new eggs, for the silk producers
became suspicious of them under the influence of egg producers
who followed traditional methods. But results speak louder than
false propaganda; the second year there was more demand for new
eggs than the government could supply.

In order to reform the land tax system a general survey was made
of agricultural land in the province, and this continued for many
years following. In contrast to the drastic methods adopted by
the Communists in their dealing with agrarian problems, these
were tackled in Chekiang by the mild means of a general 25 per
cent reduction of the land rent paid by the tillers to the owners.
As a rule the tenant farmers paid about 25 per cent of their main
crop as rent; the reduction lowered this figure to 18.75 per cent. As
the rates of land rent had existed through centuries and the method
and basis of calculation varied in different localities, the tenant

farmers of some localities were much benefited, while elsewhere the rule for reduction caused great friction between owners and tenants. Lawsuits streamed in to the Land Rent Reduction Commission. There was so much confusion throughout the province that after some years the scheme was finally abandoned. Shen, the moving spirit in rent reduction, was assassinated for causes still undetermined.

Later, a campaign against illiteracy was launched. After some six or seven years the number of short-term schools to teach the reading and writing of the more commonly used characters had increased by thousands alongside the regular elementary schools.

A new experiment was made in the educational system of the province. The National University of Chekiang was organized with the writer as president. The university was not only to take charge of higher education but also to control the public school system in the province. The office of commissioner of education was abolished and the president of the university was made a member of the provincial government. Two other provinces followed suit with their respective university and school systems. After two years of trial, internal troubles and political complications grew in the other provinces, and the whole system was accordingly abolished in 1929 during my term of office as national Minister of Education. Thus the person by whose hands it was sent to the grave was the one who had nursed it to grow with much work and thought.

I stayed a full year in Hangchow and the next year went back and forth between Hangchow and Nanking, where I was appointed Minister of Education of the national government while concurrently holding the presidency of the University of Chekiang. In 1929 I gave up the latter post and stayed in Nanking for another year, when I was forced to resign from the Ministry of Education as a result of disagreement with some of the elder statesmen regarding a question of educational policy.

CHAPTER 20

THE RISE OF THE KUOMINTANG TO POWER

AFTER the fall of Peking the country was once more a political whole. The capital of all China was moved to Nanking and remained there. Peking, meaning "North Capital," was changed to Peiping, "Peace in the North," an old name of the city before it was known to the world.

Peking had been the capital of five dynasties—the Liao, King, Yuan (Mongol), Ming, and Ching (Manchu)—over a period of more than a thousand years, and now ceased to be the capital. But it still remained the center of culture and art. The official dialect or language spoken by many of the educated classes in China in addition to their local dialects, used in broadcasting stations and taught in schools, had its home in Peking.

There were two main reasons why Nationalist China shifted the capital from the Yellow River Valley in the north to the Yangtze Valley in the south. The first was that the revolutionary spirit had permeated the latter area, which was therefore fertile soil where it was easier for the new spirit to take firm root, while the Yellow River Valley was the home of the reactionary warlords. Secondly, the Yangtze Valley was the seat of China's financial power, which could provide the government with necessary funds.

Nanking had been the capital for the Taipings, from 1851 to 1864. When they were dislodged from their last stronghold the city was devastated, and has never recovered its past glories. There were more ruins, wheat fields, vegetable gardens, and orchards than streets with buildings in that walled enclosure. The streets were narrow, rough, and filthy, the electric light no better than vegetable-oil lamps. A foot messenger was often speedier than a telephone call.

In the earlier periods of history this city on the bank of the Yangtze was a center of culture and refinement, especially in the time of the southern dynasties. Its life of wine, women, and song dwelt in the memories of generations of literary men, poets, and artists. The Ching-huai Canal, connecting lakes of luxuriant lilies, traversed the city crowded with singing houseboats lit up by painted lanterns and lavishly decorated with articles of art. On either bank of the canal, as a boat sailed leisurely by, there unrolled before one's eyes endless rows of restaurants, and rooms elaborately furnished with painted columns and bamboo screens for literary, artistic, or musical entertainments. The air was laden with enchanting tunes and soothing scents that flowed out from behind the bamboo screens.

Such was the city in days of old. But Nanking was of strategic military importance. In every major war in the country this city was destined to suffer devastation. After every conflict its glories passed into memory, and from memory it was rebuilt upon its ruins when peace came. And from the memory of the past, as it was recorded, I have depicted a part of the old life of Nanking.

Since the Taipings, however, it has never recovered its ancient beauty. It is as if the successive restorations were only copies, done by some vulgar artist, of the original picture; after repeated copying the color of the original was lost and only vulgarity remained. From time to time, in periods after the Southern Sungs (1127–1276), scholars of puritanic bent or stoic leanings objected to the type of effeminate refinement which grew up along the Ching-huai, now but an empty name with pleasant associations. But we must aver that the wrong lay not in enjoying the refinements of life but in the neglect of work and duty which should go with enjoyment. If there were only work and no play, Jack would be a dull boy. The stoic ways of living which came into vogue with the philosophers of the Sung Dynasty bequeathed to China generations of dull Jacks who knew neither play nor the right sort of work. They killed art, and with art, life. They attacked bad morals, but countenanced that abominable and most immoral institution, the foot-binding of women. Compare with this life in the Tang Dynasty (618–905), when work and play went hand in hand and a healthy civilization shone like the brilliant sun upon all its neighbor nations! Think of the Tang dances (mind you, there was no foot-binding then), music, sports, poetry, painting, and calligraphy; and then of its great generals and their glorious armies. During the Tang period Chinese civilization reached its zenith. After the Tangs came declining days. In the time of the Northern

Sungs art persisted but the martial spirit waned, until finally the philosophers of the South Sungs with their asceticism and moral speculation killed the arts both of peace and of war.

The Ching-huai Canal still ran through the city of Nanking. The houseboats and the apartments were there, too. But the forms, the quality, and the content were all changed. The refinement of life had disappeared with the flowing waters of the Yangtze, into the Yellow Sea.

When the Nationalist army entered Nanking a new spirit was born—a spirit of reform and reconstruction. Modern science was to revitalize the arts of days past. Upon the debris of the partly ruined city a modern town was built with asphalt roads traversing all sections. Trees were planted and parks designed and developed. Automatic telephones, light, and water were installed. An aerial map was made from the seaplanes of the American gunboats stationed at Nanking. On the basis of this map a new city was planned. The Commission of City Planning, of which the writer was a member in his capacity as Minister of Education, worked for more than a year with an American architect of wide experience in Chinese architectural design in the enchanted city of Peking. The commission planned to retain as far as possible the grandeur and beauty of Chinese architecture together with the convenience and hygienic installations of a modern city.

Old, dilapidated buildings were torn down to make way for new roads and houses. Commerce began to prosper. Modern theatres multiplied to accommodate the growing population. The canal and the lakes were dredged and old temples and other public buildings repaired.

The Central Museum was built to house a part of the treasures from the Palace Museum of Peking, and an underground safety vault constructed for them, of reinforced concrete, in a hill which would be immune to air bombing. For the directors foresaw the impending Japanese aggressions against the new capital. As the situation in the north grew worse and war clouds hung thick over this side of the Great Wall, the more valuable treasures of Peking were moved by hundreds of trainloads to Nanking, and before the fall of the new capital to the Japanese all had been transported for safekeeping to caves in the mountains of the interior.

The gigantic steel gate of the museum vault, with its intricate combination locks, was a piece of American ingenuity which humbled the Japanese. As reported from the occupied city, they worked on the locks for several days and finally gave up.

The buildings of the Ministries of Communications and of Railways were of reinforced concrete with modern lighting system, ventilation, and conveniences. But their architectural design was altogether Chinese, with enamel tiles, painted columns, artistic windows, and other exterior decoration. These two imposing buildings stood opposite each other on Chung-shan Road, the main artery of traffic in the new metropolis, as monuments to China's old glory adapted to modern needs. Other buildings were planned and designed, but on account of the war they all had to be postponed.

The Sun Yat-sen Mausoleum, with blue enamel tiles and white marble columns, stood on the Purple Mountains outside the city overlooking the hilly valley and the winding Yangtze. Flights of granite steps led up to the tomb of the father of the Chinese Republic. The mountains were reforested with trees from various parts of China. Flowering plants and fruit trees decorated the gentle slopes. An athletic field and stadium with a swimming pool were built at the foot of the mountain.

A new model village was built in the rolling valley. A general plan was first laid out by the government, with roads, drainage, telephone and lighting systems, and school buildings. In the short space of a few years new houses sprang up like mushrooms, with ample space around them for Oriental gardens. Trees grew and plants flowered; the birds sang and streams flowed. Old ways of living gave place to a new life in which science and art, work and pleasure, nature and human endeavor, went hand in hand.

Such was the nucleus which, it was hoped, would grow and some day transform every corner of the land. It was a modest beginning but had already borne fruit. For the new village movement had within a few years reached a number of cities and their surrounding areas. It was only a matter of time and further economic development for the new villages to change the mode of living of young China.

We could not very well expect that all trouble from the warlords would end with the downfall of Peking. Their seat of government was gone, but their real power was entrenched in the provinces.

The country was vast and communications poor. These conditions and the unsettled state of mind in the country afforded them good opportunities to nurse their ambitions. At any favorable moment they were always ready to snatch more power; they lurked in the provinces like germs in the blood, ready to attack when the body weakened. In ten years, from the time his victorious army entered Peking to the eve of the Sino-Japanese War, Generalissimo Chiang Kai-shek had not a day's rest in his effort to unify the country.

Like the Roman generals who bound their ancient empire together by roads, he was not unmindful of the need to build more roads and railways and air lines. With Nanking as a center, highways, railways and airways were made to radiate from the capital to the provinces. A part of the communication system had existed before the Nationalist government came to power; with this as a basis it built new roads to make connections and extensions. Air lines were established to distant cities. From the new capital one could fly to Peking, Kaifeng, Sian, and Lanchow in the north; to Fuchow, Canton, and Kunming in the south; in the west to Hankow, Chungking, and Chengtu.

New railways were built to connect Hankow with Canton and Kowloon, just opposite Hongkong. If the Japanese had not at this time started trouble in Manchuria, a continuous journey would have been possible in 1931 from either Hongkong or Shanghai to Paris by rail. A through train ran from Shanghai via Nanking, Tsinan, and Tientsin outside the Great Wall, and via Mukden to Tsitsihar in north Manchuria, by Chinese railroads built parallel to the Japanese-owned South Manchurian Railway. A branch line from Tsitsihar connected with the Trans-Siberian Railway. The progress of unification in China and the building of these parallel lines prompted the Japanese to try to take Manchuria, or the "Three Eastern Provinces," at a stroke—which became known to the world as the "Mukden Incident" of September 18, 1931.

Along the coast the gap between the Chien-tang and Tsao-ao rivers on the Shanghai-Hangchow-Ningpo line was filled, but the laying of track was suspended when war broke out. The new line between Soochow and Hangchow, however, was completed before hostilities began. Another new line from Hangchow running west to Kiangsi was finished just before the war and during the war was prolonged farther west to Hunan, where it connected with the

Canton-Hankow Railway. The line was also further extended to Kweilin, capital of the southwest province of Kwangsi.

Highways were extended more rapidly. The Nanking-Hangchow highway was built during my sojourn in Nanking and I had the pleasure of going through it before it was opened to traffic. It traversed the richest sections of Chekiang and Kiangsu Provinces. As the car wound its way along Tai Lake one felt like stopping for a few days to sit under the pine trees and watch the sails rise or vanish over the horizon in the sunset. The fishermen cast their nets and drew up shining carp from the water. Tai is one of the five largest lakes in China, irrigating millions of acres of fertile land in the two most populous and cultured provinces of the country.

This highway also passed through a bandit-infested region, but the bandits disappeared when the road was opened because troops could be rushed to the spot.

Local troubles sometimes brewed as fast as construction progressed. At times the railway and highway lines had to run a race with disturbance in areas without modern roads. The rebellion in Fukien Province a year before the war was frustrated by central troops rushed down through the then newly built Hangchow-Kiangsan Railway and along the roads also newly built, from Hangchow to that province. More roads meant less rebellion and less banditry, aside from the easy flow of products from one locality to another.

Communication is the key to modernization and reforms and to the discovery of possibilities of future development of the country. Thus the Nationalist government began its reconstruction program with the building of roads and railways. This was also the way to secure the unification of the country; any local rebellion could be put down easily if good roads were available. Again, better and more communication means more travel and quicker exchange of ideas. Beautiful scenery hitherto hidden in inaccessible parts of the country suddenly opened to the appreciative eyes of scholars, painters, poets, and lovers of nature.

Under the influence of the Nationalistic government the provinces themselves began to build more roads. Existing roads were fast extended after the Kuomintang came to power. During the war, troops were freely shifted on these roads from one province to another. A year or two before the war a motor trip was made from Nanking to Kunming—that is, from the east coast to the southwest frontier city, the starting point of the Burma Road.

In the field of administration an attempt was made to increase the efficiency of official business. New filing systems for official documents were devised and put into trial use. The form of language in official documents was simplified.

A civil examination system was again inaugurated, but to the disappointment of those who had seen the old Imperial days, without the pomp and honors that had greeted the successful candidates.

A new code of civil law was drafted. The status of women was raised to the same level as that of men. Daughters were to inherit property of their parents as hitherto only sons had done. Freedom of marriage was granted to the parties concerned when they came to legal age. A mutual agreement of the parties concerned is sufficient for legal divorce.

The school curriculum was standardized and the proportion of science teaching increased. Physical training was emphasized. New laws were promulgated governing the universities, and the Central Research Institute, Academia Sinica, etc., were established to carry on research in science, history, economics, and engineering.

The obnoxious internal customs system of *likin*, which we shall see more of in the next chapter, was abolished. Government finance was put on a sounder basis. National currency was standardized, government banks reorganized. The circulation of silver was later suspended and only government bank notes allowed to circulate; during the war we began to realize the importance of this move, for if we had had to rely upon bulky silver as the medium of exchange it would have been well-nigh impossible to carry on the long years of war, while if the shift had been made in wartime it would have caused great confusion.

From 1927, when the capital was established at Nanking, to 1937, when the Japanese army fired its first shots at the Marco Polo Bridge, only ten short years were allowed to the Nationalist government to do its job. During these ten years intermittent rebellions and other obstacles retarded the progress of reforms and reconstruction, yet in this brief time 7,300 kilometers of railway were constructed, in contrast to 8,300 kilometers during the last fifty years. More than 100,000 kilometers of highway were built, and 33,000 kilometers of new telegraph lines were added to those already in existence. Yet naturally there could be only a moderate beginning in each phase of construction in so short an interval, and so it must be considered.

After the Kuomintang came to power the struggle with the Communists continued. While they lost control in the cities, their influence spread in the country districts and worked among the peasants. From 1928 to 1934 agrarian uprisings occurred in more than two hundred hsien, scattered among eighteen provinces, where landowners were "liquidated" and the land distributed among the peasants by the same drastic methods witnessed in the early days of the Russian Revolution.

The stronghold of the Communists was in the province of Kiangsi, where they occupied fifty-nine districts. After several years of fighting between Nationalist forces and Communists in that province, the latter withdrew to the northwest corner of the country and later established their capital in Yenan. There they gave up their more violent measures and as an expedient adopted a moderate policy of agrarian reform—a modified form of the Kuomintang program of land rent reduction which we have seen.

Meanwhile the popularity of Generalissimo Chiang Kai-shek among the people became very great—so great that warlords and others on occasion were forced by popular sentiment to submit to his moral force as the national leader.

One extreme and dramatic example was the Sian affair. In this instance the Generalissimo flew to Loyang and then to Sian on an inspection trip. Many political and military leaders went there later to discuss national problems with him and get orders from him. Then something undreamed-of happened. In the stillness of night shots were heard near his quarters. Armed soldiers pressed in, searching for him. As a man who had gone through many battles, he was always alert and got away from the place, but he was found and delivered into the hands of General Chang Hsueh-liang, on whom he had lavished much time and kindness, helping him to develop. The incident reflected, though in distortion, the desire for national unification in order to resist Japanese encroachments.

When the startling news was broadcast to the whole country,

people were distraught and worried, and women and children wept. Telegrams came from every part of the country to Sian urging the young general to use his better judgment. Madam Chiang Kai-shek and Dr. T. V. Soong risked putting more prizes in the hands of the crazy young general and flew direct to Sian. In the face of strong public opinion the young man faltered and finally sent the Generalissimo and his lady safely to Loyang.

Before his safety became known there had been a dancing party held in the barracks of the U.S. Marine Guards at the American Embassy, at which members of the various embassies and legations were present and I also was a guest. A Tass correspondent asked me why I did not dance. I told him that I was worrying about the safety of our national leader. He said calmly, "Don't worry. He'll come out pretty soon. Nothing will happen to him." I looked at him in a high state of expectation and said, "I hope your prophecy will come true."

The next evening about dinnertime my telephone rang. "Hello, this is the Central News Agency. Generalissimo Chiang Kai-shek arrived safely at Loyang and flew to Nanking." The news seemed too good to be true—I could not believe my own ears. I telephoned Dr. Hu Shih who was at dinner with a party. Cheers reached me across the wire.

In the Chih-hsiang Theatre at the Tung-an Market, where the extras first circulated, waves of applause swept the audience, to the indescribable embarrassment and perplexity of the actors, who were unaware of the happy tidings. In about half an hour the stillness of the gloomy winter evening in Peking was suddenly broken by the gay sound of firecrackers, while stars of fireworks splashed joyously in the dark sky.

A friend of mine, on a train from Nanking to Shanghai, wondered at the noise of firecrackers as the train approached Soochow. At the station the happy news reached the passengers, who felt like setting off a few themselves to let out their pent-up emotions; none were to be had at the station, so the schoolgirls on the train began to sing instead.

The warlords had wrought havoc in the country for a quarter of a century, and people longed for some national leader to rise and sweep away these obstacles to national unity. They had found him in the person of Generalissimo Chiang Kai-shek. His difficulties were enhanced by the double task of dislodging the remnants of the snarling "tigers" from their lairs in the provinces, on the one hand, and building up adequate forces to resist Japanese invasion on the other. But public opinion was solidly behind him in carrying out his great task.

Part V

SOME ASPECTS OF CHINESE LIFE

CHAPTER 21

THE "LEAKAGE" SYSTEM

FOREIGNERS coming to China for the first time used often to meet with the annoying practice of petty "squeeze" among their servants and cooks and naturally felt that something must be wrong with China. But they would presently be informed by old China hands, familiar with the China of Imperial days and the later regimes of the warlords, that the practice of "squeeze" was not only to be found in servant circles but also among those higher up. "Squeeze is a national system," they would say and cite concrete examples to illustrate their point.

This reference to happenings of bygone days that lingered in their memories would focus the eyes of the newcomers on remnants of the dark side of Chinese life which are fast passing, and the effect has been to throw a veil over unprejudiced minds in their effort to see the living, new China of today. This is very unfortunate for foreign observers who have tried to understand China, and unfair to both this and the last generation of Chinese leaders, who endured hardships and sacrificed their lives for reforms in China's national life.

I propose now to paint a dark, vivid, and real picture of Chinese economic life in the past, without exaggerating or minimizing —which I hope I can do even better than the old China hands.

Anyone who witnessed the downfall of the Imperial regime must be aware that one of the main factors which caused the Manchu government to lose control of the country was its decrepit system of public finance. Large numbers of public servants were paid only nominal salaries and left to finance themselves by *Lou-kwei*, or the "leakage" system. This practice deprived them of any sense of public morality and caused them to countenance corruption as a matter of course. The Imperial government connived at the irregular gains of its officials, and the officials in turn connived at those of their subordinates. The poisonous sap circulated in the whole tree of state, reaching to every twig of every branch and every leaf on each twig. It flowed through all the roots of the tree and every rootlet.

From the government offices through which public revenues passed, the government required only certain fixed amounts to be forwarded to the national treasury. The officials in charge of the revenues could, by various means and all sorts of excuses and plausible reasons, attach a variety of fees to the regular taxes. In this way, for every tael of silver that flowed into the government treasury at least the same amount or even more would be diverted to "leakage" funds. In the later years of the Imperial regime more wine leaked into private cups than remained in the public barrel. The government, finding itself parched as a fish in a dry pond, pressed hard for more money—whence still more "leakage" for public servants and heavier burdens for the people.

Failing to realize funds by taxation or other means, such as offering public offices for sale, the Imperial government resorted to borrowing from foreign sources by awarding them concessions for building railroads or opening mines. This was to quench thirst by drinking poison. It may be remembered that the nationalization of railways in Szechuan Province, as a preliminary step to awarding the building rights to foreign concerns, pulled the trigger for the Revolution of 1911.

But as to the "leakage" system and how it worked. China was then divided into some twenty-two provinces, comprising about two thousand hsien. The chief executive of the hsien was the magistrate, who took charge of all financial matters and concurrently filled the role of administrator of justice in his district. His salary—not more than a few taels a month—was nominal. All expenses incurred by the holder of the office had to be paid out of "leakage" funds. When higher officials of the Imperial government passed through his district he had to entertain them and secure for them all the "necessities" required for their travel. To the entourage of any higher official he had to offer "presents," usually in the form of money.

On the banks of the Yaokiang River just outside the city wall of my native Yuyao stood a welcome pavilion at which the magistrate welcomed passing officials of higher rank. One sunny afternoon

some forty years ago I noticed crowds gathering at a distance, near
the pavilion. I joined them and watched the landing of the Imperial Examiner and his entourage, on their way to Ningpo to
hold civil examinations in that prefecture. On the previous day the
magistrate had "caught," or requisitioned, many houseboats from
the people and the one set aside for the Imperial Examiner was
loaded with sealed cases, their contents known only to those who
had prepared them.

I watched the party change boats. The Imperial Examiner
stepped into the most prominent; the sails were set and the little
flotilla with the officials and "leakage" gifts on board floated down-
river with the ebbing tide to the seaport city of Ningpo. Under
that inspiration I said to myself that from now on I must study
hard, so that some day I myself might be an Imperial Examiner
blessed with such mysterious gifts as lay hidden in those cases.

Regular "gifts" had to be presented to the secretaries of the civil
governor (*fantai*) of the province. Failing that, a magistrate could
not expect them to speak kind words for him to the governor and
would find them faultfinding in his official relations with the governor's office. Added together, the amount required for plain sailing in his career was by no means small. Human nature also made
him not unmindful of the necessity to provide for a rainy day. And
he had his family and followers to support.

Candidates for magistracy who had pull were covetous of the
districts with large revenues. I remember that in the hsien in which
we lived during my school days no magistrate had ever held office
for more than a year. The regular term of office was three years, in
which a magistrate could realize approximately a hundred thousand dollars. In those times this sum was considered very great. So
the governor appointed acting magistrates, whose term was usually one year. In this way there would be more chances for expectant magistrates to share the profit.

When a magistrate retired from office after the expiration of his
term and paid an official call on the governor, he was usually asked
by his superior whether his district had been a good one, meaning
how much he had got out of the "leakage" funds. His friends and
relatives also asked him the same question by way of starting a
conversation.

The higher the rank of the official through whose hands the

government revenues passed, the more "leakage" flowed into his private coffer. The taotai of Shanghai was known to reap a profit of some 100,000 taels a year. Governors and viceroys of rich provinces and the powerful princes and grand ministers in Peking usually enjoyed large yearly incomes.

The system was upheld even by the great statesman and scholar, General Tseng Kuo-fan, who put down the Taiping Rebellion for the Manchu Dynasty. In one of his letters he argued that "leakage" was indispensable to the smooth running of the government; the expenses incurred by an official were great and he had a family and relatives to provide for. The system was countenanced by scholars as well. In his diary a famous scholar-official who lived in Peking during the Hsien-feng and Tung-chi period complains that Viceroy Chang Chi-tung presented him with only a small "gift." A later entry reads something like this: "Went to Tao Ren Pavilion in the afternoon to sip tea. Chang Chi-tung entered. I pretended not to see him and left the place." This may be safely interpreted to mean that the famous viceroy had offended the prominent scholar by presenting him with too small a gift from his "leakage" funds.

During the Imperial regime promising candidates could keep servants with very little pay or none at all. The servants would stick to their masters through thick and thin for years, hoping that some day when luck fell into the laps of their masters they too could share the "leakage" with their lords. When luck did come, master and servant alike would strive to make it still leakier, so that each and all could have cupfuls of this wine to their hearts' content. If luck failed to appear they would keep on waiting until the last ray of hope was gone. Under pressure of starvation some unfortunate masters found relief in the rope, with which they ended their lives. In Hangchow during my school days the news circulated by word of mouth that an expectant magistrate, idle for years, had hanged himself on a New Year's Eve when his creditors pressed him hard for the money he owed them.

The poisonous sap penetrated even to the households of the well to do. The cook would poke "holes" in his vegetable and meat baskets in order to make them "leak." Servants got something from the purchases they made for the household—especially in Peking the shops always added a certain percentage to the price for the servants who made the purchase.

The practice of "leakage" even went abroad and found its way into the household of Napoleon. Napoleon had a Chinese cook who served his master very faithfully. On his deathbed this great French general remembered his faithful servant, saying, "Treat him well because his country will be one of the greatest in time to come. But the Chinese love money. Give him five hundred francs." On the other hand, the Dean Lung Professorship of Chinese Literature in Columbia University was established in memory of a Chinese laundryman with the money earned by a lifetime of washing. Before his death Dean Lung handed over a bag of gold to his master and asked him to do something good for China. The master, adding a sum to it, established the chair in memory of the patriotic laundryman.

The practice of "leakage" permeated the entire system of likin. And likin, like a gigantic octopus with tentacles reaching to every communication line in the country, sucked the blood out of the trade and commerce of the nation. It had been installed during the Taiping Rebellion to raise war funds for the support of the Imperial army. The Taipings were gone, but the obnoxious system was there to stay.

It worked this way. Anyone who knew how to "squeeze" the people would bid—say two hundred thousand dollars a year—to government agents for the right to run the likin at a certain station or a number of stations established at points on the highway where merchandise passed from one city to another. The person who won the bid would become likin commissioner at that station or group of stations and had the right to assess duties on the goods passing through. If he could realize a sum of three hundred thousand dollars within the year, he would turn over two hundred thousand to the government and keep the remainder for himself and his partners. So he would make most goods dutiable in order to swell his private fortune.

Once I saw a boat loaded with watermelons passing under the bridge at a station. It was stopped by a long bamboo hook from shore and several inspectors jumped down and began to thrust iron rods into the melons. The owner begged them to desist and promised to pay any amount they demanded. The "duties" were paid; the poor farmer sailed on.

I remember how small traders and farmers hated likin. Everybody would have liked to smash the stations to pieces. Once a group of young scholars going by boat to take an Imperial examination passed by a likin station, ignoring the order to stop. The inspectors detained the boat and began to search their belongings. The scholars leaped ashore, entered the station, and smashed everything they could lay their hands on. Only the flag, emblem of the authority of the Imperial government, was left drooping in the air with its inscription: "To Collect Likin by His Majesty's Orders." Triumphantly the scholars departed under the gaze of the admiring crowd.

After the Revolution of 1911 the "leakage" system was gradually suppressed, and the system of likin was abolished later on. Higher salaries were paid to officials. But cases of corruption were still frequent. The practice persists among servants in the form of petty "squeeze." A lady once scolded her cook for being too greedy in getting his "squeeze," and got into a quarrel with him. Someone remarked that he was as greedy as a hungry wolf, to which he replied, "If one were not greedy, he would not become a cook."

In one of the embassies in Peking the ambassador's cook charged ten cents for an egg, while his secretary's cook charged his master five cents. "Why should I have to pay more for an egg than the wife of our secretary?" asked the ambassador's wife. "Madam, the ambassador receives a higher salary than the secretary," was the reply. Owners of cars often found their gas tanks "leaky," because the drivers helped themselves to cupfuls of gasoline. Unwarranted repairs made bills for maintenance mount up.

Since the Nationalist government came to power in 1927 China has been endeavoring to check the occasional corruption in the government. Severe punishment has been meted out to offenders. However, the legacy from centuries of the "leakage" system, which existed even before the Manchus, is difficult to discard totally within a few years or even a generation. Under the leadership of Generalissimo Chiang Kai-shek official corruption has been reduced to a few isolated cases. With the introduction of a modern financial system and the gradual enlightenment of public conscience, China has done much in checking these malpractices. As the technique of government improves with time, she will attain the level of a modern, well-organized country in which more efficient methods of taxation and effective control of public finance will be devised.

The Chinese have always trusted in the intrinsic good of human nature, believing that evils arise only from perversion of that good through negligence or lack of proper education. It was the decrepit system of public finance that caused China's trouble in this respect, not lack of a sense of moral responsibility. But the system had such a demoralizing influence on public practice that we still suffer from its effects.

Concrete examples have shown us that the remedy lies in building up a good system to supersede the bad ones. It is not sufficient merely to abolish the bad. The customs administration organized by the British for China was free of the bad influence of "leakage." Employees were properly trained and adequately paid. Ample pensions were given them after retirement. Patronage was little known. The control of this important branch of national revenue by foreign governments as a guarantee for the payment of indemnities and foreign debts has been humiliating and extremely dangerous to national integrity, but the adequate system of revenue built up as a by-product is an unintended blessing to China.

The postal administration was organized under the Western system. It has been running efficiently since its inception—even long years of civil war did not disrupt its work. Ever since the Japanese aggression started it has been marvelous to see letters circulating in the occupied areas as freely as in Free China. Mail carriers have constantly crossed the firing lines to deliver the mails entrusted to them.

The salt administration is another example. Even during the long years of Japanese aggression the people have been adequately supplied with this daily necessity.

The Huang-ho Commission was well known formerly for its "leakage" system; indeed, the famous Shantung and Honan cuisines were the product of the rich appetites and well-lined coffers of the gluttonous commissioners of the Huang-ho works. In the same way, Yangchow cooking became renowned through the epicurean salt merchants of Yangchow.

With the formation of a Huang-ho Conservancy Board with modern trained engineers in charge of the conservation work, the "leakage" system itself was cast into the river and flowed down into the Yellow Sea. The gluttons disappeared with their system; only the art of cooking remains. Yangchow delicacies, too, are still admired by men of good taste, while the innovators who introduced them are gone and forgotten since the introduction of the salt gabelle, a modern, well-organized system of salt administration.

With well-organized administration, a well-trained and well-paid personnel, tenure of office ensured and adequate pensions provided after retirement, the good that is in human nature has full play.

It may be said that these successes have depended on foreign assistance. But let me ask: Are they due alone to the good morals of the foreigners—or rather to the good system they have introduced into China? Without personal integrity no such system would work, yet could we depend on foreign morals alone to obtain the desired results? Could a handful of foreign experts on top be powerful enough to check the irregular practices of hundreds and thousands of Chinese personnel? It is through the co-operation of the rank and file of Chinese employees under a good system that the customs, salt, and postal administrations have been successful. This is what Mencius, disciple of Confucius, has said: "Good morals alone will not make a good administration; systems alone will not carry the work to the desired ends."

The modern banking system and railway administration in China are also commendable examples. The banks and railways on the whole run efficiently and are free of gross maladministration of funds.

Modern universities in China are further examples of honest administration of funds, aside from their stand for intellectual honesty. Teachers have worked hard, through privations on account of the abnormally high cost of living during the war, to maintain their standards of scholarship. The majority of students coming under the good influence of the teachers and the university organization cannot but form healthy ideas and correct habits as regards honest and efficient administration of public funds, along with the modern training they have received. And we must remember that in their hands the future of China lies.

Above all, the attitude toward the administration of public funds has basically changed. In the old days the "leakage" system was connived at or even admired. At present it is disliked and reviled by all intelligent people. This change of public sentiment will have an important bearing, given modern methods, upon the future handling of funds in all spheres of public administration.

It is more difficult to eradicate the practice of "squeeze" among servants, cooks, and chauffeurs. Perhaps it will take a generation or two to alleviate the economic status of these people; until that is done, we cannot very well expect that they will drop their bits of "sweets." Perhaps by then it will be difficult in any case to find people to work as household servants. Yet in my six years of sojourn in Kunming during the war I have met with one cook, one man servant, one maid, and one chauffeur in our employ who never "squeezed." Our present cook and man servant have a spotless record as regards money matters.

Let the reader turn the leaves of a textbook of European history to the period just before the French Revolution; let him glance through the constitutional development of England or the history of India in the times of Warren Hastings; he will readily agree with the writer that the "leakage" system of China was but a mild form of corruption. Yet, along with other forces, it did gradually sap the vitality of a reigning dynasty, once very powerful, and render it in the end financially anemic and politically impotent. Finally the Manchu Empire crumbled like a house of cards before the moral force of Dr. Sun Yat-sen.

CHAPTER 22

SOCIAL STRUCTURE AND SOCIAL PROGRESS

IT HAS been a common belief that China's four hundred million people were as loosely connected as the sands of the sea. It would be nearer the truth to say that her great population is—or was— segmented into many small self-governing units. Chinese democracy has consisted of tens of thousands of such units, loosely knit together by a common language, a common culture, and common ideals of life achieved through centuries of cumulative effort. These units, large or small, developed on a basis of family, trade, and tradition. Individuals were bound by these common ties to each self-governing group and so were more intimate with the members of their own group than with a broader society. They understood local problems better than national ones. This was the fundamental reason the constitutional National Assembly failed to work, and this was why the people allowed themselves to be governed by warlords. It was the frame of mind that gave birth to the nationwide idea in Imperial days, often quoted here, that "Heaven is high above and the Emperor is far away."

Individuals, unless they broke with society in some way, were always part of the unit, but the units were not well cemented by any effective national organization. This was a strong point as well as a weakness in China's national life—a strength because it made China democratic and enduring through ages of war and invasion, and a weakness because it made her central authority impotent and rendered her vulnerable to the attack of invaders.

The existence of these units in Chinese life has its historical background. They came into being by the slow work of centuries. As the Chinese gradually moved into the less populated or unpopulated areas, they went in groups to form separate colonies which grew into self-governing villages or communities. The vast Chinese Empire was built up by centuries of peaceful colonization of outlying territory by just such social clusters. In recent years, by a study of the dialects of China, we have been able to trace the path of this development. The Cantonese dialect is found to be closely related to the spoken language of the Tang Dynasty. We may reasonably infer that the predominant part of the population of Canton are descendants of the Tangs. Later arrivals, forming their own distinct groups, spoke a quite different dialect known as *Hak-ka,* which shows the language characteristics of recent centuries. Even along the Yangtze Valley the slight difference in dialect in various localities affords a subtle record of the stages of colonization.

The migration of the Chinese population to the south was hastened in the tenth century by the downfall of the Tangs when north China was devastated by invaders from outside the Great Wall. The southern provinces, especially Kwangtung, Hunan, and Chekiang, which were not vulnerable to the successive invasions and were less affected by intermittent wars, became reservoirs of Chinese culture destined to irrigate the vast territory of New China in the last fifty years.

If a reform was to be truly effective in the direction of national unity and coherence, it had to touch the age-old local units by effecting some sort of change in the family, the trades, and tradition. And inversely, since these units were knit together by a common language and culture and common ideals of life, any modification of culture and ideals through the common language would be bound to affect the life of these social clusters and consequently of the country.

China was first set on the road to change when foreign manufactures began to affect the trades. Thus one of the three strands that bound her society was loosened. That was the early stage of change when she first came under modern influence, and the process was unconscious. Then the introduction of modern ideas through books and newspapers and the school system further weakened the already slipping knot by loosening the strand of tradition. The last remaining element, that of family ties, had finally to give way with the other two.

The loosening of these three ties which bound people to their local units caused years of disturbance. Individuals groping for new effective bonds created trouble of many sorts. The students were the first to be affected by the new ideas and it was they who started the trouble; workers in the new industries lost their old trade bonds and they, too, joined the students in troublemaking, as we have seen. The internecine wars of the warlords, the failure of constitutionalism, and the existence of the demoralizing "leakage" system neither prevented the disintegration of the old social organizations nor retarded social progress to any great extent. The troubles caused by the warlords were but ripples on China's vast social sea. The undercurrent went on swirling under the surface, with or without them, or the debased National Assembly, or the "leakage" system. These were evils in the superstructure merely; the self-governing units themselves remained temperamentally peaceful and morally clean.

In the long course of history, especially since the latter days of the Tang Dynasty, China has been weak in national defense because her invaders have all been organized on a war footing while she was organized on a basis of peace. Defense forces have had to be drawn from peaceful communities and maintained by a central authority which was a mere superstructure above a peace-loving society.

The Chinese under the leadership of the Mings overthrew the Yuans or Mongols not so much through their own military might as because of the failing strength of the Mongols. Through long years of wars on two continents the military force of the descendants of Genghis Khan had spent itself. Under Chung Chu, second emperor of the Ming Dynasty, China succeeded in organizing a strong army which conquered a great part of Manchuria during his reign; but this military power gradually weakened after his death. When the warlike Manchus rose outside the Great Wall the Mings were helpless in the face of Tartar invasion, and the Ming Dynasty gave way to the Ching or Manchu Dynasty without much effective fighting. After more than a century in China the Manchus in turn were contaminated by the peaceful spirit of the Chinese, and when the Western Powers attacked China with gunboats she was again helpless.

Studying the past, Japan assumed that history would repeat itself and on this assumption began her continental campaign against China in 1894. Up to that year she was right. But Chinese history then began to shift its course as China learned the "tricks" of Western civilization. Japan was either unaware of this change or tried to nip it in the bud. In either case she did not hesitate to launch a new continental campaign some thirty years later, and was surprised to find that a stumbling block had risen in her way.

This was China's social progress. Japan had seen at the top the weak and corrupt Imperial Peking government whose financial strength had been sapped by the "leakage" system; later she saw on the surface the warring warlords; but she was blind to the undercurrents which had slowly but persistently moved in China's immense ocean during the last fifty years.

In the old days organized national ties had existed in secret societies. The members lived outside the village units, gathering around large cities and along commercial routes. Their main purpose was mutual protection against oppression, but this sometimes degenerated into illicit trade. They were powerful in time of internal rebellion but not of much use against foreign aggression. They lacked new ideas and the notion of social progress was alien to them.

But now, on the fringes of the many thousands of self-governing units in the country there had gathered people imbued with national ideas as against local prejudices and newly learned patriotism as against family loyalty. These individuals hummed like honeybees round a hive and gradually gathered in clusters along the edges. More and more individuals sneaked out to join those outside. As the clusters grew in size, they began to make intrusions into the hive and affected the life of the whole colony. At the same time they began to organize themselves into a national union, so to speak, and took China as their common hive.

Such was the growth of China's modern national institutions. The process was hastened by the rapid extension of communication: steam navigation, highways, railroads, and airways. Educational associations, chambers of commerce, labor unions—scientific, engineering, and political science societies and other bodies—all were organized on a national basis. Political parties, whether the Kuomintang or those whose views were opposed to it, all led the people to think along national lines. The universities took members of the family and molded them into leaders of the nation. Schools instilled national consciousness and patriotism into the formative minds of the new generation.

In spite of continuous civil wars, even before the unification of the country the number of public schools had multiplied in all the provinces. Private citizens established private schools as a way of expressing their patriotism. These millions of elementary school graduates, entering thousands of local self-governing communities, spread ideas of patriotism even to the humble hamlets of the interior.

Once, traveling in the interior during the fight along the Great Wall, I saw a solitary small boy playing soldier. He took a tree for his imaginary enemy and stabbed it with his dagger. Then he imagined that his enemy struck back. He made gestures of defending himself, then fell to the ground with his eyes closed and whispered to himself, "I die for my country." Evidently he was defending the country against the Japanese invasion. During the later war, after a few of the Chungking people had deserted to the Japanese, way back in the hinterland I saw a little boy digging a small grave with a spade. When the work was done he put a sign on the grave: "The Traitor." In one mountainous region, where the nearest school was miles away, a mining engineer saw small boys writing on the walls of their village: "Long live the Three People's Principles of Dr. Sun Yat-sen." These instances show the growth of the national bonds that were taking the place of local ones.

Under the influence of the new education, organized into a national school system, children all over the country now made paper airplanes and sailed them in the air. They made toy water pumps and built toy automobiles. They began to be mechanically minded —a good groundwork for future industrialization of the country.

The growth of light industries in recent years has drawn more and more individuals from the local units and they have begun to associate into a national body instead of local guilds. Radio has brought new ideas to the people through the air. Customs, superstitions, dialects, folksongs, religions, domestic industries, and the economic condition of the tottering local trades and of the suffering farmers have been investigated and studied scientifically from data gathered by institutions of higher learning and learned societies. China has begun to know herself through scientific research.

The turmoils of half a century had set the people thinking. Their attitudes toward life began to change. They tried to create a new

stability out of chaos by forming effective national bonds to hold
China together in the face of invasion and by working for the
progress of the country. This new social and national consciousness
was not yet strong enough to face modern warfare with full force.
But it was formidable enough to offer stubborn resistance, with
indomitable will.

CHAPTER 23

ENCHANTED CITY OF PEKING

As PARIS has inherited the spirit of the ancient Roman Empire, Peking has inherited that of the Chinese Empire of the old glorious days. Paris is the city of cities in the West, Peking in the East. Of Paris you feel that it is not only a city of Frenchmen but also your own; so Peking is not the city of the Chinese alone but universal. In both Paris and Peking one says, "This is my city, where I would like to live."

I lived in Peking for fifteen years until the Evil One dislodged me in 1937. As I look back to the old days there even the annoying dust of Peking is rich in pleasant associations. I miss it and long for it. In the early morning when the rising sun cast its beams upon the paper windows, with shadows of creeping vines dancing upon them, you would see a thin layer of dust sprayed evenly upon your mahogany desk from the night before. It was a pleasure to dust it off carefully with a feather duster. Then you would dust the brush-holder carved with landscapes, and the carved ink stone once owned by famous scholars of past centuries who dusted and washed it centuries before you. And you would do the same for the porcelains of Chien-lung, the bronzes of the Chow Dynasty, the oracle bones of the Shang period—used for divination four thousand years ago—and other timeworn treasures. Even the books, printed long before the West knew anything of the art and lying peacefully on your shelves, did not escape your attention. Let your fingers touch the covers; you would find that the dust did not grudge its favor.

Then you felt that you had done well your morning's preliminary work. The sunlit windows with their dancing shadows now smiled before you. The spotless desk with its ageless pieces of art displayed before your eyes beckoned you on. With a tranquil mind and contented heart you set to your day's work.

In such an atmosphere of antiquity you might read of the period when Confucius taught his disciples; or when the Nestorians came to the glorious empire of the Tangs; or the Jesuits made their astronomical instruments at the Ming court; or Buddha preached his doctrine of eternity; or Napoleon carried his campaign into Russia and drank oil from the street lights; or Genghis Khan sent his invincible armies to the Danube basin, founded an empire on two continents, and made Peking the capital of one of his sons. In Peking one could read history in its true perspective. For this city was as grand as nature itself and as old as history. As a capital it has witnessed the rise and fall of five dynasties—dynasties came and were gone, but Peking remained.

The palace buildings were all rectangular and symmetrically arranged like an armchair, with a vast rectangular courtyard in the middle in which stood proudly the giant incense burners of gilded bronze whose smoke, when incense was burning, streamed to the sky. Bronze deer stood in rows and pairs of crouching lions of stone or bronze guarded the entrances. Over a hundred of these courtyards with imposing buildings on three sides were fitted together like the squares of a chessboard in the Forbidden City, which was shut in by rectangular yellow walls with yellow-roofed towers standing out against the sky at the four corners. The Mongols began it, the Mings rebuilt it, and the Manchus improved it to its present form.

The yellow enamel tiles of the roofs shone under the brilliant sun in a speckless blue sky. At dusk or before dawn the triumphal towers of Wu Men—the main entrance of the Forbidden City—silhouetted against the pale sky, looked like castles in the air. On a cloudless moonlit night they made one feel that he was near some fairy palace of the moon which he might admire but not reach.

Before the little Emperor Pu-yi, who reigned over this city within the city of Peking, was ousted from the Forbidden City by General Fung Yu-hsiang in 1926, semimonthly audiences were granted to the remnants of Manchu officialdom. Attired in the quaint old Manchu costumes the officials clustered around the back doors of his toy empire seeking admittance.

A few days after the coup d'état I went into the palace to witness a government committee sealing, house by house, the doors of the halls. A few of the eunuchs were still retained, from whom I got quite a bit of information about life in the palace and stories of the doings of emperors and empresses, princes and princesses, of bygone days.

One story was about the large looking glass which ran from the ceiling to the bottom of the wall. The Empress Dowager loved to sit opposite it so that she could see for herself how stately she was. One day the governor of Shensi was granted an audience by Her Majesty. As he entered the door he saw her in the mirror and bent his knees before the image, kowtowing.

"What did the Empress Dowager do? I suppose she was angry," I said.

"No, no. She smiled and said to him kindly, 'You are seeing me in the mirror.'"

I met some of the eunuchs who attended the princes at the palace school for princes and found them to be all illiterate. Imperial household regulations forbade them to have an education, so that they would remain ignorant of what was taught in the school.

Perched on frames hanging in the veranda, red, yellow, and blue parrots talked the language of the princesses who had spent much time in teaching them. "Please come in. Guests coming. Bring tea . . ." said the blue one to me, and the red and yellow ones echoed, "Bring tea! Bring tea!" This was the first time I ever saw a blue parrot. Goldfish—black, white, red, and gold varieties— many of them almost a foot long, darted in the palace ponds, their periscope eyes looking skyward while their multiple fan-shaped silken tails waved gracefully in the water.

The living quarters of Pu-yi looked vulgar. A cheap-looking long foreign table stood in the middle of the hall with a few ugly chairs at either side. A pair of pink glass vases decorated the table. It was more like a second-rate country inn in America than the residence of an emperor of China. All the fine furniture and art treasures had been pushed aside and bundled up in the background. The vulgar Western civilization of the treaty ports had invaded the palace; nothing could be more out of place. Cheap magazines were scattered about. Half an apple, freshly cut, and a newly opened box of biscuits lay on the table. Apparently the Emperor had been taken by surprise and left the place as it was at the moment.

When the sealed doors were subsequently opened for a methodical checking over of the art treasures, the variety of beautiful objects was amazing. There were watermelons carved out of jade which looked like real ones, porcelains the color of "blue skies after a shower," bronzes that had witnessed thirty centuries of peace and war, and Imperial seals of jade which had set their mark on many an important document.

Among the famous paintings of the Tang, Sung, Yuan, Ming, and Ching periods were landscapes depicting the beauty and harmony of nature which invited you to step in and enjoy a tranquil life; horses that looked ready to trot out from the picture; fish that seemed to be swimming in water; geese hissing and honking as if painted in sound; bamboo shadows that appeared to bend in the autumn breeze; lotus leaves fresh with morning dew; orchids that seemed to pour forth their mild scent into the air. Great painting in China meant to render not the likeness alone but the motion, sound, color, characteristics—all that would stir the imagination and evoke feeling. In other words, it tried to paint the spirit of the subject.

For two years the committee, with a staff of over a hundred persons, ransacked every recess of the vast palace for treasures of art and checked many hundreds of thousands of articles accumulated through generations of emperors. Some of the storerooms were sealed with spider webs and others had dust ankle deep, a sure sign that they had been a no-man's-land for a century or more. Some treasures had lain there unnoticed for many, many years, no one knew how long.

At long last the palace was thrown open to view and the Palace Museum established to exhibit its treasures. The public, especially the younger generation, opened their eyes at the riches and wonderful achievements of Chinese art through the centuries. Peking was already a center of art; connoisseurs were many and artists not lacking, and with the opening of the Palace Museum the city was much enriched. Things heretofore secluded in the depths of the palace were now revealed for anyone to see—things previously accessible only to the royal family were now open to the common people.

As science is the expression of the mind in knowing and searching for the laws of nature, art is the expression of the heart in feeling their reality. Art is an expression of the life of the people who create it, and makes life richer and more enjoyable. Science is the product of the activity of the mind in satisfying its intellectual interest, and creates material prosperity. In modern civilization the two must join hands to make life complete.

There was a chain of three lakes—the South, Middle, and North "Seas"—to the left of the Forbidden City, with camel-back bridges spanning the creeks between them, trees centuries old along the shores, lilies growing luxuriantly in the water, and pavilions perched on the surrounding heights with golden enamel tiles, vermilion columns, and artistically painted beams. A fish caught some time ago in the lake, so the story has it, bore a gold plate with the sign of "Yung-lo" of the Ming Dynasty (1368–1643).

In the Middle Sea was Yun Tai, an islet surrounded by lotus where the Emperor Kwang-hsü was imprisoned by the Empress Dowager after the unsuccessful reforms of 1898 and where he died broken-hearted in 1909. On the island was a group of palace buildings with spacious courtyards. Moss-grown trees stood high above the yellow tiles of an intricate system of halls, pavilions linked together with winding corridors of vermilion beams and columns. Miniature hills with rocks and caves brought mountain scenes into the Imperial gardens. How much the unfortunate Emperor enjoyed life in his beautiful prison only Kwang-hsü and those who were with him could tell. During the long days of his lonely existence he was perpetually tortured by ailments of mind and body until death relieved him.

Water was formerly conducted into the lakes through stone conduits connected with springs in the Western Hills. Parts of these pipes still lay along the highways. The drainage system in Peking was a great engineering feat of the old days. Underground aqueducts resembling modern subway tunnels were constructed to drain the sewage from the city. During the latter part of the Manchu Dynasty they were all choked, but the system of yearly inspection of the drainage was still retained to the last days of the regime. In the early days inspectors were ordered to walk through the tunnels to see whether any section needed repair. Later, when passage was obstructed by deposits of dirt, they deceived the eyes of their superiors by a cunning method of cheating: two inspectors in uniform climbed down at one end of the aqueduct and stayed there, while another pair in identical uniforms, hidden at the other end, appeared as the inspector general rode by on his horse. The example illustrates how the spirit of the system had evaporated through years of stagnation while the system still remained as a symbol. This happened in many departments of the Imperial government in the later years. It was small wonder that the government of Imperial China had become a mere symbol.

Peking was a city of trees. In the spacious courtyards and gardens of private residences were moss-grown trees which shot heavenward with a wide spread of branches and luxuriant leaves. If you stood on Coal Hill or some other height, the city seemed to be built in a forest. Wide streets running parallel and crosswise like the lines in a checkerboard traversed the "Bois de Boulogne" of Peking. By an old Imperial rule trees might be planted but never cut down in the capital. With the years people forgot about the rule but had acquired the good habit of loving trees—an instance in which the spirit got into the veins of the people while the system was forgotten. Here lies a secret of China's regeneration.

Few of those who have lived in Peking will fail to retain the pleasant memory of its palaces and other public buildings with their gleaming tiles under the cloudless blue. Imperial parks and gardens were blessed with junipers planted in rows and squares centuries ago and filling the air with soothing scent. Restaurants with exquisite cuisine were always ready to satisfy the wants of the epicure. Curio shops displayed antiques and jades, catering to connoisseurs. Public and private libraries preserved centuries of wisdom on their shelves and in archives. Most remote of all were the oracle bones which threw light on that misty era of Chinese history, the Shang Dynasty (1766–1122 B.C.). And there was the awe-inspiring Altar of Heaven, which made one feel the grandeur of nature and the sublimity of the spirit of man.

Only yesterday, comparatively speaking—in 1898—the modern National University of Peking was founded as a direct successor to the centuries-old Imperial Academy, *Kuo-tse-chien,* in an atmosphere of centuries of accumulated culture. This institution served both as a center of the old culture and a fountain of new wisdom. Scholars, artists, musicians, writers, and scientists came to Peking to develop their minds and enrich their hearts in the congenial atmosphere of the ancient city. There the inspiration of the past, the influence of contemporary thought, and hope for the future flowed into one inseparable stream of wisdom, and the youth of the country came and drank at its fountain.

CHAPTER 24

LIFE IN THE FOUR CITIES

HANGCHOW was the city of natural beauty; Shanghai that of foreign manufactures; Nanking, of revolutionary spirit; Peking, of the golden age—of art and leisure. In my childhood I was reared in a small village in Chekiang, lived among the farmers and craftsmen and played with their children. During my boyhood I was educated in the city of Hangchow and later in Shanghai. When I returned from America my work required that I live, first in Shanghai, then in Peking, then in Nanking and Hangchow, and finally again in Peking until the beginning of the war.

As to their geography, Peking stands in the northern plain not far from the seaport of Tientsin, in the Huang-ho (Yellow River) Valley. It is a northern city, while the other three are southern cities of the Yangtze basin. Hangchow is situated on the banks of the river Chien-tang, where Hangchow Bay begins to spread its broad waters out to the ocean. In the old days Hangchow and Peking were connected by the Grand Canal, 2,074 kilometers long, which crosses both the Yangtze and the Yellow River. The Canal is still partly navigable to the present day.

Northeast of Hangchow, Shanghai perches on the banks of the Whangpoo River, which empties near the mouth of the Yangtze into the Yellow Sea—a body of water which is an integral part of the Pacific, different only in name. Nanking lies a little inland, farther north and west of the other two, along the southern bank of the Yangtze. Not far down the river from it the Grand Canal crosses the Yangtze at Yangchow, where Marco Polo resided as magistrate under the Mongol Dynasty. The four cities are all connected now by railways. Generally speaking, they all border on the Pacific.

The southern cities of the lower Yangtze Valley have approximately the same climate. Spring and autumn days are very pleasant. Sprouting willows are signs of the coming of spring—joyous spring seekers pluck the budding branches and bring them home to decorate their doors as symbols of welcome. When the leaves turn red they tell the coming of fall, and the crimson leaves in the setting autumn sun lend inspiration to poets. The damp season falls in spring, when there is plenty of rain; during the other seasons sunshine and rain are about evenly distributed. Summer and winter are not severe.

The soil is fertile. Rice is the chief product. Sericulture is a family industry. Fish, shrimps, crabs, eels, pork, mutton, beef, vegetables, and fruits abound. Out of these materials the famous Yangchow cuisine was created.

Shanghai was the financial center of the Yangtze Valley. It owed its growth to the commercial and industrial activities of the foreigner. Foreign capital was the foundation of its economic structure and foreign merchants and capitalists its aristocrats, before whom all the Chinese living in the city bowed their heads. These foreigners lived a life by themselves. Even if they had been there for several decades, China remained to many of them a *terra incognita*. They lived in beautiful mansions with spacious gardens and were served like lords by obedient Chinese servants. The masters got rich by exploitation and the servants got their modest share of profit by petty "squeeze." Their clubs excluded the Chinese worth knowing; their libraries excluded the books that were worth reading. Their minds were full of arrogance, ignorance, bigotry, and racial prejudice, but were closed like clams to such science and art as the great masters of their own people had created and were creating, and to the new ideas and new movements that were growing in China or in their own countries. Their life had no higher ideal than the amassing of money.

Second in rank to these foreigners, the Chinese compradors shared their masters' ignorance and their money. Compradors of foreign banks and concerns were held in high esteem by the Chinese merchants. When they looked up to their masters and opened their mouths for a bone, their compatriots wagged their tails sympathetically, their mouths watering. The compradors, like alchemists, spent their time turning coppers into silver, while their foreign masters transformed silver into gold. They spent a part of their silver in getting concubines; their masters were much smarter and spent only gold on their "friends."

The third class of people in Shanghai were the merchants and shopkeepers. They waited on the doorsteps of the compradors to buy foreign manufactured goods. When they made money they sent it back home to buy land. Occasional visits to their families, who as a rule lived in their native villages, towns, or cities, brought "inspiration" to the provincial folk, and thus more relatives came back to Shanghai to share their business.

I can speak of these things that existed in Shanghai with intimacy and without exaggeration, for many of my relatives were merchants and some were compradors in that city. I know well their mode of life and their ways of thinking; I also knew quite a few foreigners there and have heard many stories about them. Enlightened foreigners, especially the Americans whom I knew well, shook their heads with knit brows when we talked about Shanghai.

The fourth class were the factory workers. They were surplus farmers or those who had given up farming to come to the great city to make more money. They were slum-dwellers.

The fifth and last were the rickshaw coolies, who came from the poor districts north of the Yangtze. These human animals pulled and ran like horses on their two hind legs, with small carriages rolling after them. This cheaper and handier means of communication kept Shanghai constantly in motion—the coolies kept the blood circulating in the city's business veins.

These five classes of people together formed what came to be called the "Settlement mind"—the mentality which grew in the Foreign Settlement of Shanghai. It is a mind which worships power and admires superficialities. Power, whether financial, military, extraterritorial, or in any other form; superficiality bordering on vulgarity in painting, calligraphy, singing, music, and every phase of life. These reigned supreme in Shanghai. *Hai-pai*, or the "Shanghai School," was the epithet invented for this kind of mentality; the opposite is *Ching-pai*, or the "Peking School," which admires the arts in their deeper meaning and strives for perfection. Shanghai was a financial sea but an intellectual desert.

People were all busy as ants at their hoarding. The more they piled up, the more they were admired. In Shanghai both Western and Chinese civilizations were at their worst. The Chinese misinterpreted the West and foreigners misunderstood the Chinese; the Chinese hated the foreigners, who in turn despised the Chinese, both with reason. But they had one thing in common—their equally deculturated state; and one mutual understanding—hoarding. These two elements welded Chinese and foreigners together in a common brotherhood of money. "You exploit me, I squeeze you."

There were oases in the desert, and in them lay the redeeming feature of Shanghai. In the first decade of the century extraterritoriality here afforded a refuge and clearinghouse for revolutionary ideas and literature. The seeds of the theory of evolution and the ideas of democracy were first sown in these oases and blown far and wide to the intellectual centers of China. While in other parts of China they grew into giant trees, in international Shanghai they remained dwarfs. In the 'twenties a rapid growth of Chinese industry took place in and around the Settlement, protected from the exploitation of warlords by the same extraterritoriality. When returned students came into financial and industrial power, the Chinese began to put into use foreign tricks of management and production, learned, however, more often directly from Europe and America than from the foreigners of Shanghai.

The life of Peking must be painted in other colors, as we have already seen. Aside from beautiful palaces and Imperial gardens, one's first impression was that there seemed to be only two classes of people in the city: those who pulled rickshaws and those who were pulled in them. But when you lived there longer you discovered that there were various classes among those who rode. It would be difficult to find any "top" classes; there were simply people of various professions coexisting side by side in a good, neighborly way. In the old days the Manchus were born aristocrats, but these had now vanished into the multitude. All men were born equal and their differences were of their own making. The only aristocracy was that of learning—the painters, the calligraphers, the poets, the philosophers, the historians, the literary men, and in recent times also the scientists and engineers.

The connoisseurs of art who could put their finger on the genuine amid the counterfeit; the craftsmen who made a thousand and one articles of art; the booksellers who were living bibliographies and the seal carvers who could make you feel your name worth preserving in artistic seals; the rug designers who beautified your floors and brightened up your living quarters—all lived side by side in the enjoyment of knowing or making things for the enjoyment of others. Knowledge and crafts were the keynote of life in Peking.

All could find some leisure in the day to enjoy beautiful things in many different ways. You might drop into an old, dingy-looking bookstore, converse with the man in charge and glance over the books on the shelf; you would feel that your mind was being led into the treasure of knowledge of the past and of the present. You might spend two or three hours there if you liked—when you left you would be invited courteously to come again. You need not buy unless you wanted to.

You might go into a curio shop if you felt like it, to look over all the beautiful things, both genuine and clever imitations, and enjoy them to your heart's content. You would be always welcome whether you bought or not at the time. But once you became interested you would very likely spend the last dollar you had counted on for supper.

You might go to a theatre and hear the singing of some of the great actors. It was perfect in every detail, touching the strings of your heart, which vibrated with every note. Or you could go to the Palace Museum and admire the treasures of art created by geniuses of the past. In this atmosphere of arts that always strive after perfection and the deeper meaning of life there grew up the mentality I have just mentioned which came to be called Ching-pai.

If you preferred you might go to the Imperial Gardens and sit under the moss-grown trees sipping tea, or upon the ancient rocks on one of the artful little miniature hills, watching the geese swimming in the pond. On holidays one could go by donkey, rickshaw, or automobile to the Western Hills to see historic spots and breathe air laden with the fragrance of hoary pines.

In seeking wholesome pleasures scholars, artists, craftsmen, scientists, and engineers all united in their enjoyment of old Peking. At work, they carried on their activities in widely diverse fields. The scientists worked in their laboratories to make contributions to the stock of human knowledge, the engineers went back to their slide rules and drawing tools, the scholars buried themselves in books to reconstruct from the past ideas and ideals for the future.

The craftsmen produced more beautiful goods; the artists, having drawn inspiration from nature and from the past, cast their mental images on paper or in other materials with their deft fingers.

Years of trouble and war had left Peking undisturbed. Governments had come and gone but the fine old city remained the same. As we have seen, the name was changed to Peiping when the capital of China was removed to Nanking. Peiping, however, still remained Peking and has a good chance to be the capital again in the future. With the shift of the capital a portion of Peking went to the new seat of government—some of the scholars and artists, the architectural design and treasures of art—but the atmosphere and flavor of Peking remained unchanged. Railways and airplanes kept the blood of the two cities interflowing to mutual advantage.

Nanking is different. It is a city that had to be built upon ruins. In the new capital there reigned a spirit of building up the new structure and tearing down old remains. In Peking, people were nurtured on old glories while they cast their minds into the future. But Nanking had no past to rely upon except memories; everything had to be built anew. Therefore in the collective mind all was thinking, planning, and work, and life kept pace with these activities. Everybody was busy attending meetings and carrying out orders. The atmosphere was always tense. The leisurely spirit of Peking could not have flowered in Nanking.

On the streets pedestrians hustled, rickshaw coolies dashed by; even the inert donkeys fell in with the rapid flow of traffic with hurried steps. Every month new streets shot through old blocks and new houses sprang up like mushrooms. Everywhere was growth—rapid growth.

Even pleasure had to be secured through hard work. Restaurants served delicious food in congested corners, waiting for new quarters under construction. People planned gardens and waited impatiently for the trees to grow. Things you wanted had to be improvised. Without constant constructive activity you fell out of line and were left behind; you had to keep up with the spirit of the time. After some six or seven years of hard work Nanking became a new and prosperous city. Old ruins were fast disappearing while the spirit of thinking, planning, and work was constantly growing, and it radiated to other cities in the provinces and into the future of the country.

Your mind ran ahead into the future to catch up with the spirit of progress in the world. But your steps were necessarily slower —too slow to keep pace with your mind. You can plant trees but you cannot make them shoot skyward overnight; railways and highways must be laid yard by yard; policies of reform have to be carried out day by day. Then, you would think, what is all this hustle and bustle for?

What people sometimes felt about their effort may be summed up in words current and typical in those times: "Discussions ended with no decisions, decisions ended with no actions, and actions ended with no results." It was not really as bad as that. But one thing was certain: people felt their work did not measure up to the efforts made. And that was the spirit of progress.

Hangchow had something of all three of the other cities, yet it was different from them all. It was like Peking in its old culture, for it is the capital of a province of scholars; yet it lacked the grandeur of the former capital of China. Like Shanghai it was tinged with commercialism, yet more lightly, while the absence of foreign overlords left the city freedom for self-expression. It was something like Nanking in its spirit of reforms and reconstruction. But it was provincial-minded, as Peking and Nanking were national-minded. Hangchow is the city of a province in China, while the others are cities of China.

The great asset of the city is the West Lake, which not only supplied the richness of nature but retained the pleasant associations of generations of poets and scholars who once lived there. Hangchow's shortcomings also lie in its historic scene. For its people so treasured the lake that they could not look beyond its horizons; they fooled themselves into thinking it greater than the Pacific Ocean and as alluring as the veriest Paradise on earth. They were, in fact, hypnotized into believing the proverbial saying: "In the heavens you have Paradise and on earth you have Soochow and Hangchow." Just forget Soochow, they would think; Hangchow is here and Paradise is with us.

So Hangchow is West-Lake-minded. If you stayed there too

long you were in danger of being engulfed, like the lovers of the South Seas; you would grow and wither there, and become complacent in life.

But the spirit of reforms and reconstruction emanating from Nanking awakened Hangchow from its slumber. Rubbing its eyes, it began to see the possibilities of future development of the province and the part it was to play in the rebuilding of China.

Peking, too, had its broad and tranquil water view. Outside the walled city, from the tops of the Western Hills, one had a bird's-eye panorama of the valley with the river Yunting winding its gentle way through vast tracts of cultivated land. The pagodas in the city were visible to the east. To the west the Marco Polo Bridge spanned the river where it lay like a sleeping dragon undisturbed through peace and war. Under this long, historical bridge the muddy, loess-laden water flowed steadily, day and night, month after month and year by year.

The name "Yunting" means "perpetual stability" or "everlasting peace." Was peace everlasting? The Chinese cherished that hope, and so we gave the river its name and then did little to make the peace secure. Finally it slipped from our hands and vanished into the flowing water under that very bridge. For at that bridge, on July 7, 1937, the first shots were fired by the Japanese army in the undeclared war which ultimately set all China aflame. Japan had become intoxicated with the cup of seeming success. And in the Japanese magic box the flames of China were transformed into a streak of lightning that blasted Pearl Harbor on December 7, 1941.

Part VI

WAR

CHAPTER 25

MANCHURIA AND KOREA

IN THE summer of 1918, some nineteen years before the outbreak of actual war between Japan and China, I made a trip with a friend, Huang Yen-pei, to Manchuria. As this is the area where Japanese aggression in China began, it will not be inappropriate to describe how it appeared in those early years.

We took a train from Shanghai to Nanking, and thence, from across the Yangtze at Pukow, went by the Tientsin-Pukow Railway to Peking. From Pukow north, for two days and a night, the train traversed a vast plain. The dry dust, the arid yellow soil, and the cornfields in this enormous plain of the northern section of the country, which I was visiting for the first time, contrasted greatly with the humid black earth, winding creeks, rice fields, and hilly valleys of the south in which I was born and reared.

I wondered whether the difference in geographical surroundings between north and south had much to do with the difference in physical and mental make-up of their respective peoples. The eastern coastal provinces of Chekiang and Kiangsu, where my ancestors had lived for generations and indeed for many centuries, were the regions in China which, down the long avenue of history, had produced great numbers of scholars, artists, and statesmen. But northern Kiangsu, together with that part of northern Anhuei through which we now traveled, struck me as the poorest part of the country, where deforestation was extreme and the frequent floods of the Huai River played havoc among the population.

Then we came to the Yellow River Valley—to Shantung, the northern coastal province where people were tall, muscular, and hard working, but much crowded through overpopulation—and finally to Peking. From the capital, of whose parks and palaces, museums and gardens, I then had my first glimpse, we continued to Mukden by the Peking-Mukden Railway, passing through Shanhaikwan Pass, the coastal terminal of the world-famous Great Wall of China which, like a gigantic dragon, runs hundreds of miles from Kansu to the coast, separating China proper from Manchuria and Mongolia. Before the train went through the pass we heard cicadas singing in chorus on the leaves of summer trees, just as noisily as in every other part of China. But as soon as we crossed the pass, all the trees were silent, without those singing homopterous insects. They lived and sang only inside the Great Wall!

We came at night into Mukden station, in the Japanese settlement of the city. The streets were dotted with Japanese shops and looked like a small city in Japan. Penetration of the Japanese in Manchuria was already a fact—nothing short of victorious war could stop it. Historically Manchuria, together with that vast territory to the west called Mongolia, had been the center of China's troubles. From time to time the peoples of these great areas—the Huns, the Mongols, and the Tartars—made inroads inside the Great Wall and wrought havoc there. The Japanese were to be modern Tartars after entrenching themselves in Manchuria.

We saw a number of officials working under General Chang Tso-lin, the local warlord in power, and learned much about Manchuria from them. We wanted to interview the general but were advised by friends not to do so. Mukden, former capital of the Manchus before they conquered China some three hundred years ago, was the capital of Fengtien Province, over which Chang Tso-lin ruled. We visited the Imperial Manchu mausoleums near the city, where Manchu emperors were buried before they came inside the Great Wall.

From Mukden we traveled by the South Manchurian Railway, owned and operated by the Japanese, to Kuan-cheng-tse, which was later—after the Mukden Incident of 1931—renamed Shinching, or Seijo, and made capital of the Japanese-made puppet empire of Manchukuo. Here the penetration was very evident. Japanese shops were everywhere to be seen.

On both sides of the railroad endless miles of luxuriant wheat nourished in the virgin soil of Manchuria bore witness that this tremendous area of north China beyond the Great Wall was the richest portion of China and could well support the tens of thousands of immigrants that flowed yearly from Shantung and Hopei Provinces into this northernmost part of the Chinese Republic. To

cut off Manchuria from China was to deprive her of lebensraum
and suffocate the provinces in the Yellow River Valley.

Kuan-cheng-tse was the terminal of the Japanese-owned South
Manchurian Railway and the starting point of the Chinese Eastern
Railway, formerly owned and operated by Tsarist Russia. This
company had inherited a legacy of corruption from the tsarist
regime and the line was operated by a gang of corrupt White Russian employees. People who bought tickets had to fight for a seat
on the train, while free riders occupied comfortable compartments.
Theft was rampant. One passenger who slept with his shoes on
in an upper berth next morning found one of them gone. He
stared at his shoeless foot and wondered how the shoe could have
been stripped off without his knowing it; and I wondered what
was the earthly use of stealing one shoe without the other. All
passengers kept a watch on their belongings after this strange
incident. As a precaution my companion hid his supply of rubles
in the pockets of his underwear and slept with his Chinese gown
on. The next morning the rubles were gone. On our return trip,
at Harbin station as I was talking to a Chinese customs official—
an American—through a window of the train, I felt somebody
meddling with my hip pocket. Before I could turn around my own
rubles were gone.

The dilapidated city of Harbin, international metropolis of the
extreme north, was a meeting place of East and West. Poor
Chinese and Russian children in rags played together in the
streets and intermarriages were frequent. Children spoke a sort of
hybrid language, part Chinese and part Russian. The free mixing
of the poorer classes of inhabitants of Harbin was something novel
to me. The bigoted foreigners of Shanghai looked down upon the
poorer classes of Chinese as something that would contaminate
them. Perhaps this was because few poverty-stricken Europeans
ever came to stay in Shanghai.

The streets of Harbin, once well paved, had gone unrepaired
for years. The carriages in which we rode bounced up and down
on the rough ground so badly that comfort was a negligible factor—we had constantly to grasp at something to avoid being
thrown out. The sewers were choked up. After a shower the
streets turned into rivers in which the water often came up to one's
knees. We met a number of people from south China who were in

trade there. All the merchants did prosperous business in that frontier city by speculating in wheat, soy beans, and minerals. So long as their business was good they had no time to worry about the dilapidated state of the Russian-developed city.

We went to Kirin, capital of Kirin Province—one of the three provinces of Manchuria—and were impressed with its beautiful scenery. The city is situated on the banks of the Sungari River. Climbing to the temple on the hill in the city and looking down over the widest part of the river, one saw that it was like a lake, and I was reminded of West Lake at Hangchow. The river was rich in fish. The best fish I ever tasted was whitefish from the Sungari. In old Imperial days this delicious fish found its way only to the tables of the Imperial Court and the princesses and grand ministers. Ginseng, the life-sustaining drug that China treasured, was also indigenous to the province; large quantities found their way every year inside the Great Wall to all the provinces.

We paid a short visit to Tsitsihar, capital of the province of Heilungkiang. There we experienced an abrupt turn of summer to winter. Overnight we noticed that the green leaves began to wither and drop from their branches. This was the northernmost city within Chinese boundaries; we could go no farther unless we went on to Siberia by the branch line which connected with the Trans-Siberian Railway.

Returning to Harbin, we chartered a steamboat and sailed down the gentle Sungari to Fuchin Hsien. For two days and a night we enjoyed the mountain scenery on both sides, while mountain islands wreathed in virgin forest appeared here and there in the winding river. The evening was blessed with a brilliant moon in a clear sky, the air crisp in the northern summer night. The moon was reflected from the water, which broke into ripples of silver as our boat plowed calmly through. Often the Sungari itself appeared to have ended in a lake, with dark forested mountains rising ahead of us against the moonlit sky. But as we drew near the river suddenly opened to left or right, and as our boat changed its course and curved gradually around the mountains, the river seemed to straighten out and roll down ahead beyond the horizon.

Fukchin, or Fuchin Hsien, was a city of granaries. The wheat and soy beans produced in the surrounding hundreds of square miles all were brought to this frontier city. In the winter it was

defended against possible attacks of bandits—the "Red Beards"
—by walls built round it with bricks of ice which melted away
in summer when the defense was less necessary. Everyone carried
a gun and knew how to use it. The new stock of Chinese in the
frontier provinces was primitive, full of fighting spirit, and not
burdened with the overrefinements of old culture. What a contrast with the overcivilized stock inside the Great Wall! Before
the war we drew our best fighters in the Chinese Air Forces from
this strong stock from the virgin soil of Manchuria.

Our final destination was Lu-pu Hsien and the plantation of a
friend of ours. This district was situated at the sharp end of that
spearhead of land where the Sungari and Amur rivers meet and
flow concurrently into the Huen-tung—the lower part of the Amur.
We went by small boat down the river, arriving at dusk, and were
put up for the night in a small lonely hut with thatched roof. A
section of the broad brick bed was already occupied by an old
woman and a cat, the remainder being set aside to accommodate
us. Two pigs lay comfortably on the mud floor, snoring occasionally. Mosquitoes and bedbugs annoyed us the whole night.

Long before dawn we set out for the plantation. A party of four,
we trotted on horseback in single file through miles of woods and
wheat fields. Before we reached our destination the sun had begun
to come up over the horizon. Mountains were barely visible in
shady outlines on the Russian side of the Amur Valley. Horseflies
began to gather and the animals bled profusely; I was riding a
white horse, whose coat showed streaks of blood running down.
We did our best to chase away the flies with a horsetail duster. At
about six in the morning we came to a plantation run by a Dane.
We were told that a band of Red Beards had visited the place a
week before. The walls were riddled with bullets.

We arrived at our destination at about eight. The plantation
yielded fairly good profits for the first few years of cultivation in
that virgin soil, but bandits were the real problem. A few months
earlier the "Little White Dragon" and his band had paid them a
visit and carried away a large portion of the cattle and poultry. The
bandits were on friendly terms with the people on the plantation,
apparently, and exchanged their bad guns for good ones. "After
all," said the manager, "the bandits are really not so bad, but if

the Japanese should get control of this part of the country it would be the end of us all."

This was the final point of our northern journey. At the southern tip of the Manchurian mainland we also visited Dairen and Port Arthur, both Japanese-leased territories. Dairen was a commercial port through which soy beans were exported in immense quantities. Port Arthur was a naval base, the key to Manchuria, over which the Japanese fought the Russians in 1904. The defeat of Tsarist Russia had resulted in a transfer of the lease to Japanese hands. With railways starting from Port Arthur and Korea and running through south Manchuria, the Japanese had already got control of the heart and veins of the Chinese Three Eastern Provinces.

We wandered about the naval base for a day and climbed many hills trying to get a bird's-eye view. Finally, on top of one of them, in the slanting sun we came across a stone monument inscribed with the famous lines of the Tartar general who conquered the Sungs in 1276: "March an army of a million men to the West Lake and mount, on horseback, the first peak of the Wu Mountains." At Hangchow, overlooking the lake, the Sungs had established their capital in 1127. To follow in the Tartar's steps was the dream of Admiral Togo and his people after the Russo-Japanese War. And after some thirty years the dream came true, when a Japanese army entered Hangchow after the fall of Shanghai.

Korea was the springboard by means of which Japanese imperialism leapt to the mainland of Asia. It was over Korea that China and Japan clashed in 1894. The Sino-Japanese War for control of that ancient kingdom was the starting point of Japan's aggression on the continent. It opened a new chapter of China's history—the chapter which was to see China's reforms, revolutions, wars, sufferings, humiliation, and eventual westernization and modernization.

After our trip to Manchuria we turned off to Korea. Crossing the Yalu River which forms the boundary line between China and her erstwhile protectorate, we arrived by train at Chemulpo. From there we proceeded to Seoul, capital of the country.

The Japanese governor general of Korea resided in the capital. His imposing, Western-style office building was located right in front of the royal palace, as if put there purposely to insult the Korean kings. The kings were gone, but the palace remained to endure the humiliation of being put back into the background.

The royal palace looked exactly like the Chinese Imperial Palace in Peking, but on a very much smaller scale, rather like a toy palace. In the old times, when the Chinese Imperial ambassador condescended to call, the king had to descend from the granite steps to meet the honored guest in the courtyard. If the ambassador had an Imperial Edict to deliver, His Majesty had to bend his knees in receiving the Imperial favor.

At the back of the palace was a Chinese pavilion in which the princesses performed the ancient Chinese dances of the Tang Dynasty. In Korea as well as Japan, ancient Chinese customs still prevailed. Their pronunciation of Chinese words, their customs, dances, music, and ways of living could all be traced back to influences of the Tang era. As I stood in the pavilion gazing up at the mist-mantled hills of Seoul, my mind reverted to the glorious times of that dynasty (618–905) when Chinese civilization shone as brilliant as the sun in a clear sky, casting its beams far beyond the horizon upon such lands as Japan, Korea, and Indo-China. The offshoots of Chinese civilization grew, were preserved and later rejuvenated in Japan, whereas in Korea and Indo-China they grew and withered. The mother country of this glorious civilization had changed its manners, customs, and ways of life as the waves of invasion swept over it. Japan, which succeeded in building up a new civilization in the last century by the introduction of Western civilization upon a foundation of Chinese Tang culture, had gobbled up Korea, and as appetite grew with eating, was on the way to swallow up China, her teacher and benefactor. But Japan taught China a lesson in her turn: how to build a strong new nation upon a foundation of old civilization. Hence China's reforms, revolutions, westernization, and modernization.

While I mused thus over the past and the future, sunshine was peeping through the clouds and the mist was fast fading from the Seoul hills. The Korean who had taken me there, an old Chinese scholar, was standing by in silence but now called my attention to a dinner engagement. We left the pavilion and passed the spot where the Princess Ming was assassinated, presumably by the Japanese for her sympathy toward China. "I know what you have been thinking," said the old scholar. "It is too late for my country now. Our kings preferred dances to the affairs of state. But China, which is your country and may be regarded as mine, has a bright future. I am old now. Brother, you are young. Do your best for China."

The dinner was ready at the Chinese Consulate General, formerly the residence of China's special ambassador. What had happened behind the doors of this historic mansion during the quadrangular love affairs of China, Tsarist Russia, and Japan in courtship of the Korean lady, only those who participated knew. History gives bare outlines only; personal records, if any, remain yet unpublished. Matters have had to be left to the imagination of posterity.

Life in Seoul was being fast engulfed in Japanization. Japanese bazaars, banks, shops, and restaurants occupied prominent sections of the streets. Managers of big business, government officials, and teachers of the more important schools were all Japanese. The life of the vanquished people was fast receding into the background, like their palace. Here and there you would see Koreans squatting complacently on the sidewalks with long stick-like pipes in their mouths, puffing to their heart's content, and women walking leisurely by with heavy loads on their heads. Some of the old type of school, in which Confucian classics were taught, had been left to struggle for existence. I went into such a school, which had one old scholar of the classics as teacher and a dozen pupils squatting around him on the matting. The Koreans and Japanese still kept the ancient Chinese way of squatting on their heels on the floor. It was slightly heated from beneath even in summer and was kept as clean as a bed. The pupils had to learn the Chinese classics by heart as I had done in childhood. Although they used the same textbooks they pronounced the words quite differently. Like the Japanese and the Indo-Chinese, they had been influenced by the Tang pronunciation.

All the people wore padded cotton stockings even in summer. I asked the reason and was informed that the earth was cold in the northern country. Yet they all wore white linen gowns which were quite cool.

The Koreans as well as the Japanese and Indo-Chinese loved Chinese landscape painting, calligraphy, and poetry. But each of the three peoples retained their own individual characteristics. As it was with their arts, so it was with their lives. Korea and Indo-China had come more under the Ming influence in later centuries while Japan, beyond the sea, escaped it. Moreover, the seafaring people of Japan were highly adventurous and therefore kept the martial spirit of ancient China, while the Koreans and Indo-Chinese were touched more deeply with that complacency that tinged Chinese life in later centuries. The system of civil examinations which conferred so much honor upon scholars in China found its way to Korea and Indo-China, but stopped at the gates of Japan.

In its relation to China the younger generation in Korea was undergoing a change under the pressure of Japanese-controlled modern schools, in which the sacred person of the Mikado was worshiped, the virtues of the Japanese exalted to the skies, and the vices of the Chinese amplified to monstrous proportions. If the attitude of young Koreans toward Japan was hatred, toward China it was contempt. While the older generation lamented the passing of the good old ways of Chinese culture, the young people were made to think that they were now the blessed subjects of the Mikado's glorious empire.

CHAPTER 26

WAR CLOUDS DEEPENING

IN OCTOBER, 1930, after my resignation from the office of Minister of Education in the national government, I had gone back to Peking—now called Peiping. Again I was entrusted by General- issimo Chiang Kai-shek, then President of the Executive Yuan (the title of the executive branch of government), with charge of the National University of Peking.

The number of student demonstrations was very much reduced. When the capital was moved to the south the focus of political ac- tivities went with it. There was not much left for students to dem- onstrate against except for occasional outbursts provoked by Jap- anese aggression, which had started in Manchuria and was now fast extending inside the Great Wall.

On the morning of September 19, 1931, as I was sitting at my desk in the Chancellor's office of the university, a telephone call brought me the fatal news of the previous day. Japan had delivered a blow at Mukden and the Chinese troops had evacuated the city to avoid a clash.

I have tried to show, little by little, some of the steps in this movement from the beginning; to put its further development in a nutshell, let me sum up in the following story:

After the Sino-Japanese War of 1894, China began to adore Japan. She daubed her face and rouged her lips, ready for Japan to make advances. But her hero returned her love with contemptu- ous smiles. As a small boy I once wrote a little essay in which I said, "China and Japan are of one race and one language." My Japanese teacher, Mr. Nakagawa, scrawled along the margin: "No, no. These two countries are not of one race. Poor China is to be sliced like a melon by the Powers. What a pity it will be!" This rebuke thrust like a knife into my little heart. I remember how I wept that night for the future of my country.

If she could not win the love of her hero, China still hoped that Japan would at least remain a friend. But her hero suddenly turned a dagger on her in the form of the Twenty-One Demands. It barely missed her. Then she began to realize that this hero was, after all, but a villain in the disguise of Bushido, or the spirit of chivalry. When he came in turn to make love to her, she was always in a defiant mood. For by now she knew very well that what he was after was her rich dowry of natural resources.

Then the act of strangulation began. The villain put a rope of economic "co-operation" round her neck and tried to make her believe it was a necklace. On the fatal night of September 18, 1931, when everyone else was asleep, all of a sudden he tightened the rope.

She woke from slumber in dismay and ran away as fast as she could. But the cord around her neck was an endless nightmare rope which grew longer and longer as she ran, yet remained always in the grip of the villain-sorcerer at the other end. She was frightened and screamed. The American Secretary of State, Mr. Henry Stimson, called on Great Britain to join the United States in a forceful note to Japan. Sir John Simon, speaking for his country, refused. Stimson thus stood alone and Japan was left free to pursue the policy of strangulation.

China's lukewarm friends under the leadership of Lord Lytton came halfheartedly to the rescue. They visited Mukden, the spot where the crime was committed, and pronounced the villain guilty. But they would not untie the rope. The Italian Commissioner of the Chinese Post Office at Mukden, Mr. Poletti, in his memorandum to Lord Lytton intimated that if the Powers did not stop Japan right in Manchuria, he was sure that his own country, Italy, would poke her fingers into Ethiopia. But what weight could be attached to the words of an insignificant postal commissioner?

"Sorry, my young lady," said the neighbors. "We can do no more than declare our sympathy with you."

Sympathy she got, but help there was none.

A few months later I made the trip back to the south. The afternoon of January 28, 1932, I went to Shanghai station to take the train back to Peiping. As I entered a sense of utter strangeness stole over me—the station looked as quiet as a deserted village. A station guard told me that there was no outgoing train. "It looks as if the Japanese are ready for a blow," he said. "You had better leave here right away. Something may happen any minute."

That night I was suddenly wakened by the roar of cannon, followed by the rat-tat-tat of machine guns. I jumped from my bed and followed the stream of guests to the roof of the hotel. The sky was red with the glow of fires that leapt out here and there from the vicinity of the station. Japanese aggression seemed to have followed on my very heels from north to south. The next morning I went up again to the roof and my heart ached with the sight of the *Commercial Press* Library on fire. Several Japanese bombers kept on bombing the building of the *Commercial Press*. The dark smoke rose heavenward, carrying with it scraps of scorched paper which floated in the sky and sailed idly over the roofs. The print still visible on some of the fragments read clearly *"The Commercial Press."*

The Japanese had opened an attack on Shanghai. It resulted in the bitterest fighting before 1937, but China was finally forced to accept terms under which Japanese troops were permitted to remain in the city.

For seven years, from 1930 to 1937, I was at the helm of the university, endeavoring to steer that ship of learning through the rough seas of Sino-Japanese conflict. With the aid of many friends—particularly Dr. Hu Shih, Mr. V. K. Ting, and Mr. Fu Shih-nian—the university sailed smoothly with only an occasional trimming of her canvas.

The standard of science teaching and research was raised. A serious study was made of Chinese history and literature. The faculty had ample time for research and the students were led to direct their attention to study; the whirlpool of revolutionary activity and student demonstration was gradually transformed into a center of learning. During all these years there was only one demonstration worth recording. As the Japanese forces drove rapidly inside the Great Wall the students in Nanking and Shanghai clamored for war. Demonstrations on a large scale were frequent in the capital and the students in Peiping wanted to join the movement. One day a crowd of students tried to take a south-bound train at the East Station. Being refused entrance to the train itself, the boys and girls lay on the track day and night to prevent it from leaving the station. At length a few hundred were allowed to go and join their comrades in Nanking.

Seeing that war clouds hung thick over our heads, during the next years we tried to gain time by sailing along the shallows of caution, not venturing on those high seas where we would be bound to clash full-force with the Japanese tidal wave. But our caution was not timidity. When Japanese scholars, fifth column-ists in disguise, came to pay "respects" to the "center of culture" (which really meant to them the center of the anti-Japanese move-ment), we talked frankly with them. One, I remember, spoke at length about cultural relations with our professors and was told that we did not see any cultural relations between the two coun-tries but only the military ambition of Japan. "Give up your mili-tary ambition and China and Japan will co-operate well."

These men—geologists, economists, biologists, and other schol-ars—came to us from time to time seeking the "friendship" of the university. They all complained about our anti-Japanese move-ment. We told them that anti-Japanese we were not, but anti-Japanese-militarism we were. Their minds, however, were set on the strangulation of China; nothing short of a complete surrender could change their course.

Meanwhile the Japanese Kwantung army stationed in Man-churia made rapid inroads inside the Great Wall. The Chinese army fought against the intruders along the Wall, then in the northern part of Hopei Province, and finally withdrew to Peiping and its vicinity. Wounded soldiers streamed in and all the hospitals were filled. A hospital was established supported by faculty mem-bers. Wives and young co-eds acted as nurses. Here I came into close contact with the fighting forces and learned their psychol-ogy. In conversations at their bedsides the soldiers showed no sign of weakness toward the Japanese. They attributed their defeat to the lack of modern weapons, especially guns, which permitted the enemy to break through the Chinese wall of human flesh.

I wish to remind the reader that this undaunted spirit of the Chinese army built a wall of flesh and blood for the defense of their country against the steel and fire of the enemy. It enabled China to fight on and on for eight long, suffering years, with mil-lions of dead and wounded, without a murmur. China lost many battles but was still winning the war.

When the fighting was going on along the Great Wall, General Ho Yin-chin, Minister of War, came to Peiping to direct the operations. He and I wanted to effect a truce in order to gain time. I went to call on Sir Miles Lampson, the British Ambassador, to sound out his feelings as to acting as mediator. He said that Mr. Suma of the Japanese Embassy had intimated to him that the Japanese, too, desired a truce. Cables were sent to London and the reply permitted Sir Miles to act as mediator. Washington was informed through the good offices of Mr. Nelson Johnson, the American Ambassador. But the plan fell through when the Foreign Minister, Lo Wen-kan, told the British Embassy in Nanking that no one was authorized to deal with a foreign country but himself.

Then the Japanese forces broke through the defense lines along the Great Wall and swept down toward Peiping. The city was about to be evacuated.

As I was laid up in the Peking University Medical College after an appendix operation, I was not informed. But early in the morning I heard Japanese planes droning over our heads and smelt something wrong. I got permission from the doctor in charge to leave the hospital and limped to the residence of General Ho Yin-chin, who was surprised to see me still in the city and informed me that the Japanese were about to attack. I made plans to leave the next day.

Next morning at dawn my telephone rang. It was the general. "A truce has been arranged—you don't have to leave the city." At once I telephoned Dr. Hu Shih.

"Why, the Japanese planes are droning over our heads," he said.

"I have just received a message from General Ho Yin-chin to that effect," was all I could say. But the Tangku Agreement had been signed for China at midnight by Huang Fu, by the terms of which the Japanese forces were to halt after occupying the northern part of Hopei.

The Japanese, having occupied this area and established a puppet "autonomous government" there, urged the Chinese commander of the remaining Hopei forces to co-operate by establishing an autonomous government in Peiping. Rumors circulated widely in the city that the commander, General Sung Chieh-yuan, would give in to the Japanese. In this momentary crisis the university professors issued a statement that they were unconditionally opposed to the so-called autonomous movement in north China. The general, in point of fact, did not comply.

One afternoon a month or two later a Japanese gendarme called on me in the university. "The Japanese garrison in the Legation Quarter invites you to go there and talk over some matters which they wish to understand and which need explanation," he announced. I promised to go in an hour, and he left.

Before dark I went alone to the Japanese barracks in the Legation Quarter, after informing my family and some of my friends. As I entered the offices of General Kawabe I heard the click of the key which meant that the door was locked behind me. A Japanese colonel stood up and said, "Please be seated." I took the seat and out of the tail of my eye saw a soldier standing by the door with a drawn revolver.

"Our commanding general invites you to come here and wishes to know why you carry on an extensive propaganda against Japan." He offered me a cigarette as he spoke.

"What do you mean? I carry on anti-Japanese propaganda—? Nothing of the sort," I replied, accepting the cigarette.

"Then did you sign that statement opposing the autonomous movement?"

"Yes, I did. It is our internal problem. It has nothing to do with an anti-Japanese movement."

"You wrote a book in which you attacked Japan."

"Show me the book."

"Then you are a friend of Japan?"

"Not exactly. I am a friend of the Japanese people, but an enemy to Japanese militarism, just as I am an enemy to Chinese militarism."

"Well, you know, there is some misunderstanding about it in the Kwantung army. Would you go there and have a talk with General Itagaki at Dairen?" The telephone rang and the colonel answered, then turned to me. "A special coach has been prepared for you. Would you go to Dairen tonight?"

"No, I will not."

"Don't be afraid. The Japanese gendarmes will go with you for your protection."

"I am not afraid. If I had been I would not have come here alone. If you want to use force, go ahead—I am in your hands.

But I advise you not to. You will become a laughingstock when the world, including Tokyo, is informed that the Japanese army has abducted the Chancellor of Peking University."

His face changed color and he looked as if I were now a problem to him. "Please don't be afraid," he said casually.

"Afraid? No, no. Confucius has told me as well as you to remain calm in the face of danger. You believe in Bushido. Bushido would not harm a defenseless person." I puffed the cigarette calmly.

The telephone rang again, and again he turned to me. "Well, Chancellor Chiang, the general wanted me to thank you for your visit. You may wish to go to Dairen some other time—whenever you like. Thank you. Good-by." The key clicked again. The colonel helped me with my overcoat, accompanied me to my car, and opened the car door. Darkness had already fallen.

The following afternoon General Sung Chieh-yuan sent a major general to advise me to leave Peking lest he should be unable to protect me. I thanked his representative and said that I would remain on my own responsibility.

I stayed on, but nothing happened to me. Occasionally some Koreans came to the university and acted very queer—these incidents were reported to me but I did not pay much attention to them. Then the tactics of the Japanese changed. General Matsumoro was sent to Peiping as special agent of the Japanese army. He made friends with me and came to my house often. He denounced the Japanese general for grilling me at the Legation barracks, and for about half a year we were very friendly. At the end of his term of office he came in full military uniform to say good-by. He told me that he was being sent to Hailar, on the border between Manchuria and Siberia, to command a cavalry division, and said that he was afraid the war clouds were deepening and that a clash between China and Japan would be very unfortunate. "If the war should come," he said, "the Japanese army would go as far as Hankow."

"Yes, General, I agree with you. If our two countries should be so unfortunate as to come to an open clash, international complications might arise and all the Japanese navy be sent to the bottom of the sea, and the Island Empire might be reduced to a few tiny dots on the map of the Pacific Ocean."

He sighed and said, "That may be. But Japan would still be

an independent nation, while China will be destroyed by the Western Powers."

"It may be so. Next time we meet I hope we shall not embrace each other, weeping for what we have done so foolishly. No matter what happens in the future, General, let us remain friends." We parted with heavy hearts.

General Imai succeeded him. He called on me and I returned his call. We talked quite frankly along the same lines as I had talked with his predecessor. Once two members of the Japanese House of Peers called. One had formerly been governor of Formosa. After looking around to see whether anyone was within hearing he inquired in a whisper who had been the person responsible for detaining me in the Japanese barracks. I told him it was Takahashi. He shook his head and said, "Ridiculous."

The Japanese had found out by now that the university had no immediate desire to start an anti-Japanese movement and they hoped to win it to the Japanese side by making friends with leading members of the faculty. Both sides were cautious in dealing with each other and the tension between the university and the Japanese army was somewhat eased.

General Tashiro came to Tientsin as commander of the army there. The Japanese had treaty rights, with other Powers, to station troops in that city. The general came to Peiping and gave a banquet to leading Chinese and Japanese officials, military as well as civil. In a speech at the banquet he advocated economic co-operation between China and Japan. Some of the Chinese officials responded but spoke rather equivocally. On the score of economic co-operation I remained as silent as a sphinx except for occasional jokes at the table. To my great surprise a telegram came to me in code from Nanking a few days later, informing me that the Japanese Embassy had intimated to the Ministry of Foreign Affairs that the Chancellor of Peking University supported Sino-Japanese co-operation.

This was how the Japanese worked on China. The procedure seemed to be: first sweet words, then political intrigue, then intimidation, again sweet words, and finally blitzkrieg. The order might vary somewhat, but they never deviated from their fundamental course—the subjugation of China. This was also the way the Japanese went about dealing with America before Pearl Harbor.

CHAPTER 27

WAR

WHEN Peiping was Peking, the city was a center of intellectual activities and the student movement. When it became Peiping it turned into the center of Sino-Japanese conflict. During the early months of 1937 one incident after another happened in the vicinity. The arrow was drawn and must in time fly. With lightning speed it went off at the Marco Polo Bridge. On the night of July 7 the Japanese army under cover of darkness suddenly shelled the outskirts of the city from their side of the bridge, and the Chinese army stationed in the city returned fire.

I was at Kuling, a summer resort on the middle Yangtze, when the war god descended upon Peiping. Generalissimo Chiang Kai-shek had summoned a group of intellectuals for discussion of national problems in the cool Kuling mountains during those hot summer days. The sky was clear and patches of shade from the trees made lacelike patterns on the green lawns. One day after lunch, as I was resting in a one-room cottage, one of a group of houses the Generalissimo had set aside for his guests, and was looking through the window into a tall shady tree and listening to the singing of the cicadas, Chen Tsang-po, editor of the *Central Daily News*, broke the quiet of the noon hour by knocking at the door with the news that the Japanese had struck at Marco Polo Bridge the previous night. I leapt from the bed and inquired for further details. There were none.

We discussed the possibilities. As I was fresh from Peiping he asked my opinion from what I knew of conditions in the city. I told him that from my impression of the Japanese commanding generals there and their conservative views, the thing looked like another local incident. The Japanese plan seemed to be to bite off the Chinese cheese piece by piece, and I was not inclined to think they were ready to swallow the whole chunk. But by this policy of slow motion—gnawing off a bit from time to time and slowly accumulating, day after day—in a few years they would have entrenched themselves firmly in north China and it would be difficult to dislodge them. The Yangtze Valley would be at their mercy. Japan had swallowed up Manchuria by a slow process and had then come to north China. What Manchuria was to north China, so north China was to the south. The same method and the same process. That seemed to be the policy of the Japanese vis-à-vis China.

There was desultory fighting for some days. Twelve days later, as skirmishing went on outside the city, Generalissimo Chiang Kai-shek, in an address to several thousand officers from various armies in the country who were under training in the Kuling Training Center, expressed the view that the Japanese were about to launch a general war against China and we must get ready to defend the country at any cost. "But if such a general war should start," he said, "we must be ready to sacrifice . . . It will be a long war and the longer it drags on, the more we shall suffer."

It was the first time I had heard him speak in such unequivocal terms of the Japanese question. General Chen Chun, General Hu Chung-nan, and other commanding generals of the Chinese armies who later distinguished themselves at the various fronts were among the listeners. A few days after this speech Generalissimo Chiang Kai-shek returned to Nanking by air and the commanding generals rejoined their respective armies. With some of my friends I flew to the capital and tried to get back to Peiping, but northbound trains were all suspended.

In about two weeks the war was spreading like a flood in the vicinity of Peiping. General Sung Chieh-yuan fought gallantly as casualties mounted. The commander of the Japanese army, Tashiro, with whose conservative views regarding China problems I was well acquainted, fell ill and the radical younger officers got control of the Japanese forces. After a few days General Tashiro died. Was it illness, suicide, or assassination? Rumors were rampant but nobody could find out the truth. General Sung Chieh-yuan still clung to the idea of localizing the incident and urged the central government troops, which were being rushed northward, to stop at Paoting. And at Paoting, accordingly, they made a halt.

But the Japanese army, now under the direction of young officers, did not stop; Sung's forces were attacked by the enemy right and left and on all sides. One of the commanding generals died in action. Finally General Sung withdrew from Peiping and the Japanese entered the city without firing a shot.

Now the Japanese had control of Peiping. Would north China suffer the same fate as Manchuria after they occupied Mukden some six years earlier? Would Japan stop at north China for the moment, wait a few years more, and use that base for a further attack on south China? Or was she tired of waiting—would she strike at south China with a single blow and get the thing done, once and for all? Either way seemed possible. The plan of slow motion seemed on the whole more dangerous to China. All the ranking officers in Nanking and the military leaders in the provinces favored a country-wide resistance to the aggression. All China —officials, generals, and the people—stood up as one man to face the greatest calamity in history to fall upon the country.

Meanwhile Japan began to dispatch troops to Shanghai from across the sea. China at the same time rushed her own troops down the Yangtze to the same port. In that small area, face to face, were massed tens of thousands of men. A tiny spark would set off a terrific explosion in the powder magazine. It was immaterial which side should strike it first—whether by the accidental discharge of a gun by a careless soldier without orders, or by the policy of men high up in power.

The Japanese army knew very well that the men responsible for the Mukden Incident, such as Generals Honjo and Doihara, had received the highest rewards and honors for their meritorious acts. Those responsible for the Marco Polo Bridge Incident were to receive like honors, there was no doubt. Who could blame the commanding generals from across the sea for aspiring to similar rewards?

All of us in Nanking knew that the thick war clouds hanging over the whole country were bound to break into a storm. I left for Hangchow by motorcar to stay with a friend in a villa on the historic West Lake. In the serene quiet of the place I had a chance to muse over the past and think of the future. Every day, and every succeeding night, we expected a clash between the two opposing forces in that tightly congested area of Shanghai. Every now and then my friend, Wang Wen-po, telephoned to Shanghai to inquire about the situation. On August 12 the voice at the other end replied abruptly, "No news. Tomorrow at ten, at ten. That's all." The receiver was hung up.

Next morning the fatal hour struck. Smoke rose sky-high. Bombers from both sides blasted the lines of the opposing forces. A full-scale war had begun. There would be no more local incidents, no more piecemeal ways. Japan must either gobble up all China or give it up. But gobble she could not—quite, and give up she would not. It was bound to be a long-drawn-out war.

Two days later, on a cloudy afternoon, I was sitting under a willow tree watching the fish shuttling back and forth in the shallows of the lake. Peals of thunder were audible over the other side of the city. The telephone rang for me. "Hello—do you hear that?" More thunder. "Yes, it's thundering."

"No—the enemy is bombing our airfield."

Seven bombers had flown over from Formosa without escort. They were met by Chinese fighters stationed at Hangchow and five were shot down on the spot. The remaining two flew for their lives and were forced to land at some distance. The pilots were captured, and we learned that they had been told by their commanding officers that there were no fighter planes in China.

Next day the Japanese bombed Nanking. In the beginning of the war the enemy dropped only one bomb at any one place, so that all their bombs were scattered. This caused much less damage than concentrated bombing, which they learned a year later from the Russians at Changkaofen, a borden town between Manchuria and Siberia where they had a clash with Soviet forces.

My friend Wang Wen-po was a member of the Chekiang provincial government and Commissioner of Reconstruction. He had to get busy. Hundreds of trucks were taken over from the bus lines and munitions shipped to the front in them. Once a fleet of some twenty such trucks was sent to the front. It ran into the rear of the enemy and was fired upon. One truck driver got out of his car and hid in the fields; under cover of darkness he crawled on his stomach through the enemy lines and came back to Hangchow. A few days later he found another truck and dashed off again for the front.

Refugees from Shanghai poured into Hangchow. The temples were filled with women and children. Humble huts in the mountains were turned into temporary homes for fashionable young ladies. They talked and laughed as if nothing had happened to them. The Chinese were always in good humor even in time of danger.

A friend of mine, formerly a cotton magnate, came to Hangchow with his daughters and young children and lived in a temple up in the mountains. He told me that he would like to build a house for his family.

"What for?" I asked.

"I should like to stay in Hangchow during the war in Shanghai," he said.

I was surprised at his idea of the war. I told him that he had better move into the interior as the war would surely spread to Hangchow and all coastal cities and perhaps up the Yangtze as far as Hankow. He was stunned and could not believe my words. Five years later I met him in Chungking, where he told me that he and his family had left Hangchow before war descended upon the West Lake.

In Nanking a plan was afoot for the evacuation of three of the northern universities: Peking and Tsinghua Universities in Peiping and Nankai University in Tientsin. These three institutions were to combine into a union university at Changsha, an inland city on the upper Yangtze. Hu Shih telephoned from the capital and asked me to go back to Nanking to put the scheme into effect. I did not welcome the idea but was finally forced to accept the plan. There are things in the world which you do not want to do but must do in the end, willy-nilly. Like war itself: when war comes, you find yourself fighting whether you like it or not. This was my attitude toward the associated university.

Knowing that I would be unable to see my father's home again before the end of the war and that the hazards of war are difficult to foresee, I borrowed a Buick from a friend and drove home. My father, now very old, was all smiles. When I left again for Nanking I told him that China would be reborn through fire and blood.

"What do you mean?" he asked, giving me a steady look from his twinkling eyes.

"The thing is this. The war will be a long war. Hundreds and thousands of houses will be burned and thousands and millions of lives will be lost. This is what I mean by fire and blood. And in the end China will emerge victorious."

When I left him I had the feeling that most probably I would not see my beloved father again, to whom I owed so much and had returned so little. When bombs visited the native city of my boyhood days, he moved into the mountains and there enjoyed his trees, flowers, and birds. After two years of war he got up early one morning as usual and felt dizzy. He went back to bed and there his spirit fled, at the age of nearly eighty. He was but one of many indirect casualties of war. War is rather hard on old people.

I stayed at Nanking for several days and then boarded a steamer sailing upriver for Hankow. Near the docks wooden boxes containing government archives, books of the Central University library, and art treasures from the Palace Museum were piled high along the banks of the Yangtze, ready for shipment. And on the way to Hankow we met boat after boat packed with troops steaming down the river to reinforce Shanghai.

From Hankow I took the Canton-Hankow Railway to Changsha. On the way we met trainloads of troops crowded in open cars, coming up to Hankow from Canton and Kwangsi. The war was now really on a national footing, not a mere local war as heretofore. The spirit of the fighting men was high. I asked where they were going.

"Fight the Japs!" they replied with zest.

CHAPTER 28

LIFE IN CHANGSHA

CHANGSHA is an inland city. For the first time in my life I lived far away from the sea. Even in America I had stayed first in California for four years and then in New York for another five, always on the seacoast. Living in an inland city I felt a kind of dryness in spite of the damp climate and Tung-ting Lake not far away. My ideal of a place to live was in the mountains near a vast plain or on the plain near the mountains, in either case not far from the sea. Away from the sea, the sense of space in my mind seemed to fill up with solid earth. I began to feel somewhat uncomfortable.

When I arrived at Changsha Mei Yi-chi, President of Tsing-hua University, was already there. To run a university in troubled times is something of a headache. To do it during a war, in conjunction with two other institutions not lacking in the diverse personalities and idiosyncrasies common to university professors, was worse. With the worries of war and anxiety as to my family and friends in the war zones or occupied areas, it was more than my health could endure. "Headache" is a figurative term, but real stomach trouble saps one's spirit and physical vigor. In spite of frequent stomach-aches I had to exert myself to help my colleagues steer our precarious craft with its mixed crew over a rough sea.

Teachers and students of the three component institutions flocked to Changsha. Some came by sea from Tientsin, taking a British steamer to Hongkong and then a plane or the Canton-Hankow Railway; others took the Peiping-Hankow Railway to Hankow and then the Canton-Hankow line to Changsha. Within a few weeks some two hundred professors and over a thousand students had gathered around the Changsha Bible School, which the Union University rented as its temporary home. Books and laboratory apparatus were bought and shipped in from Hongkong. In less than two months the university was in full swing.

Owing to lack of space in the city the College of Literature moved to the sacred mountains of Nan-yu. I made two trips there, and these are among my pleasantest recollections of this part of the country. On one of them I wandered with friends deep into the mountains on a three-day jaunt, crossing on our way the road by which a fugitive Ming emperor passed to the southwest almost three centuries ago to avoid capture by the Manchus. A stone tablet in his memory stands there to this day, with the names of all the officials who followed him inscribed upon it. Oddly, at one of the temples we visited, a tree planted by the fleeing emperor had grown into a crooked shape looking like an old, old man taking a rest after a very long journey. We were now treading the same path, standing in the same temple. For what reason? Foreign invasion from the north, which had troubled China through ten centuries.

The first night we stopped at the Fang-kwang Temple. Here a famous Ming scholar passed the remainder of his life after the fall of the Ming Dynasty. It was a clear night—the full moon sailed low over the mountains in the empty sky. I had never seen the moon look so low and so near, as if one could poke one's fingers in its smiling face.

The second night we stopped at a monastery near the highest peak of the sacred mountains. A spring gushes from the very top of the peak, and a temple is perched there. This is the house of the Fire God and a symbol of the ancient practical wisdom that water should always be ready near fire, which may thus be controlled.

Near this temple we saw the sun come up next morning, a wonderful sight. It rose out of a sea of clouds, first sending up violet, golden, pink, and blue tints through the cloud bank and then emerging to lie like a golden ostrich egg on a white velvet cushion. All of a sudden it split into four brilliant oranges, then in the flash of a few seconds merged again into one great ball. For some moments it seemed to change color with every fraction of a second, as if with the turning of a moving-picture color camera. Then it stopped, glowed mellow gold for a few instants, and finally became a great ball of fire from which we had to turn our eyes. The icebergs of cloud disappeared and the still waves vanished. Only a thin layer of mist veiled the valleys down below. Through it one could see chimneys sending up their smoke in the mild morning sun.

Pilgrims came by thousands to the sacred mountains. Many walked from several hundred miles away. Old and young, rich and poor, all joined in common worship of the Buddha.

Changsha is the capital of Hunan Province, a center of rich rice production feeding many millions of people outside its boundaries. Fish, shrimp, eels, and turtles from the river Hsiang were abundant, oranges and persimmons bountiful. Pork was tender and full of flavor. The bean curd, China's national food for rich and poor alike, was as pure and smooth as thickened milk. The only drawback was the high humidity—there were far more rainy or cloudy days in a year than sunny ones.

Every time I went up by airplane from the city, as I sometimes had to do, I thought of the crystal palace deep in the sea where the king of dragons lives, as we all learned in Chinese fairy tales. There would still be clouds above my head, while down below mist enveloped the city like the white around the yolk of an egg. Farther up, there would be another ceiling of cloud without a streak of sun.

The people were healthy, independent, and hard working. They loved to fight. The slightest provocation would find them ready for combat, whether vocal or by fists. At highway stations one often saw signs: DO NOT QUARREL and DO NOT FIGHT. Rickshaw coolies sauntered along the streets and refused to run. If you told a coolie to run faster he would invariably say, "You pull the rickshaw—I'd like to see you run." While the temper of the people was quick, their movements were slow. Here was a case where temper and tempo did not go together.

They were frank and sincere, not easily influenced by other people's opinions. They would be either your friends or your enemies, with no halfway between. They are good soldiers. "No Hunanese, no army." It was by his Hunan army that Tseng Kuo-fang defeated the Taipings in 1864. Even now no Chinese army is found without some soldiers from Hunan. It is the Sparta of China.

The Japanese invaded Changsha three times in the course of the war, and three times suffered defeat there. The people co-operated with the national army wholeheartedly, through blood and fire.

In Changsha we had news of the war in Shanghai. For three long months Chinese troops of flesh and blood held at bay the Japanese army of fire and steel. Finally the Chinese army withdrew to save further futile sacrifice. Now the enemy converged on Nanking. An exodus of the population from the capital began—thousands of people streamed along the highway to Changsha. Trains of trucks and cars miles long poured into the city. Suddenly it was congested with refugees. Some ministries of the government moved to Changsha, others to Hankow.

Before long the Japanese army entered Nanking, where animal instincts ran wild in the Japanese soldier. Women were raped to death and fleeing people were machine-gunned at random. Military trucks ran through streams of people on the streets. The atrocities committed by the Japanese will remain forever a black spot in human history.

At the turn of the new year the Japanese army headed upriver toward Nanchang. It seemed to be approaching Changsha, while the Chinese army was concentrated around Hankow. The capital of Hunan Province was now vulnerable to enemy attack. I flew to Hankow to sound out the Generalissimo as to the removal of the Union University still farther inland. I interviewed first the Minister of Education, Chen Li-fu, who advised me to see the Commander in Chief. So I went to call on him. He agreed that the university ought to move farther west, and I suggested that we move to Kunming, which had access to the sea through the Yunnan-Indo-China Railway. He readily agreed and suggested that someone go there first to select a site for the university.

The month of January, 1938, passed in preparation for the removal. Books and scientific apparatus were packed and trucks and gasoline bought. In February, as the preparations were almost complete, I flew to Hongkong, where I took a French liner to Haiphong in French Indo-China. Thence I went by train to Hanoi, capital of the French colonial government, and from there to Kunming by the Yunnan-Indo-China Railway through one of the most mountainous regions of China.

CHAPTER 29

INDO-CHINA AND BURMA

JUST as, some twenty years earlier, I had found the ancient Chinese ways of life still persisting in Korea, so now, taking the opportunity of going to Kunming by way of Indo-China, I found there the same ancient Chinese ways. Like the Koreans, they wore a dress similar to that of the Ming Dynasty. Their pronunciation of Chinese words stemmed from that of the Tang Dynasty; villages, cities, and administrative districts bear Chinese names pronounced somewhat after the Tang fashion.

The French preferred for general use a romanization of the Annamese language, which is itself a modified form of Chinese. I must admit that it is much easier for the common people to learn. But this romanized Annamese will further widen the gap between China and Indo-China.

The capital of Annam, where the titular emperor, Pao-dai, lived, was very much like the palace of the former Korean kings and, again, like the Imperial Palace in Peking on a much smaller scale. Indeed, the court of Annam looked like a living branch of the Imperial Ming Court. The French had preserved it as a sort of living museum, while the Japanese preferred to transport the Korean king to Tokyo and make a Japanese out of him.

I was told that the first ancestor of the emperor of Annam was buried on a hill in Kunming. For he was Chinese. One afternoon, later, I tried to locate the grave but failed to find it.

While Hanoi, capital of the French colonial government, had become a French city with wide streets and imposing public buildings, the peasants lived in miserable villages which seemed to be sinking down into the earth. Liberty, Equality, and Fraternity! Colonial governments are an anachronism and bad as a system, for the governors are there for exploitation and not interested in the welfare of the governed, which is contrary to modern theory of government.

Here I wish to make one exception: the colonial government of the Philippine Islands. The Americans had an ideal—to raise the people to a higher level of civilization. The American colonial government in the Philippines established a system of public schools not inferior to American schools. I went to the Philippines in 1931. Everywhere I saw schools in which history, literature, science, and democratic ideals were taught. The United States endeavored to make the Philippine Islands a republic in the image of her own.

Britain had to depend on her colonies for her national existence; France had to be fed with riches from her colonies. Each was interested in the welfare of the governed peoples only in the sense that the geese should be kept alive to lay more golden eggs. In Korea and Formosa Japan was pressing the geese flat in order to squeeze the eggs out of them. Before the war Japan had amassed a great fortune from trade with China. But she was not satisfied; she wanted to make China a vast colony so as to be completely free to squeeze that giant goose.

The British way of keeping the geese alive was rather ingenious. They controlled the key industries and let the natives live on what was left. Let the geese feed on the corn and fish they can catch in the pond. So the geese were happy with their corn and small fish and the owners were happy with their golden eggs. The British never interfered with the customs, manners, superstitions, or beliefs of the governed peoples, and the natives could enjoy their life undisturbed except in matters affecting public health. For public health concerns alike both governors and the governed; you cannot segregate contagious disease or pestilence. Roads, too, were built and maintained, for peace and order and commerce depend upon good roads. Defense was built up only to the extent required to put down rebellions within the colony; to defend it against attacks from some other Power was left to the prestige of the British Empire, and when that prestige weakened the colony was at the mercy of a powerful neighbor. This was how Hongkong and Burma were temporarily lost, and this was why Britain was so jealous for her prestige, especially in the Far East.

Burma borders on the southwest corner of Yunnan. I went there as leader of a goodwill mission just about a year before Pearl Harbor. The British way of governing colonies was clearly evident. I saw the oil refineries, lumber mills, and rice mills—these were key industries and were under British control. Other things were left to the Burmese. Sacred cows roamed the streets in Rangoon without interference from the police. Here, there, and everywhere were temples with their gilt pagodas and monks respected by both the governors and the governed. The Burmese enjoyed an undisturbed life under British rule; the geese, swimming in their pond, were satisfied with their fish and corn, and as far as I could see showed no sign of unrest. And the owners got their golden eggs.

But the light that shone brilliantly in the homeland of the governors could not be altogether smothered in the colonies. In India Gandhi went unmolested except for imprisonment in times of crisis. Such instances would be dealt with underhandedly in the colonies of certain other European nations. But Great Britain, that land of liberty, could not help shedding some of her light through the clouds of a colonial sky. There are signs that Britain is on the road to a more enlightened policy toward her colonies. I hope that these streaks of light will be broadened to strong beams of liberty, illuminating the peoples she is entrusted to lead. British friends, give them more of that light which you have so plentifully in the British Isles. Chuck overboard the anachronisms!

As far as types of civilization are concerned, the former kingdom of Annam, now a part of Indo-China, is Chinese, while Burma is Indian. The palace of the former king of Burma at Mandalay is Indian in architectural design. The names of the cities and towns bear no trace of Chinese origin. The Annamites, like the Chinese, eat with chopsticks; the Burmese, like the Indians, with their fingers. Yet both Annam and Burma, as we have seen earlier, were formerly tributaries of China, and their loss was part of her awakening.

When Burma fell to British hands the royal family escaped into Yunnan and is supported by the provincial government down to this day, although its title is only nominal now. Its children and grandchildren entered Chinese schools and became Chinese. But they are known to the people of Tengtsung in Yunnan as descendants of the Burmese royal family, whose ancestors once reigned over the kingdom of golden pagodas and yellow-robed monks from their peacock throne in the royal palace at Mandalay.

CHAPTER 30

THE MIGRATION OF UNIVERSITIES

THE migration of universities from the coastal provinces where Chinese institutions of higher learning were originally centered to the hinterland of China was a direct sequel to the outbreak of war. Besides the three I have mentioned, other institutions located nearest to the scene of war and likely to be first affected moved gradually toward the interior. As a result there were toward the end of the war some twenty universities and colleges, with a total enrollment of about sixteen thousand students, boys and girls, newly established in Free China.

These institutions were scattered all over the interior provinces. They were housed either in temples or in the buildings of local schools. Some were able to rent private mansions when no public buildings were available. Still others had to put up temporary shacks. All brought with them such scientific apparatus and books as conditions permitted. The amount was of course negligible, yet even this scanty equipment was not infrequently ruined by the deliberate and merciless bombing of the enemy.

A large number of the students were from the occupied areas. Their support from their parents was naturally cut off; some even lost track of their families in the war zones. It may be noted, also, that some parents in the occupied areas deemed it wise, when questioned, to report as dead sons who were actually studying in Free China. The national government in Chungking consequently allotted large sums of money to care for these helpless students.

As the Japanese invasion began in north China the universities first affected were naturally those located in the areas of Tientsin and Peiping. When the two cities were occupied many students and faculty members, realizing the futility of expecting to have any spiritual freedom at the point of the invader's bayonet, went south or elsewhere to join their universities. Two combined universities were established by order of the national government then at Nanking: one at Changsha as I have related, and the other at

Sian in the northwest. The Northwestern Union University consisted of two former national universities and two colleges. It was later moved from Sian to Hanchung and has since been broken up into more or less its original components.

As the war spread to other parts of China, universities which had hitherto been able to remain where they were had now to follow our example. Thus the National Central University was moved from the former capital to the war capital of Chungking; Chekiang University was moved from Hangchow to the interior province of Kweichow; Chungshan University was moved from Canton in south China to Yunnan in the southwest.

I shall describe in some detail the former Union University in Changsha: how it was organized—or associated, to use a better term—and later transplanted from Changsha to Kunming. The story may serve as an example of the handling of other migrating universities.

As I have already related, the Union University at Changsha was formed by the association of three former Peiping and Tientsin universities by order of the Ministry of Education, then at Nanking. They were the National University of Peking, the oldest and the first government-sponsored modern university in China; the National Tsinghua University; and Nankai University at Tientsin. The presidents of these three institutions were made members of the presidium. All their faculty members and students were turned over to the Union University. Classes were resumed at Changsha by November 1, 1937, with an enrollment of approximately 1,250 students from the three universities, and an additional 220 students from other institutions which had also been moved. The latter were admitted as visiting students. The university was in fairly good shape, though equipment and facilities were meager. The spirit among the professors and students was excellent; the reading rooms were, for the most part, packed with students despite the handful of books available. But early in 1938—that is, after the fall of Nanking—things changed. Japanese planes made Changsha one of their bombing objectives. A prolonged stay in the city was perilous, so with the approval of the government, after the completion of a semester's work the Union University moved, at the end of February, 1938, southwest to Kunming.

The migration from Changsha to Kunming was made in two

groups: some three hundred male students with a few professors constituted themselves a walking party, hiking from Changsha in Hunan through the mountainous province of Kweichow all the way to the remote city of Kunming in Yunnan—a trek of 3,500 li, or approximately 1,160 miles, accomplished over a period of two months and ten days. The others, numbering about eight hundred, rode from Changsha to Canton on the much-bombed Canton-Hankow Railway, thence by boat to the British colony of Hongkong, and again by boat to Haiphong. From here they traveled by the French Indo-China Railway to Kunming, their final destination. The rail-boat and boat-rail trip required from ten to fourteen days, depending upon connections. Over three hundred and fifty students remained in Changsha to join the various war organizations.

After its removal to Kunming the title "Union University" was changed to the present name: National Southwest Associated University. As Kunming had no immediately available and suitable buildings to put at the disposal of the newcomers, the university —called "Lienta" from the abbreviation of its Chinese name—decided to locate its College of Arts and College of Law and Commerce at Mengtsz, probably the second largest city in the province, and keep the College of Science and Engineering in Kunming. When classes began in early May, 1938, there were around thirteen hundred students in the total enrollment for these four colleges of Lienta. In September of the same year the two colleges at Mengtsz moved back to Kunming, where the housing problem had become less acute as all the local middle schools had by then been moved to the country and their school buildings could be rented. The "happy-double-union" was celebrated by the founding of a teachers' college by order of the national government at Chungking. Enrollment in the five colleges, comprising twenty-six departments, increased to two thousand.

In September, 1939, Lienta again grew in size. There were by now over three thousand students. The university was fortunate, as its hundred shacks, built in the past ten months, could then be used to accommodate the growing student body. At the close of the war we had about five hundred professors, assistants, and administrative officers and three thousand students. Most of the latter came from the occupied areas and had to cross more than one firing line to reach the free zone; they went through much hardship and suffering, and others lost their lives before they could reach Free China.

My son, a student in Chiao-tung University in Shanghai, on his way to join me at Kunming met with several incidents. Once, on a dark night, with a number of friends he tried to go by small boat under a bridge guarded by the enemy and was shot at. On another occasion the party traveling ahead of his lost one of its members, who was arrested by the enemy and his head was later found by his friends dangling from a tree.

The son of a friend of mine came from Peiping to Kunming, traversing many firing lines in the north, and was shot at by the enemy several times. Often he had nothing to eat during the day and had to walk miles under cover of night. He had left Peiping with his brother, who was arrested by the Japanese guard at the station and sent to a detention camp because something was found in his pocket which identified him as a student. They had disguised themselves as apprentices of a shop. When the identity of such a person was established it was a serious offense.

It was reported that the basement of the College of Literature in the University of Peking had been turned into a dungeon in which terror reigned. I had no way to verify actual conditions there, but later met a former student of mine who had been arrested and imprisoned for two years before he managed to leave Peiping for Free China. He said that he was sent there for a "treat." The place was a living hell. Water was forced into his nose until he lost consciousness. When he came to, a Japanese gendarme by the name of Uyemura told him that he deserved the treatment because his alma mater was responsible for this terrible war in which Japan had suffered so much. "No pity!" said Uyemura in a rage. "Let the punishment fit the crime!" Three times he was thus "treated," fainting each time. In that dungeon he saw other tortures which do not befit my pen to describe. The shrieks of the girls and the groans of the boys turned that seat of learning into an inferno where Satan had his day.

While the students left in Peiping moaned under torture, the university in Kunming was blasted by enemy bombs. The bombing was done deliberately, since the seat of the university was outside the city wall with no military objective near by. Many buildings were destroyed, including the stacks of the main university library and some of the science laboratories. About one third of the university buildings were rendered useless and had to be rebuilt as fast as possible. Despite all this, the spirit of the students was wonderful. As a rule they studied hard in these trying circumstances, with meager food and poor living conditions.

This migration of institutions of learning from the seacoast to the interior has an important bearing on the future development of China's hinterland. The presence of a large number of intellectuals in various localities in the interior will exercise a strong influence upon the mental outlook of people in those localities. Moreover, students as well as teachers who have lived for a long time along the coast with only a local knowledge of the country have now had an opportunity to learn actual conditions in the interior, which has given them a better perspective on conditions in the vast country as a whole.

The migration of universities, combined with the removal of industries, both government and private, and of skilled laborers, engineers, experts, and managers, was indeed epoch-making. In the postwar period ahead of us the development of China in regions far from the coast, hitherto inaccessible to Western influence, will have a better chance than ever before.

CHAPTER 31

AT THE TERMINAL CITY OF THE BURMA ROAD

WITH the migration of the universities, I came to stay for the duration of the war at Kunming, terminal city on the Burma Road. Before Pearl Harbor I made one visit to Burma and many to Indo-China and Hongkong; all were connected with Kunming by air. After the capitulation of France, Indo-China was given over to Japan virtually without a fight. So we built the Burma Road to connect the city with Rangoon. After Pearl Harbor Burma, too, was lost to the enemy. Land communications with Haiphong in Indo-China and Rangoon in Burma were cut. Kunming was now bottled up. Lend-Lease ammunition ceased to flow into the city except by air over the "hump" of the Himalayas which separates China from the land of Buddha.

In the last few years I have visited Chungking by air many times, and once also Chengtu, capital of Szechuan Province. The hilly wartime national capital of China is situated on the banks of the Yangtze River within the Yangtze gorges. The city is built on hills. Its narrow strip of land is girdled by the Yangtze on the south and the Kialing River on the north, the two rivers merging into the greater Yangtze at the easternmost point of the narrow strip. Thus Chungking looks like a tiny peninsula. Most of the houses are built upon terraces, and dugouts were made at their back doors or under the buildings through the granite hills. For several years Japanese planes rained explosives on the defenseless city day after day, night after night, month after month. But the capital remained undaunted. Buildings were hit and destroyed and rebuilt by tens of thousands, yet comparatively few lives were lost. The enemy tried to bomb the wartime government out of its capital, but the city still stands like the pyramids, which have endured their many centuries of hardship and will stand many centuries more. Chungking embodies to perfection the spirit of stubborn resistance against the Japanese invaders.

To the west of the hilly capital, about half an hour distant by air, is the flat city of Chengtu. This walled city is as spacious as Peking. The streets are wide. The atmosphere is also somewhat like that of the former capital. The irrigation system at Kwan Hsien, established some twenty centuries ago, waters over a million acres of fertile land in the Chengtu Valley. Serious flood or drought are almost unknown. This immense, rich valley kept the people in Chungking and the army stationed in the province and adjacent districts amply fed.

When we moved our university to Kunming we had in mind the possibility of importing books and scientific instruments from Europe and America through Indo-China. But after the fall of Canton the main line for the supply of munitions was cut and shipments were diverted to the Indo-China-Yunnan route. The congestion on the railway precluded the shipment of nonmilitary cargoes. Only a small fraction of our shipments was allowed to trickle in.

Meanwhile all the cities along the Yangtze River fell one after another into the hands of the enemy, up to I-chang, not far from the Yangtze gorges. Finally that too failed to stem the tide of advancing enemy might and went under the heel of the invader.

Kunming felt the pinch of every adversity of war. What most affected the daily life of the people was the rising cost of living. When we came there, in the second year of war, rice per Chinese bushel (eighty kilograms) cost $6 in Chinese currency. When it had increased by degrees to $40 a bushel one of our professors of economics predicted that after a few months it would rise to $70. People laughed at him. But it did go to $70. The capitulation of Indo-China and the loss of Burma both severely affected the price of commodities.

The first noticeable rise in prices came after the first bombing of the city by enemy planes. The country people were afraid to come in, and fewer vegetables and meats were brought to market. The shopkeepers worried over the safety of their goods and raised prices to cover their possible loss. The embargo on certain imported goods also affected the prices of similar or allied home products. Thus the embargo on kerosene raised the prices of vegetable oils. The rise in price of vegetable oils carried with it an increasing price for lard. When lard went up, pork followed suit. One thing thus led to another. The upward run of prices naturally gave rise to a host of hoarders. Hoarding in turn aggravated the price situation. When the swing of the pendulum went higher on one side, momentum brought it high again on the other.

The thing to have done, of course, was to control prices by controlling commodities from the very beginning of the war; not try to regulate prices after it was too late. I was told by a British friend that British farmers made a good deal of profit out of the first World War, but that farm products were controlled at the beginning of this war. Since this was the first modern war on a large scale in China, she had no past experience of such problems.

The climate of Kunming is really ideal. Situated in the semi-tropical zone at an altitude of six thousand feet, the city is something like a great summer resort. But because of its size the inhabitants do not think of it as such. It is perpetual spring. The rainy season falls in summer, when frequent showers cool off the summer days. During the other seasons most of the days are filled with smiling sunshine cast upon the luxuriant growth in the fields from a cloudless blue sky.

Flowers abound in that climate and fruits are plentiful. Melons, eggplant, and citrons grow to enormous sizes. People do not have to work hard to make a living; they enjoy a complacent life and take things in leisurely fashion. Newcomers from the coastal provinces were at first exasperated by the slowness of the inhabitants, but they themselves gradually melted into that sea of tranquility.

The people of Kunming were quite concerned about the flow of thousands of refugees into the city from the coast. Many brought large sums of money and spent it freely. The local people blamed them for the increasing cost of living. The city was crowded with fashionable young ladies and well-dressed folk from the coast. In the evenings they rubbed shoulders with native citizens on the sidewalks of the main streets of Kunming. House rents rose fast. Hotels were all filled to capacity; on arrival people often found no place to stay. New houses shot up like mushrooms. Old houses destroyed by bombs were rapidly restored. Yet the population grew faster than houses could be built to accommodate it.

Within the few years of the war Kunming was transformed. The old tranquil scene was filled with truck drivers, war profiteers, contractors, engineers, and manufacturers. Munitions trucks shuttled through the outskirts of the city.

The natural and historic surroundings, however, remained unchanged. Kunming Lake, which flows into the Yangtze and over two thousand miles into the Yellow Sea, remained as placid as before. Fish and duck enjoyed their watery life as in days of old. Historic temples with quaint trees around them perched on the hills overlooking the wide span of the rippling lake. The Buddhist monks chanted their prayers as others had done centuries ago. Looking over the lake to the horizon I often wondered: If a sealed bottle with letters in it were thrown into the water, might it not be carried by the outgoing current down the Yangtze, passing through Chungking, I-chang, Hankow, Kiu-kiang, Anking, and Nanking to the sea near Shanghai? And perhaps some fisherman might pick it up and forward it to my native land of Chekiang. It was, of course, only the dream of an exile thinking of home.

A network of aqueducts, built between two parallel embankments protected by age-old spruces, conducts water to irrigate tens of thousands of acres of fertile land. The embankments are wide enough to run a horse on; one could trot leisurely along this endless trail for miles in the forest of scent-laden spruce, traversing the luxuriant fields.

In the city a stone tablet marking the spot where the last refugee emperor of the Mings was strangled to death looks tragically down the slope at the passers-by. The much-to-be-pitied emperor fled to Burma, but was taken back to China by General Wu San-kwei, the one who later, while defending the Great Wall against the Manchus, was to go over to the enemy in order to save his lady from the bandit leader. In his campaign against his own people in south China he came to Yunnan, where the captive emperor was brought before him.

"What do you have to say?" asked the general, as the story has it.

"Nothing," replied the last emperor of the Mings. "The only thing I want to know is, why did you rebel against my forefathers, from whom you received so much favor and so many honors?"

Wu San-kwei trembled at these words and ordered the captive emperor strangled at the spot where the stone tablet now stands. It reads: "Here died Emperor Yung-li of the Ming Dynasty for his country."

About ten kilometers from the city is the Black Dragon Pool. Spring water, crystal clear, oozes out from the bottom and overflows into tiny streams. Around it are temples and gigantic moss-grown trees. A scholar and his family lived here toward the end of the Ming Dynasty. When news of the emperor's death and the consequent downfall of the dynasty reached him, he plunged into the pool and committed suicide. His family and servants followed suit. The whole family died for their country by suicide and were all buried there. This is difficult for the Western mind to understand, but Chinese philosophy holds that if you cannot do anything else to save your country, death is the only way to redeem the debt of your conscience. By this philosophy the Chinese soldiers laid down their lives during this war willingly by hundreds of thousands in a battle often of simple flesh and blood against the enemy's steel and fire.

Our more or less chronological story is here ended for the time being. The following chapters will discuss some of the problems of Chinese civilization and culture, past, present, and future, and some of the persistent national problems that will present themselves in China in years to come.

From Hongkong in 1842 to Pearl Harbor in 1941 is a period of exactly one century; to tell the story of that period this volume has been written. England was instrumental in blasting China's southern gates open to world commerce. With the flow of opium and Western manufactures came the seeds of Western thought and science, which affected China's view toward life and the universe. She resisted, struggled, and finally absorbed Western culture, as she did Indian culture centuries and centuries before. England was the instrument of Fate that brought China into the community of the world.

The course China took was rather roundabout, like the winding of the Yangtze River. But in direction she remained unchanged—like the Yangtze which moves down over its course of more than two thousand miles to color the Yellow Sea, in spite of its many windings. It flows day and night, month after month, year after year, and will flow in the same way for endless centuries to come. The invincible Yangtze is the symbol of China's national life and culture.

Part VII

CHINA IN THE MODERN WORLD

CHAPTER 32

CHINA AND JAPAN—A COMPARISON

BEFORE the coming of Admiral Perry Japan was an offshoot of Chinese civilization, pure and simple. After that time she became a blend of offshoots of both Chinese and Western civilizations. Unless one understands both China and the West he is not in a position to understand Japan.

Yet there is something more. Offshoots may be similar to their main roots, but they are not identical. To render judgment upon things similar as if they were the same may lead miles away from the truth. Moreover, the blending of two civilizations may change the character of the contributing originals.

The offshoots of Chinese civilization in Japan were of the Tang era (618–905). While many of the precious elements of Tang culture had been worn away in China through centuries of barbaric invasion, they were preserved in Japan. Dancing, music, the arts, ways of living, the pronunciation of Chinese words and China's martial spirit, all of Tang origin, found living embodiment in the Island Empire of the Rising—or hereafter the Setting—Sun. If you want to know something about the Tang civilization, go to Japan. Upon a foundation of Tang culture Japan made herself great by the absorption of Western science.

However, an offshoot is but an offshoot; it has to receive nourishment from the roots of the mother tree. As soon as the mother tree in China withered, the offshoot had to depend for nourishment on the local soil of Japan. Now, Japan had every nourishment in her soil to nurse the Tang offshoots to grow, save one—originality. In this respect she failed miserably, and for lack of this one element Japan remained a dwarf tree.

After Perry's arrival she began to tap the flow of Western civilization to fertilize her land. The tree did shoot up heavenward after receiving new nourishment from this source. But again she failed in respect of that most valuable element of Western civilization—originality.

She copied. She copied the Tangs in her civilization. She copied England in building up her navy. She copied Germany in training her army. She copied America in developing her industry. She copied the nineteenth-century Western anachronism of building a colonial empire—a bit too late. She copied Germany's blitzkrieg by hitting at Pearl Harbor—a bit too far. Japan is a wonderful copy which is almost as good as the original but falls short in reproducing the spirit behind it, something rather elusive. Her copybook is closed now, I hope, forever. She grew on copying, became strong on copying, and I hope will not commit hara-kiri on copying.

I admire Japan for her genius of exact aping—something China was unable to do, for she was too clumsy for that. But China made up for it by the possession of originality. She created and created until her energy was sapped by centuries of barbarian invasion, famine, and disease after the downfall of the Tangs.

In parallel fashion, America is an offshoot of European civilization. But here the case is different, for the early colonist from England brought with him the seeds of a love of freedom, which is an expression of originality in ideas. So America created and created till she became the most highly industrialized nation in the world: the most materialistic and at the same time the most idealistic and humanitarian. In the combination of these great opposing elements into one unity lies the greatness of America.

The martial spirit of Japan, of which the Japanese are very proud, is embodied in Bushido, the way of chivalry, which she incorporates into what she calls vaguely Yamato, the "spirit of Japan." Bushido as revealed in peace is an intense loyalty to one's country; in war it means to fight to the last man. Japan has forgotten that what she calls Bushido is nothing more than the martial spirit of ancient China. The very word shows the Tang origin. The modern Chinese pronunciation is Wu-shi-tao—in Cantonese, Mu-shi-do, very similar to Tang pronunciation, whence the Japanese Bu-shi-do.

With strict discipline and efficient organization, and with a thorough application of modern science, Bushido became a mighty weapon of war with which Japan won victory in the Sino-Japanese and Russo-Japanese Wars and ultimately hoped to conquer China and the world. Out of it grew a will to power; upon this foundation she built up a military empire which recognized nothing but power.

The secret of the phenomenal success of Japan in world power lies in reforms along Western lines made by hereditary ruling classes nurtured in the martial spirit, with a strong aptitude for copying and an intense loyalty to leaders and to their native land. They had at hand a people whose supreme virtue is to follow their leaders and obey orders. So the reforms of Japan since the beginning of the Meiji period have moved in a constant and unchanging direction.

Reforms in China, on the other hand, have to start from the bottom. There have been no hereditary ruling classes, no aristocracy but the aristocracy of learning. The vast country has to be whipped into unity of purpose by learned leaders from among the common people. Thus the process is necessarily slow and follows a zigzag way. Political leaders such as Sun Yat-sen and intellectual leaders such as Chang Pin-ling, Liang Chi-chao, and Tsai Yuanpei have all been scholarly men drawn from ordinary backgrounds. From the common people they came and to the common people they went with their great gifts of social and intellectual vision.

Modern Japan has been built up by ruling classes, modern China by the common people. It is therefore much easier to be a leader in Japan, where a leader dictates to the people; in China he has to educate and really lead them—a much more difficult art, which requires a good deal of resourcefulness and originality.

China was comparatively slow in making reforms, but once she made up her mind to it she always tried to find their deeper meaning. In the course of the last hundred years, as we have seen, she began by making cannon balls, from which she was led to political reforms, thence to social reforms and to the introduction of ideas from the West. She wanted to strike at the core of everything. She penetrated deeper and deeper to the heart of Western civilization. She recast her old beliefs and constructed new ones until they became part and parcel of her life. She is a scholar, a moral philosopher, an artist. Her civilization and culture have grown out of her life and she could not be satisfied with Western ideas until they were thoroughly assimilated into that life. In contrast to Japan, therefore, China's thought is modern but her social and industrial structure still lags behind. This is something inherent in the philosopher, the dreamer.

China is broad-minded and democratic and possesses originality but she lacks organization, discipline, and the martial spirit. She is a country of scholars, where learning is most honored and culture most treasured. Yet the military might to defend herself within her own boundaries is something that China has yet to achieve. In China's strong points her weaknesses lie.

So it is with Japan. The Japanese is a warrior and an efficient administrator. The adopted Western civilization has been but a military superstructure which made Japan a militarily potent nation but did not touch the deeper life and thought of the people. While her structure is modern, her spirit and ideas are medieval. This should not surprise the reader, since the feudal system actually existed in Japan until only yesterday—the beginning of the Meiji period. Its abolition took place almost simultaneously with the introduction of Western civilization, while China abolished feudalism before the Christian era.

By elevating the martial spirit to the highest plane which it is possible to maintain by strict discipline, Japan has sacrificed the creative spirit which, in the long run, is the heart of a culture and the sure foundation of a nation. The creative spirit is something one cannot ape. The more one relies on imitation, the more one is apt to lose his creativeness. The more strict the discipline for war required of a people, the more that people will lose the creative spirit.

In the assimilation of Chinese culture, as with the Western, Japan was only partially successful. For example, of the two important moral precepts which are the guiding principles of life in China—loyalty and considerateness—Japan learned loyalty, an indispensable virtue in a feudal state or a militaristic nation, but failed to understand considerateness, which is the virtue of the scholar. She stuck to her own ideas stubbornly or faithfully but refused to consider other people's viewpoints. The narrow-mindedness of the Japanese, of which even they themselves are conscious, deprived them of the leadership necessary for a continental colonial empire. They had ambition and military might but no statesmanship. The Japanese see things very clearly within certain limits but are blind to major cultural movements of the world. They are bigoted, intolerant, and inflexible under the cover of extreme courtesy.

On the other hand, the two virtues went hand in hand in China. She is faithful and at the same time considerate. China does not feel that faithfulness to her own ideas precludes the existence of other points of view. She always tries to imagine herself in the position of others. That is considerateness, of which Japan was not capable. So she failed to understand China.

Japan has acted like a strong little boy who tries to take a ram by the horns. It snorts, jumps, arches its back, and butts at him until he is forced to let go or is laid flat on his back. Then he wonders why the creature should act that way. Poor boy! Think what you would do if someone took you by the ear—try to see yourself in another's position—and you will understand China.

Another important factor that has made the Japanese a war-loving race is the belief that Japan is a divine country, born of gods and living and conquering by divine will. This is not easily understood either by the West or by the Chinese. But it is a fact that the Japanese believe it reverently. The Chinese believe in gods, but they take them as the guardians of morals, not of war. For the Chinese the gods have nothing to do with the rise or downfall of an empire. But to the Japanese the rise of Japan was the will of the gods.

From time immemorial the ruling classes of Japan have believed that in war the gods are always on the side of Dai Nippon. When the Yuans or Mongols failed to conquer her, they thought the gods had protected her with their divine power. The typhoon that destroyed Kublai Khan's Mongol fleet was an act of the gods. The reigning dynasty of the Mikado, the Japanese have believed up to now, is of divine origin and its emperors the direct descendants of gods.

A Chinese graduate of Tokyo Imperial University, later a professor in a Chinese university, has done an illuminating piece of historical research to show how Japanese imperialism grew out of this religious-patriotic fervor. Expressions of it in the everyday life of the soldier are not lacking. During the war Japanese soldiers almost all carried Buddhist or Shinto charms for protection in battle. I saw many such charms brought back from battlegrounds by

Chinese soldiers, who finally came to regard them as an indispensable part of enemy military equipment and paid no more attention to them, except to joke about them occasionally.

After one battle between the American Air Force and the Japanese invaders I acted as guide to a party of American officers and soldiers who drove in jeeps over miles of rugged mountain paths to a crashed Japanese bomber. In the pockets and on the bodies of the dead pilots we found the usual Buddhist and Shinto charms, smeared with blood and riddled with bullets. An American captain pulled a cloth charm from the dead pilot and asked me what it was. I told him.

"What's the use of it?" asked the captain.

"For divine protection," I replied.

"No protection, though—" he turned over the cloth and tried to make out the indecipherable signs on it, "—you get me?" And he threw it on the ground casually and forgot about it. Like this American officer, the Chinese had come to dismiss lightly these tokens of invulnerability. So it is with the world.

On the day of that aerial battle I saw seven enemy bombers spinning down from the skies in white smoke. The other search parties brought back from the wrecked planes many similar talismans, besides cartridges, maps, and scientific charts. A curious combination of medieval superstition with modern science. But to the Japanese it is no superstition; there is a living divine force which spurs them on to fight for their country, protected by the gods. The charms are but the symbol of that divine power.

After the fall of Hongkong a Chinese couple—a Mr. and Mrs. Huang whom I know well and who understand the psychology of the Japanese—presented an image of Buddha to a Japanese soldier who entered their house. Crossing the harbor to Kowloon the little boat he took capsized and all on board were drowned but himself. He came back to them to express his gratitude, for he believed that the image had saved his life. But to the Chinese way of thinking the image had protected the couple from being molested by the enemy, while the escape from drowning was mere luck.

The world does not know much about Japanese religious fanaticism in war because the Japanese themselves have not said much about it in their propaganda. While in China modern science has sapped the old beliefs and is a disintegrating factor in relation to them, in Japan it became merely a powerful weapon of the gods to weld the country together in a war of aggression. This psychological background of intense religious patriotism has made the Japanese warlords unamenable to reason, the Japanese soldier a hard nut to crack, and Japan herself a menace to the world; such is the result of fanaticism combined with modern science.

To have such a fanatical neighbor would be a headache to any country. And Japan has been much more than a headache to China during the last fifty long, troubled years. Only utter defeat and unconditional surrender could make Japan come to her senses. The inevitable fate awaited her, and we must now hope that it will have its bitter but salutary consequence.

When the gods of the Allied nations have fulfilled their mission, Japan—as I can imagine—may be a picturesque and peaceful country, with enchanting mountain scenery, pretty gardens wreathed in *sakura* blossoms, attractive pavilions with ladies in beautiful kimonos; and an industrious, courteous, and docile people, in whose ears will ring no voices of gods urging them onward to war and to conquest.

Then, and not until then, will peace reign in Japan, in China, in the Far East, and in the world.

CHAPTER 33

CHARACTERISTICS OF CHINESE CULTURE

EAST and West are different because their cultures are different. Yet you will find similarities in both. These parallels, no matter how close, will not make two cultures alike; the peculiar characteristics of each still render one different from the other. In the West varying culture traits make the Germans different from the English and the French from the Dutch. Yet there are characteristics common to all—common ties which hold the Western nations together culturally under the loose name of "Western culture." These again differ from the Eastern nations. Similarities or contrasts of culture, therefore, are not to be judged by outward parallels but by the fundamental character of each.

In this chapter we will examine the characteristics of Chinese culture under three headings: (1) the absorbing power of Chinese civilization, (2) morals and intellect, and (3) the practical wisdom of the Chinese people.

1. The Absorbing Power of Chinese Civilization

SOME forty years ago, when I was still in school, we were constantly told by foreigners and progressive Chinese alike that China was like a solid rock which absorbs little or nothing. That is to say, Chinese civilization was stagnant and petrified and China was incurably conservative. She loved and lived by her own ways. Nothing could effect a change in John the Chinaman.

This appeared to be all right but proved all wrong. From the opening of the treaty ports until after the Sino-Japanese War in 1894 China appeared to resist Western influence. However, during previous centuries she had absorbed many of the outlandish things which from time to time made inroads upon her life.

In music, the so-called "national" Chinese music of the present day is played on instruments mostly of foreign origin. Forms of the fiddle, flute, and harp were introduced from Turkestan centuries ago. We also kept the ancient Chinese harp, but only a few understand its music and still fewer can play it.

Various foods have been introduced to the Chinese dinner table from foreign lands: watermelons, cucumbers, grapes, and peppers came hundreds of years ago; sweet potatoes, peanuts, and Indian corn have appeared in recent centuries. In late decades the Irish potato, tomato, cauliflower, cabbage, and lettuce have found their way into Chinese cooking. Tenderloin steaks of the West, chopped very fine and served with bean sauce, have kept delightful company with Chinese dishes. Tomato soup with tender shrimp meat and hot fried rice hissing euphoniously in it was an innovation. Dinner in China is sometimes topped off with ice cream, American coffee, and Sunkist oranges, together with fruits of native production. Oranges grew originally in Chinese soil, traveled to America, received their education in the Luther Burbank school of California, and returned to their native land with a new title—something like the B.A. or PH.D. brought back by Chinese students from American universities. Chinese oranges also went to Germany many, many years ago, where they turned into apples—for the Germans called orange *apfelsine,* Chinese apple.

Spiritual or intellectual nourishment from any quarter that was worth the trouble of absorbing China was always ready to welcome. During the Ming Dynasty the Jesuits brought to China astronomy, mathematics, and the Bible. An Imperial minister was converted and his residence in the Siccawei district of Shanghai was made a center of Catholic activities. From the Jesuits the Chinese learned Western astronomy and some became Christians because of it. The Siccawei Observatory has been a guiding star for shipping along that coast ever since the opening of the treaty ports.

Huang Chung-hsi, a great Ming scholar living during the end of the Ming and the beginning of the Ching (Manchu) Dynasty, was one of the admirers of Western astronomy brought by the Jesuits. He said: "Learning has been preserved in foreign lands while China has lost it owing to the lack of proper care." He once told a friend that "so far as astronomy is concerned, we are only babies in comparison with the Western scholar." Which shows how open-minded great Chinese scholars were.

The fact is that China has endured many vicissitudes of fortune in the course of her centuries because of her great capacity for absorption. No civilization in the world could sustain itself without taking in alien elements from time to time in one way or another. I think it needs no historian to prove that point. The interdependence and mutual influences of Western civilizations are so obvious as to require no argument. But the interaction of Eastern and Western civilizations is less apparent. I have been told by Professor Joseph Needham of Cambridge that the expanding properties of gunpowder influenced the discovery of steam power, and that the idea of good in human nature, of the Confucian school, influenced the Encyclopedists in France. A number of things have trickled from time to time into the West from the East. But I would like to leave it to the West to tell us.

We did not absorb more than music, foodstuffs, and things of similar nature through our western and northern frontiers by land because there was not much more to absorb. The races in those regions had little spiritual or mental food to offer. For the latter we turned to India. In the field of arts Chinese painting and architecture were influenced by Buddhism; in Chinese philosophy Buddhist thought played a very important part, and it even affected the style and vocabulary of Chinese literature.

Centuries before the Jesuits the Chinese had assimilated the moral aspects of Buddhism, but they left the system of otherworldly philosophy alone. After centuries of sojourning in China, with tens of thousands of Buddhist temples and monasteries occupying the best sites on mountains as well as in cities, its basic philosophy and religion still remain foreign to the Chinese mind. The scholars befriend or tolerate it and the common people worship it as one of the religions in China. Nevertheless it remains foreign. To the practical-minded Chinese its metaphysical system is not palatable. It exists in China because there are moral teachings in it and in time of distress one could find moral refuge in it. The Chinese only wanted to absorb foreign elements into their own system of thought, to be enriched by them; they would not surrender their own system to an alien one.

Out of their virtue of tolerance the Chinese had an ingenious way of dealing with any system they could not absorb into their own. They would take part of it and leave the rest to co-exist with the indigenous products. Thus a portion of her teeming millions would take in the imported system and become Buddhists, Mohammedans, or Christians, and all lived side by side in a good, neighborly way.

But to go back to the introduction of Western civilization during the last half century. In the matter of clothing the process of westernization in the past thirty years has been still more striking. Felt or straw hats have taken the place of old types of headgear; cut hair has banished the "Chinaman's queue" as you have seen it in old pictures. Women wear bobbed hair with permanent waves. Short skirts and silk and nylon stockings have given Chinese women a chance to show their pretty and well-developed legs. As regards their feet, they have indeed gone through a revolution. Western shoes have relieved the agelong agonies of foot-binding, with subsequent improvement in their bodily health. Healthy mothers bring forth healthy children—the effect upon the coming generation has been remarkable. Our children are not only healthier as compared with children of days gone by, but more active— quicker in movement and keener in mind.

In social affairs both sexes intermingle more freely in contrast with the old customs of segregation. In civil law marriages no longer have to be arranged by parents; young men and women have the right to find their lovers and choose their own mates. Coeducational institutions are rather the rule than the exception.

As regards dwellings the old superstition of feng-shui that affected the choice of sites for buildings has given way to modern theories of architecture. While the old artistic styles are still preserved for their beauty and grandeur in some cases, air, light, convenience, comfort, and hygienic conditions are first considerations. Flush toilets, baths, and a steam heating system are installed in modern houses. Stiff-backed chairs and hard beds have given way to sofas and spring mattresses.

Chinese food is rich in its variety because it is always ready to absorb alien elements. Western food is comparatively simple because it is, I think, not so ready to take in foreign materials. Tea was indeed introduced into Europe from China centuries ago. Spices were introduced from the East, and in search for a shorter trade route to India Columbus happened upon America. Worcestershire sauce, I am told, was developed from Chinese bean sauce. Aside from these, Western food has remained untouched by Eastern influences. Chop suey houses are found by the hundreds in America and Americans are quite fond of chop suey but know few other Chinese dishes.

On the other hand, China keeps on absorbing more and more alien elements, sometimes sensibly and at other times rather indiscriminately—not only food but clothing, shelter, ideas, social customs, and so forth. In most cases the process of absorption is through unconscious rather than conscious action. It is something like the absorption of nutriment from the soil by the roots of a tree: they absorb and cannot do otherwise. It is the nature of a growing tree to absorb, or it would cease to grow.

The introduction and absorption of alien civilization from China's western frontiers were accomplished in the course of many, many centuries, during which foreign elements came into the country only in trickles. Therefore she took them in gradually and slowly digested them. It was for the most part an unconscious process; it did not change the main course of Chinese civilization, but was something like the attraction of a magnet for iron particles. They cluster around it, but the magnet does not change its position.

Western civilization, on the other hand, came to China's eastern frontiers by sea in torrents, in all its fierceness, speed, and magnitude, and in the short span of some fifty years. To try to absorb Western civilization—with all that the French and industrial revolutions had contributed to it—was like gobbling up many days' food supply at one meal. Naturally China suffered some discomfort —not to say unbearable stomach-ache. Thus Western civilization at one time became so distasteful to China that she feared it, cursed, kicked the table over, and turned from it in despair, only to find more food being pressed on her. The reaction against Western civilization was a reaction against food after a stomach-ache through much overeating. The abortive reforms of 1898 were but a case of overeating. The Boxer Rebellion of 1900 was a violent case of acute and complicated indigestion. China was forced on the operating table, to be operated on by Western doctors—the allied armies of eight nations. For that she had a handsome bill to pay—450,000,000 taels—and in the operation almost lost her life.

The doctrine of Chang Chi-tung that "Chinese culture is fundamental and Western civilization is supplementary" is no more than to say that a sound stomach is more important to health than the foods it is to take. So China tried to move cautiously, measuring her steps instead of lengthening them. But the tides of Western civilization would not wait for her. They lashed her eastern shores, overflowed into the rich Pearl and Yangtze Valleys, and rapidly extended to the Yellow River Valley. She had to go on taking more imported food in spite of her recent serious upset.

By 1902 the students, who had the best appetites, caught up with the spirit of the times, and revolution—against established authorities, educational, political, and moral, as well as intellectual—became the catchword of the rising generation. Burdened with a legacy of the past which seemed to them at the time no more than the dead hand of a bygone civilization, the receptive mind of youth took so enthusiastically to Western ideas as to offset the influences of tradition.

Soon after the opening of the five treaty ports, China had established arsenals, dockyards, machine shops, schools of foreign languages; had translated books on elementary sciences and sent students to study in America. Being defeated in various wars of self-defense against Western Powers, she started to build a navy. A small navy was built, indeed, only to be destroyed by Japan in 1894. Japan could not endure to have China have a navy.

Failing this, China went a step further by taking up the reform of government, army, and education. The Imperial government at Peking began to prepare for the adoption of a Western constitutional form of government; it established new systems of education, organized modern armies and police, and sent large numbers of students to study abroad. This may be regarded as the first conscious effort in history to absorb a foreign civilization on a large scale, and it had far-reaching consequences in China's national life.

The reforms in education were the most important, because they were the best planned, with most foresight, and dealt directly with the rising generation whose minds were least fettered by traditional ideas. Later, when the students of one school generation grew up and came into power, they adopted more Western ways and consequently those of the succeeding generation were in a better position to absorb more new ideas. When these came to power in their turn, they went still further in westernization and more new measures were introduced into the government, army, and schools. Thus each new generation was more modernized than the previous one.

The 1919 student movement in Peking, the emphasis upon science and modern democratic ideas by professors of the National University there, and the literary revolution sponsored by Professor Hu Shih, were the beginnings of conscious effort to absorb Western thought, hitherto limited mainly to the industrial and political spheres. This effort came nearer to the heart of Chinese culture and with it a new leaf was turned in the cultural history of China. For by this means China has been trying to catch up with the advancing tides of the world. Chinese civilization, with compass pointing to the West, has gradually shifted its course to meet the main currents of Western civilization, and in the next fifty years, while still retaining its own characteristics, it will flow in the common channels of the coming civilization of the world.

So far China has already received much benefit from westernization. The freedom of women to be on equal terms with men in social activities, to marry and remarry, and to have their feet unbound has been gained though the influence of Western respect for women. Western medicine has prevented plagues which wrought yearly havoc among the teeming millions. Painless operations have relieved the suffering of thousands of people. Machinery and inventions have improved means of production and contributed much to the enjoyment of life. And it goes without saying that modern weapons of war have also helped people to kill more, and to be killed. Modern science has widened the scope of knowledge; scientific methods have been carried into the study of Chinese history, philosophy, and literature. Above all, the old superstitions in which people used to live are giving way to the enlightenment of scientific truths. The greater our capacity to absorb Western ideas, the more our civilization will be enriched. Poverty and disease, twin curses of Chinese national life, will gradually disappear in proportion to the extent and thoroughness of China's modernization. To me, in this respect, modernization and westernization seem inseparable, if not identical, since the process of modernization began in the West and has gone forward without interruption. So China cannot get one without getting the other.

In a way, modernization has been as much imposed upon the West as westernization upon China. Wherever the spearhead of modern invention passes through, it changes the means of production, creates problems of distribution and control, and thus gives rise to new problems. Men must adjust themselves to changing conditions; the constant changes of environment and adjustments of man to them impose a progress on him. Imagine yourself looking down on Europe after the French Revolution; you would see that there had not been much visible change on the surface of that continent since the Roman Empire. But if you took another look half a century after the industrial revolution the changes would be quite noticeable. After still another half century you would find networks of railways covering the surface of all Europe and America, too, with trains crawling on them like thousands of centipedes. Here and there factories with chimneys sticking up would cluster in the large industrial centers like fantastic beehives. Steamboats carrying manufactured goods would be shuttling in and out of harbors, ready to bear the finished products of the factories to all the corners of the earth.

These same steamboats half a century ago brought to China the lucifer matches, clocks, kerosene lamps, toys, and other useful and ingenious foreign articles that I played with in childhood in that tranquil village. The innocent and unconscious absorption of these curious things was the beginning of the great change that was to bring China in line with the trend toward modernization—with all its accompanying sufferings, turmoils, and perils, and with the rapid disappearance of the pleasant, tranquil life of old China.

Heretofore the absorption of foreign elements, conscious or unconscious, had enriched the life of the people and led to no complications. With the absorption of modern Western manufactures and systems or ideas, trouble began to spring up. Like the modern sulfa drugs, they cure diseases but sometimes cause serious reactions, which may prove fatal. To absorb Western civilization with less violence of reaction is the problem China has yet to face. It calls for experiment and scientific research, which again are western products—machine tools to make all modern machinery, mental, social, or industrial.

2. *Morals and Intellect*

WHEN for the first time I read the Greek philosophers in the ethics class in California I began to feel, as I have said before, that Chinese thinkers in ancient times were enclosed in an atmosphere of morals, while the Greeks possessed the quality of all-piercing intellect. As I read more books on Greek life and culture it became more clear and convincing to me that some such striking contrast did exist between ancient Chinese and Greek thought, and that among other causes this was probably the main one for the divergence in development of Eastern and Western civilizations. Perhaps this assertion will seem rather too sweeping, but as my experience grew with the years I could not see it otherwise, and I still believe it to be so.

After my return from abroad I constantly tried to drive home to the minds of my people the importance of the development of intellect. The names of Socrates, Plato, and Aristotle appeared in my lectures and writings so often that I was caricatured by tabloid papers in Shanghai as "a man with mouthfuls of Plato and Aristotle." Seeing that I was not carrying the public with me, I gave it up as a bad job and changed my tactics to preaching the study of natural science. Instead of leading people to the source of the current I reversed the process by letting them see the current first. Naturally they would go back to the sources later on.

My compatriots, children of ages of practical sense, had rebuked me for forgetting the true nature of my own people.

A prominent Chinese scientist once was asked why China has not developed natural science. He offered four reasons: First, the belief of Chinese scholars in Yin, the negative, and Yang, the positive, as complementary principles of the universe. Second, the belief in the Five Elements—metal, wood, water, fire, and earth—as the constituents of the universe, and the application of this analysis of the material world around us to human life, even to medicine. Third, the Chinese rule-of-thumb ways, which are an enemy to accurate calculations. Fourth, the aversion of scholars to using their hands or doing manual work.

All these may be obstacles to the growth of natural science; but quite aside from them I do not believe that natural science would have grown up. It could not, for our attention was not directed along that line.

My people are most interested in things practical—something useful to them. I often noticed in America that when people were shown something they were apt to say, "That's interesting." The response from my own people in like case would be, "What is the use of it?" This shows the truth of the common Chinese saying that the virtuous see virtue while the wise see wisdom in the things they come in contact with. A difference in mental attitude produces different manifestations of interest. The use of a thing interests my people more than the thing itself.

Chinese thinkers see all things in their relation to man, to moral applications, to artistic or poetic sense, or to practical use. The scientific thought of ancient Greece found its origin in Egypt and Babylon. Babylonian astronomy and Egyptian geometry, like astronomy and mathematics in China, aimed at practical applications. But the intellectual quality of the Hellenic genius was to seek the *general truth* in these sciences by generalizing and formulating their principles, a process which paved the way for the discovery of natural law.

For the Greeks there were two worlds: the world of the senses and the world of reason. The senses deceive us; therefore the philosopher should not trust his sense impressions but develop his reason. It was not for its practical use that Plato insisted upon the study of geometry, but in order to develop the faculty of abstraction and train the mind to correct and vigorous thinking. Applying these powers to ethics and politics, Plato laid the foundation of Western social philosophy, and by their application in studying the reality of concrete things Aristotle laid the foundation of physical science.

For Aristotle trusted reality as seen through the senses. His was a great systematizing intellect which has left its imprint on nearly every branch of knowledge. For him, to know properly involved a correct use of the senses as well as of the reason; the advance of science depends upon development of both speculation and observation. From applied mathematics Aristotle deduced certain general laws, the study and exploration of which provided a form of mental gymnastics through which he disciplined a powerful and penetrating intellect. And by means of the same well-exercised intellect and right use of the senses, he created a system of knowledge which has been the foundation of modern science. Logic and the theory of knowledge were outgrowths of these same intellectual exercises which systematized Western thought.

Chinese thought is centered upon the development of human relations. We are interested in natural laws only so far as they are capable of serving as guides for human conduct. The *Great Learning*, one of the Confucian classics, taught us a system of knowledge to which I have alluded in an earlier chapter. It starts with the search for truths in things, from which we gain our knowledge. Knowledge is the power by which the mind is developed.

So far the story is intellectual. But as it goes on the shading of moral sense begins to grow. Mental development is for personal culture, which in turn will serve as the foundation for a well-ordered family life. The latter is the foundation of a well-governed state, which in turn will serve as a step toward international peace. From the rudiments of knowledge down to international peace this forms a complete scheme of practical moral idealism. To the Chinese, world peace is not something to be dreamed about but a practical moral scheme. For national prosperity is invariably bound up with peace between nations. A type of knowledge which does not lead to this end is but secondary or trifling.

For such an attitude toward learning, to ascertain whether the earth goes round the sun or the sun round the earth is but trivial.

Or again, what is the use of bothering with the expansion of water in a boiling kettle, as Watt did if we are to believe the story? The Chinese would be more interested in the hissing sound, which suggests making tea in preparation for guests. It is poetic.

The drop of an apple to the ground is only natural. The Chinese would moralize it. They would say that when a thing is ripe, it drops. When you do things in a proper way they come to their natural conclusion. There is no use in puzzling about it. Should the apples in your garden shoot up to the sky, it would set the Chinese to fearing that some great calamity might fall upon the people; as would the appearance of a comet, or some other perversion of the familiar order of things. It would take a Newton to think along the line of the attraction of the earth.

Thus with my own effort to preach. What is the use to China of those figures of Greek antiquity or their teachings? In my people's eyes natural science is useful only because practical uses come out of it. The Greek philosophers are remote even from modern natural sciences. What earthly use is there in them? The Chinese are in sympathy with the usefulness of science but recoil from the idea of science for science' sake. "Learning is for the sake of its use," is an accepted dictum among Chinese scholars.

With such a mental attitude it is small wonder that China has not developed pure science, an elaboration of intellectual interest rather than of practical considerations. We built the Great Wall and the Grand Canal and developed a system of irrigation; the grandeur of our architectural design, our palaces and temples, has inspired world-wide admiration. These works are among the greatest engineering feats the world has ever known. But they were not developed from a foundation of pure science and therefore, however remarkable they were, no further development was possible until modern engineering came to the rescue. For without pure science the applied science of modern engineering could not attain its present high plane. The discovery of the compass and gunpowder by the Chinese has served useful purposes in the world. But it was a Western mind that observed the principle of explosive expansion in gunpowder and applied it to boiling water, thus making possible the discovery of steam power.

In China discoveries stopped at their immediate practical use. We did not, like the Greeks, try to venture into generalization; nor, like modern Europeans, did we try to get universal laws from particular discoveries—a trait inherited from the Hellenic world in its improved form. Once the useful purposes of an invention were served, we stopped there; therefore Chinese science traveled unaided and without the guiding light of scientific thought. The development of science in China was arrested because we were too practical-minded.

I do not mean to say that the Chinese do not think logically. But their minds were not aided by systematic mental gymnastics. This defect has been reflected in Chinese philosophy, political and social organization, and daily life. It has become more glaring as the rest of the world came to live under the light of modern science in an industrialized society.

Besides being practical, our people are imbued with a sound moral sense. It may also be said that because we are moral we are practical. For morals refer to conduct, which is necessarily judged by practical results. There will be no such fanciful ideas or speculation about conduct as the Greeks had with physics and metaphysics.

At times we may venture beyond that practical moral way of thinking, but the antennae of our minds recoil as soon as we feel we are getting away from the sphere of human relations, and stop right there. A Sung philosopher of the twelfth century once stepped over the moral bounds by speculating on the formation of mountain ranges and on the finding of seashells on the tops of mountains. He observed that the waves of the mountain ranges indicated the fluidity of the mountains many thousands of years earlier, while the shells bore witness to the fact that their peaks must once have been at the bottom of the sea. But when and how the fluid suddenly coagulated into mountains, and how the bottom of the sea was raised to such a height, he had no means of discovering. There he stopped, fearing shipwreck if he should venture too far. There have been similar instances of observing nature both before and after this philosopher, but Chinese thinkers were always scrupulous, in their mental excursions, not to drift too far away from the camp of human relations.

That the Chinese are not a nonintellectual people needs no proof as it is so evident; but their intellect was exercised within the sphere of morals and practical uses. Thus they set limits to their own intellectual activities. Like silkworms, they wove their moral cocoons with threads drawn from their own minds, as it were, to encase themselves. And they loved their encasement and felt comfortable in it. Chinese life is a life of contentedness. Stability is aimed at in Chinese philosophy. Progress? No—it will create discontent, which will destroy stability. The Chinese is contented with his immediate world and has never wanted to speculate far and deep in nature. China has not produced natural science because she did not want it.

The Greeks were quite a different sort of people. Aristotle's mind ventured high up into the heavens, low down beneath the earth, and far away beyond the corners of the land. The universe was material for the exercise of Greek intellect. To the Greeks the mere use of the intellect was a pleasure. They did not care much about whether it was practical or had anything to do with morals or human relations. "What do I get by learning these things?" asked a pupil of Euclid. "Give him sixpence, since he must make gain out of what he learns," said Euclid to his servant, as the story runs. Even with morals they developed a system of ethics, looking into the validity of moral laws through intellectual inquiry, and this was how Socrates got into trouble, being accused of poisoning the souls of young people with dangerous questionings.

Out of Greek ideas about nature and love of intellectual exercise in systematic thinking—flowing intermittently through the Renaissance, the Reformation, and the French Revolution and receiving great impetus from the industrial revolution, through which it gradually improved its instruments and technique—natural science has grown to its modern stage. The practical considerations of science were never neglected in its later development in Europe. Frequent inventions and discoveries gave further impetus to scientific research. Scientific generalizations and applied science marched shoulder to shoulder. So the influences of pure and applied science react one upon another to their mutual benefit.

When modern science began to trickle into China after the opening of the commercial ports, it was its practical value that attracted the attention of the Chinese scholars. They built arsenals and dockyards. Incidentally they translated books on elementary science. They were not interested in whether the sun goes round the earth or vice versa; it was immaterial to them, since the alternatives had no practical consequence in their relation to man. More than a century earlier, when the Jesuits brought mathematics and astronomy to the court of the Ming emperors, scholars were interested because these sciences would mend the deficiencies then found to exist in the Chinese calendar. For the calendar is indispensable not only for reckoning days, months, and years but also for sowing and harvesting.

Around the beginning of the twentieth century the theory of evolution was brought into China. Chinese scholars at once saw the practical moral significance of it. With the application of a natural law of "struggle for existence," "natural selection," and "survival of the fittest," they came to the conclusion that nations in the world were struggling for existence, and through natural selection only the fittest would survive. Would China be the fittest and would she survive? She must struggle—struggle for existence. As to the validity of the theory, they had no particular interest and no scientific background to start an investigation, anyhow. Right away they threw a moral cushion over the intellectual undertaking of Darwin. At once they moralized it by saying, "The flesh of the weak is the food of the strong." Being a weak nation, China had to worry about her flesh. Countrymen, arise! It is your duty to your country to look out for the "cannibal" nations around us!

Another phase of the theory of evolution was taken up in its application to history. History goes round in a circle, the Chinese scholars believed. Under the influence of Darwinism they recast their old belief into a new faith that history forges ahead, or else recedes, or remains stationary. This change in the conception of history exercised a paramount influence upon the minds of Chinese scholars in regard to progress.

The conceptions of Yin and Yang and the Five Elements undoubtedly grew out of naïve observations of nature. They were good enough for rationalizing the conduct of nature and man. No minute calculations were necessary, much less the use of the hands. I presume that if Chinese scholars were interested in manual work, they would apply it to making useful or beautiful objects of art rather than to experiments in the scientific laboratory. People would still think and do only along the lines where their interests lay. The magnetic needle will only point in the direction of the magnetic pole.

Such an attitude of mind is of course no fertile soil for pure science. However, slowly but steadily China is modifying her attitude —from applied science she has been led to pure science, from pure science to new ways of thinking, and finally to actual modification of her attitude of mind. We have opened windows in the walls of our moral universe and looked into the gardens of a new intellectual universe where the fruits of science and invention abound.

This modification of mental attitude has set a new value upon nature—nature as the pure scientist sees it and not only as the moralist or poet sees it. The universe to the modern Chinese is not only a moral one as the ancient Chinese saw it but also an intellectual one as the Greeks saw it.

The moralist studies nature with a view to finding its laws for the benefit of human relations. The scientist studies it with a view to finding its natural laws for intellectual interest—knowledge for the sake of knowledge. China's absorption of modern science has penetrated through these moral bounds of her universe and the minds of the modern Chinese are reaching further and further out to search for truths. Their thinking has been becoming more adventurous, like a ship sailing in unknown seas, exploring for hidden treasures. In other aspects this intellectual release has caused the minds of the younger generation to adopt a critical attitude toward traditional ideas—make critical inquiries into morals, government, and social customs—with far-reaching consequences. While men of the older generation have been very much alarmed at the possible destruction of their tranquil moral abodes and have lamented the passing of the good old days, the younger generation has busied itself in building a new intellectual edifice.

All that, I think, is one of the most valuable contributions that the West has made to China.

Inversely, as the Greeks found with the Babylonian and Egyptian sciences, a study of Chinese sciences may yield profitable contributions to the modern scientific world. A modest beginning made in recent years in the scientific study of Chinese architecture, medicine, and economic botany has yielded fruitful results.

Civilizations are built around different systems of the universe as men conceive it. The Chinese conceived a moral universe, around which they built their civilization. The Greeks conceived an intellectual universe, around which they built theirs. European morals as they are today have been drawn from Christianity—a moral universe as revealed through God. On the other hand, the Chinese moral universe is as revealed through nature's ways. The Christians have endeavored to build a kingdom of heaven on earth, while the Chinese were content with trying to build a kingdom of peace and stability.

Chinese morals are derived from nature; Christian morals from divine power; for the Chinese the gods are but part of nature, while to Christians nature is but the creation of God. On these grounds it is plain that the conflicts between Christian dogma and science were bound to be very serious, as Western history has proven in abundance; while the conflicts between science and Chinese moral precepts would be mild since both started from the same ground—nature—only traveling in different directions.

It has been said that Christian thought is heavenly or godly, Chinese thought is worldly, and Greek thought unworldly. It is this unworldly thought that has led men to the discovery of the natural laws which are the foundation of modern science and hence of modern invention. The unworldly thought in the applications of science has brought prosperity to the world, if not peace and stability.

The development of European civilization, as I see it, is a struggle at various times between the Christian moral universe and the Greek intellectual universe. The Renaissance, the Reformation, and the French Revolution were but the bursting out of a submerged intellectual universe under the domination of a moral one —these various movements were only different phases of the same current. Finally came the industrial revolution in which the same intellectual universe, continuously developing through centuries, came to the surface in an overwhelming torrent and swept aside everything in its way. Its spearhead had already taken China unawares before and during the time of my childhood; it pierced our moral universe, burst out later to destroy the stability of Chinese life, and thus furnished the materials for the writing of this volume.

One universe cannot be expected to produce the fruits of another. The fruits of the tree of science ripen in intellectual gardens alone—within the system of Christian dogma or that of Chinese moral precepts no science could have been produced.

Though, indeed, we find much scientific thought in Mencius in ancient times, this is a nonessential part of his philosophical system. Such thoughts are but satellites to a planet; his system is fundamentally moral.

For science grows out of man's whole being, a burning desire for unworldly truths; a fearless, ever-searching intellect with unbiased spirit continuously reaching out for truth, and an indomitable vigor of mind and body; in other words, it grows out of the very soul of man in his intellectual world. No mere side interests or occasional excursions of the mind into nature, or lukewarm desire to understand it, could ever crown man with the glorious garland of science.

In China, under the influence of modern science, there is growing up a new moral edifice stripped of superstition and false analogies to nature; tested through intellectual inquiry and supported by findings of social science based upon methods adapted from physical research to the investigation of society.

On the other hand we must not forget that the old Chinese moral edifice, built up through centuries of vicarious experience and generations of continuous effort, by such various means as the Confucian classics, literature in general, the graphic arts, music, the family, theatre, gods, temples, even toys—this moral structure has made Chinese people trustworthy, their society stable, and their civilization enduring. Such moral precepts as loyalty, honesty, love of parents, truthfulness, benevolence, righteousness, moderation, and broad-mindedness have contributed much toward the moral emotional make-up of the Chinese people. Intellectual honesty that grows out of modern science will reinforce these virtues that have grown out of ages of moral teaching.

Side by side with the new moral universe, a new intellectual edifice will be raised to house the achievements of the creative genius of young China. On the stem of the Confucian system of knowledge, which starts with the investigation of things, or nature, and leads to human relationships, we shall graft the Western system of scientific knowledge, which starts with the same investigation of things or nature but leads the other way round to their inter-relationships.

As in the West, the moral universe will co-exist in China with the intellectual, one for stability and the other for progress. Can we strike the happy mean?

3. *The Practical Wisdom of the Chinese People*

LEARNING is for the sake of its use. What is this use? It comes under two main principles. First, whatever has to do with the elevation of moral sentiments in the masses and with the cultivation of right moral attitudes in the individual. Second, whatever will contribute to national prosperity and the people's livelihood. These principles are the summary of ages of teachings from the sages and scholars. Whatever they say and teach has come eventually to these. Scholars learned them and diffused their learning to the common people. The common people, under this influence, through ages of accumulated effort have gradually and unconsciously developed a mentality, as the reader will readily see, of common sense and practical wisdom. They have kept on asking what is the use of this or that in the light of these same principles.

When trains and steamboats came to China, people were ready to ride on them because they went much faster. They used kerosene oil because it gave more light. Telephone and telegraph facilities transmit messages without the necessary delay of mail or foot —or even house—messengers. Clocks and watches give exact time without looking at the sun. People bought Western manufactures because they served useful purposes in daily life.

When missionaries came they established schools and hospitals. What wonderful people they are, said the Chinese: they heal the sick and educate the children of the poor. When the Chinese assembled to listen to the preaching of the gospel, the eyes of a number of them were usually directed toward the hospitals or the schools. Through the leaves of the Holy Bible they peeped at the useful things of Western manufacture the preacher had brought to China from his homeland. My father made friends with a local missionary because he repaired our water pumps and gave us cough drops and quinine powder. He was honest and friendly in dealing with his neighbors. The last is important because the Chinese are both practical and moral. What about the religion they taught us? Oh—that is a good religion. It teaches people to be good. What about their God? Oh, yes. Their God? He is a good God. Put him in our temples beside many other good gods. We'll worship him, burn candles and incense before him. But He will not sit in your temples beside your idols. Well, we'll make an idol for him. No, that can't be done. He is omnipotent and omnipresent. God is in you, not in the idol. Yes, yes. When he is not in me, maybe he likes to be in an idol. No. He is in heaven. Yes, I know he is, as all the other gods are. Maybe he wants to take a trip down to earth and use the temples as his hotels. Then we can worship him there. No, He is the only God—when you worship Him you cannot worship other gods.

Then our people would hesitate and say, you worship yours; we will worship ours. "There it is if you believe it so; it is not there if you do not believe it." Herein lies China's wisdom of religious toleration.

Modern legal sense as the West understands it is not developed in China. Avoid the courts if you can. Let us settle our disputes without going to law. Let's compromise. Let's have a cup of tea and sip together with friends and talk things over. It is much less expensive, much less troublesome, and much fairer. What is the use of going to law? You often see stone tablets on the highways near a hsien capital bearing these bold letters: "DO NOT GO TO LAW."

This may be the reason for the nonlegal-mindedness of the Chinese. But as modern industry and commerce grow, society will grow in complexity, and laws for governing the complicated social relations will be necessary. When laws become a necessity, the practical wisdom of the Chinese will see to it that we are more legal-minded. But would it not lessen the burdens of the courts if people should settle their cases by sipping a cup of tea?

Do not do unto others what you would not have others do unto you. Critics say this is negative, while "Do unto others what you would have others do unto you" is positive. Yes, that is true. But the Chinese prefer the negative, from practical sense. You may like onions, so you try to force them upon others. That is positive. Onions may taste good to me, but others may not have the same feeling; they may fear them as ladies do rats. If you were not a lover of this obnoxious vegetable, would you like others to impose it upon you? No, of course not. Then why should you impose it upon others? It's negative, but it's more sensible. For the positive way, if you persist, will lead to trouble, while the negative way will avoid it.

Love your friend, be fair to your enemy. Of course it is a higher ideal to love your enemy. But how many in all history have ever loved their enemy? It looks like hitching your wagon to a star—it is something unattainable. It is practical idealism to be fair to your enemy. So the Chinese prefer it to pure idealism.

Is there any use in music? Yes, it is very useful. It can bring the feelings of an individual to harmony. It can raise the morals of a people to a higher level.

Is there any use in the arts? Yes, they are very useful. They will cultivate the finer sense of the people and thus raise their morals to a higher level. Landscape gardening, splendid palaces and temples, landscape painting, literature, poetry, calligraphy, porcelains, bronzes, skillful carvings, and the like all cultivate this finer sense in man.

Why must a man be honest? Because if you are dishonest and untrustworthy people will not believe and trust you. Then you will fail in business and in dealing with other people. Dishonesty simply does not pay. Not only is honesty a virtue, but its practical results are invaluable to human relations.

The Chinese love humor. Why? Because you can say things without offending people; besides, you can get a lot of innocent pleasure from it. You can get along with people better by innocent and amusing suggestions. Humor makes company more congenial and life more enjoyable.

Perseverance is one of the great virtues necessary to success. If you keep on filing and filing, you will break the steel. If you keep on grinding and grinding, you will shape the precious stone.

In the scenic Western Hills of Peking, one summer afternoon, Professor John Dewey, Dr. Hu Shih, and I watched a Sisyphus beetle pushing a tiny mud ball up the slope. It pushed first with forelegs, then with hind legs, and then with its side legs. The ball rolled up and up until some mishap occurred which set it rolling down to where it started with the diminutive Sisyphus riding on it. He repeated the process but met with the same failure. Again and again he tried. We admire his perseverance, said both Hu Shih and I. Yes, but his lack of intelligence is regrettable, said John Dewey. Thus the virtuous see virtue; the wise see wisdom. There are different aspects in the same thing. The eminent philosopher is truly a loyal son of the West, while his disciples are truly loyal sons of the East. The West pitied Mr. Sisyphus' lack of head, while the East admired his heart.

The Chinese people are contented with their lot. If a Chinese lives on a frugal diet, takes a humble house, and has enough clothes to keep warm, he feels satisfied. This attitude toward a simple way of living keeps China's millions contented and happy, but it precludes progress as the West understands it. Unless China is industrialized, she cannot lift the people to any level of material prosperity. Perhaps for years to come her countless people will have to be content with their lot.

The Chinese people are devoted to nature, not in the sense of finding the natural laws but in the sense of cultivating the poetic, artistic, or moral sense of lovers of nature. To be under pine trees steeped in the moon and listen to streams flowing gently over the rocks gives one a placid mind and a tranquil heart. To see spring flowers in bloom makes one feel the universe filled with the spirit of growth; to observe autumn leaves falling serves as a warning of the approach of declining days.

From nature the Chinese learns the sublime nature of man. In Peking there is the Altar of Heaven, built of white marble somewhat like a great theatre, but terraced upward toward the center, which is raised higher than the surrounding terraces. At this altar the emperors of the past worshiped heaven. On one clear moonlit autumn night, when the sky was blue without a speck of cloud upon it, the full moon shone directly upon my head and the marble terraces were flooded with silver light overflowing into the vast space around me. I stood at the center of the altar and all of a sudden felt as if heaven, earth, and myself merged into one vastness.

This experience of sudden sublimation made me understand why the Chinese regard heaven, earth, and man as one and inseparable. By believing in their unity the Chinese elevate man from the pettiness of daily life to the higher plane of sublime spirit. The vastness of space, the brilliance of the sun, the placidity of the moon, the multitude of stars, the luxuriant growth of plants, the rotation of the seasons, the timely rains that nourish the crops, the winding rivers that irrigate the fields, the dashing tides that reveal the power of nature, the high mountains that touch the sky—each and all furnish rich materials in cultivating man's sublime spirit. Of nature man is born; to nature man owes his life; from nature he learns his ways of good living. Nature and man are one and inseparable.

Nature is so good, so kind, so sincere, and so generous that man in his own very nature—which is but part and parcel of greater nature—must be good, kind, sincere, and generous. Here comes the belief of the Chinese that human nature is all-good. Evils grow only out of the perversion of good. This is why great Chinese teachers and statesmen always trust the good that is in man. Great statesmen like Dr. Sun Yat-sen and great teachers like Dr. Tsai Yuan-pei always take any Tom, Dick, or Harry for a good man until he proves the contrary. And they are always ready to forgive and forget. Herein lies their greatness and broad-mindedness. It is proverbial that a statesman's mind is so broad that you could row a boat in it, while a scholar's heart is as resonant as a hollow in mountain regions that echoes with every vibration of sound.

Nature is China's national teacher. Upon nature she built her moral universe, and thus her culture and civilization. Since Chinese civilization furnishes only inadequate means to control nature, she follows nature. Here lie the differences between East and West. It is the duty of the moralists and poets to follow nature; it is the duty of the scientist to control it. Under the influence of Western civilization the younger generation is changing—changing from a poetic and moral appreciation to a scientific study of nature. Hereafter China will understand nature not only through feelings and empirical observation but through the intellect and scientific research. China will know nature more intimately and control it more effectively to bring prosperity to the nation and better the livelihood of the people.

At the same time, science will not destroy the sense of beauty in nature as some people think it may. As I write I look out through the windows and see in the gardens the old pine trees and bamboo groves, fresh after a rain, and over the bamboo trees I see the Yangtze River gracefully winding its tranquil way past the hilly city of Chungking. The sense of the beauty of nature gives me peacefulness of mind and tranquility of heart. But if I think of the plants botanically, I see in them the growth of the cells and the circulation of the sap, which does not lessen my sense of beauty at all. If I look at the river geologically, I see through its silt-carrying waters to its bed, which millions and millions of years ago may have been just dry land or even the bottom of a rough sea. Thinking in this way, the beauty of the gentle Yangtze remains in my mind just the same or even with richer associations. That a knowledge of the working of their cells should destroy one's sense of the beauty of pine trees or bamboo groves is unthinkable. It makes me feel that nature is even more wonderful and beautiful with a scientific outlook.

From love of the beauty in nature and a feeling of her irresistible force, a strong fatalism grew up in the minds of the Chinese people. In spite of all human efforts, nature will stick to its invariable course. Thus flood and drought are beyond human power to control, and people have learned to submit to Fate. Since it is Fate, they may just as well take it good-naturedly. What is the use of making much fuss over Fate? This is why one finds many a toiler in China with a smiling face. Misery is a fate—why not take it in good humor?

Here is one secret of why the Chinese people have had so great a capacity to stand hardship and suffering during the years of war. Do your best, perform your duty, and let Fate take care of the rest. "Enjoy Nature's way and be contented with your lot." The placid autumn moon, the tender June breeze, spring blossoms, winter snows, all are in store for your enjoyment, rich and poor alike.

CHAPTER 34

MODERN CIVILIZATION

MODERN civilization originated in Europe; American civilization is but its offspring. Chinese civilization, which developed from its own sources and is of a very high order, is regarded as ancient—China began to be modernized only with the influx of modern influences from Europe and America. In the last fifty years she has been going through the metamorphosis of coming up to date, with its accompanying agonies. She has been forced into the modern world step by step, by the tides of westernization, as we have seen in these pages.

"Modern civilization" is an ambiguous term. It yields various impressions. It may mean more and better weapons of war for men to massacre each other with, until it destroys them all. It may mean better means of production, to support more millions in comfort and luxury and create a higher standard of living. Or the term may be used for the science and invention that have made both modern warfare and a high standard of living possible. It may represent the mentality which searches for objective truths in order to enable man to control nature. It may refer to better communication, and better organization in mobilizing resources and wealth. It may signify democracy to the democratic countries or totalitarianism to totalitarian nations.

Part or all of these may be called modern civilization—as to what is most essential or most truly typical no two people seem to agree. Then what has China been doing during these fifty troubled years? She has trodden in the dark. Sometimes she has seemed to be walking into a trap, as a fly will, by licking the sweetness that leads it along the path of doom. At other times she seems to have been cornered by a group of armed gangsters who forced her into submission. This she resented, and afterward tried to get weapons to defend herself. All in all, she has struggled and muddled and finally began to see light in what is called Western civilization, with its good as well as evil, blessings as well as curses.

What are the goods and blessings she should try to absorb, what evils reject? Here, too, there seems to be no agreement, whether among individuals or groups. The evils she has taken in may later prove to be laden with blessings. Thus from the evil of opium, forced upon China by superior weapons of war, she got the seeds of modern science. The goods she has adopted may prove to be accompanied by unsuspected evils. For example, by relying too much on system and organization we forgot the virtues of individual integrity and responsibility. There are cases where new systems and organizations have failed in their work for lack of due emphasis upon these qualities.

The standard of living was raised for the few who lived upon the exploitation of many. Thus automobiles were imported and used without making an effort to manufacture them. It takes thousands of farmers, each raising hundreds of bushels of rice, to produce the means of exchange for one imported car. Modern conveniences in modern towns, such as electric lights, radios, flush toilets, and other comforts, must be paid for by the sweat of millions of tillers of the land. In lifting our standard of living we are impoverishing the country by an unfavorable trade balance. Yet the standard of living must be raised, and accompanying evils must be remedied by scientific agriculture, farm machinery, and an irrigation system for increased productivity.

These again will give rise to new problems. We have suffered much from modern civilization, yet we still need more of it. If we take too much at a time we vomit it forth again violently as in the case of the Boxer uprising of 1900; if we take too little it is ineffective. This seems to be how modern civilization goes in China. Yet China must muddle along with the world, willy-nilly.

In the West, during the last hundred years, one invention has led to another, one idea to another, one step in progress to another, one prosperity to another, and one war to another. Only peace did not lead to another peace, but to war. This is how the world has forged ahead in the name of modern civilization. Must China fall in line with the rest of the world?

If there should be another war, as the world so much fears, it seems probable that it will start again, like the first World War, in eastern and middle Europe; or like the recent cataclysm, in the Chinese Three Eastern Provinces, known as Manchuria. The people of middle Europe want lebensraum elsewhere, while as to Manchuria, outside peoples want to find their lebensraum there. The former, being a densely populated area, tends to spill its troubles, while the latter—a vast vacuum—sucks trouble in. Either is a potential source of war, in which, if it comes, the whole world must again be involved, to its incalculable disaster.

In safeguarding the powder magazines of the East, responsibility will inevitably rest upon the shoulders of China. Therefore the political, social, economic, and industrial development of China during the next twenty or thirty years will have a determining effect upon the peace situation of the world. A strong and prosperous China, co-operating with the major Powers of the West, could eliminate the danger to a very great extent if not entirely. It is to the mutual interest of the Allied Powers and of world peace in general that the Western Powers should co-operate with China, say for a period of fifty years, in the development of her natural resources; and for the coming twenty years, perhaps, in the work of her economic and social rehabilitation.

Before Western influence made inroads into China, her troubles for many centuries had come solely from Manchuria and the neighboring region known as Mongolia. When Japan became a world Power after the Sino-Japanese War, she contended with Tsarist Russia for control over that vast territory, a conflict which culminated in the Russo-Japanese War. Japan's scheme to use that part of China as a steppingstone to control of the whole country led to the Mukden Incident. If history since the downfall of the Tangs has taught us anything, we may be reasonably sure that the Three Eastern Provinces will still be a trouble center for China and a cause of worry to the world until China herself is strong and prosperous and the vast vacuum of Manchuria is filled.

In building up a modern democracy and industries China needs time and favorable conditions for experiment. These conditions are peace and security. Internal peace depends upon unification of the country. Security depends upon international understanding. China will have security only when Manchuria becomes a center of peace.

We shall have to start anew in creating our future by making that vast territory a focus of peace instead of war. In that important work I hope the world—especially America, Britain, and Soviet Russia—will co-operate with China. With their co-operation the task must be crowned by complete success, a blessing for China in particular and for the world generally.

In 1921 I was elected an unofficial observer to the Washington Conference by the Chamber of Commerce and educational associations in Shanghai, and supported by Dr. Sun Yat-sen's Nationalist government in Canton. In the following year, 1922, I went to Europe for a visit to the source of modern civilization. It was very soon after the first World War. One could see that every country in Europe was busy planning postwar rehabilitation and the major victorious Powers were occupied in trying to make peace more enduring. But no one seemed to realize then that they were all helping to sow the seeds of a next war.

France was tired and longed for a permanent peace. Her eyes looked over the Rhine, whence came the danger to her national existence. Her defensive mood was later embodied in the Maginot Line, which she thought would make her immune to German attack. Like the first emperor of the Chin Dynasty (246–207 B.C.) who built the Great Wall to defend China from the attack of the Tartars, France built the Maginot Line. And as trouble for the empire of the Chins came not from outside but from inside the Great Wall, so it was with the French Republic and her "impregnable" barrier.

England was busy with the economic reconstruction of Europe and endeavoring to maintain the balance of power on the Continent. Germany, defeated, was licking her wounds. Tsarist Russia was utterly ruined and a new political experiment was under way in that gigantic Republic of Soviet Russia. Such was the political aspect of Europe after World War I.

America, unwilling to pull European chestnuts out of the fire, had withdrawn from that much-troubled continent and summoned the Washington Conference, at which the Nine-Power Treaty was penned, the Anglo-Japanese Alliance superseded, and the Shantung question settled; this, to save Japan's face, was negotiated outside the conference. The Twenty-One Demands, superseded by the new treaty, were thus unostentatiously sent to the grave. Tsingtao, a seaport in the peninsula of Shantung, had been awarded to Japan at Versailles and the complications which grew out of the award were known as the Shantung question. Indignation at this move gave rise in China to the student movement which had such far-reaching repercussions in Sino-Japanese relations, as well as in political and cultural developments in China, during the following twenty years. In America it troubled public men who had sympathy for China and became a knotty political problem. Both the Republican and Democratic parties more or less committed themselves to right the wrongs done to China by the ill-fated Versailles Treaty; thus while America withdrew her fingers from Europe she dipped them deep into Pacific waters. The result, twenty years later, was Pearl Harbor.

Without the active participation of America in the League of Nations of which she was the author; with a defensive psychology on the part of France, whose only desire was to avoid trouble; and with Britain's main interest focused on maintaining the balance of power on the Continent, the League became toothless. It barked a lot but never meant to bite. Yet any problem that member nations could not handle among themselves was handed over to the League. So it became a dumping ground for international difficulties. When China was unable to meet her difficulties vis-à-vis Manchurian problems she, too, dumped them on the League, of which Japan was a member. In the case of the Mukden Incident France was not interested. Britain was concerned only so far as the balance of power in the Far East was involved, but she was afraid of being drawn in. The League, therefore, had scarcely even the nerve to bark at Japan. Its few mild yelps might indeed be construed as connivance.

The League, however, made an invaluable contribution to our experience. Learning from its failures, the world may profit in planning the coming peace. Born of American idealism, it died of conflicting interests and the ambitions of member nations, especially the major Powers.

So matters developed in the course of some twenty years after the Versailles Treaty. The seeds of war sown at Versailles grew in every corner of the world like weeds, which eventually caught fire and set the whole world aflame.

But politics are but a passing show destined soon to vanish into history. What will always remain is the fundamental problem of culture. It is undeniable that Europe has produced modern science and organized democracy, which have brought to mankind more blessings than evils.

Germany appeared to me a country of telescopes, microscopes, and test tubes; her inventions and discoveries multiplied by leaps and bounds. In Shanghai foreign manufactures of superlative quality became known as *Jahming huo*—"German goods." The Germans were masters of material things but fell short in human relations. This, as I see it, is why they often got into trouble in dealing with other nations. Their sight was focused through the microscope or the telescope, which concentrated their view either too near or too far to perceive human behavior or feelings. They could not very well put international relations or human feelings into a test tube to observe their reactions. In the broader realm of human activities the Germans often failed to grasp the essentials or shortcomings of human nature. They had highly developed special senses in which other nations did not excel, but they were short of common sense. Their special endowments gave them the scientific thoroughness which has made so many special contributions to the world, and their lack of common sense brought misery alike to their own country and to others.

The British were just the opposite. They were a nation of common sense and masters of human relations. Their views on world affairs and policies relative to them were flexible and adaptable. They never let the cord stretch to the point of breaking. If a stronger force pulled at the other end of the rope, the British would loosen it a little to save it from snapping. If the other side was weaker they would keep on drawing the cord to themselves until it slipped from their opponents' hands. But the British would never let go their end of the rope—they would stick to the last, irrespective of consequences. In relations with other countries and in colonial policies this trait of the British people was seen everywhere.

Hand in hand with flexibility and adaptability went such other British traits as tolerance, moderation, considerateness, fair play, and an attitude of compromise. They never went to extremes in their views, and were always trying to understand other people's view in order either to bring themselves to it or to bring others to their own. They loved freedom of speech and thought, disliked hard and fast rules which might prove unadjustable to varying conditions.

The British are reserved to the point of brutal coolness, a trait disliked by other peoples and often the cause of suspicion. It has lost the British many a friend among other nations. But when you know them better, or rather when they know you better, you want to make friends with them.

Some or all of these traits together made English democracy possible. For democracy is not something abstract, something that has dropped from the sky. It consists of the best traits there are in the people who have succeeded in it. If you run through the constitutional history of England, you will find that intolerance, persecutions, corruption, and cruelties fill its pages. Quite a number of lives, including that of a king, have been sacrificed to democracy. The experience of English democracy is worth our serious study.

One fact, however, we must bear in mind: that English democracy grew fast after the unification of the United Kingdom, and American democracy, too, developed by leaps and bounds only after the Civil War. History teaches us that unification and security must go hand in hand to make an organized democracy. For England was lucky in that her islands were small and protected by the sea. In the old days invasion was not easy. So the English enjoyed security and therefore had plenty of time for trial and error. Their national existence was not endangered by foreign invasion during the period of incubation and experiment.

A similar situation existed in America. The North American Continent is itself a gigantic island, the seas around it preventing any formidable invasion. The early colonists from England brought with them seeds of the love of freedom which grew into a great tree of liberty, sheltered from the ax of foreign invaders. In the course of a century or so the democracy of America took firm root. Not only was experiment freely made in human relations but also in things material, by which I mean scientific research. While American democracy grew out of the English model, American science owed a great debt to the Germans.

The American system of higher education is a combination of the English college and the German university; the American academic dress is, so to speak, an English gown with a German cap. In the American colleges boys and girls lived in a spirit of comradeship and free association and secured a liberal foundation of learning. Knowledge was not strictly regimented; human relationships were learned through free mingling of the student body; the sight of the younger generation was not simply narrowed into telescopes, microscopes, or test tubes; a general culture was furnished to all those who cared to absorb it.

In the university proper, or the graduate school, American students were taught methods of research. German thoroughness was admired and encouraged, but its full realization had yet to be achieved at the time of my college days. During the first World War the five colors of the former Chinese flag—red, yellow, blue, white, and black were reduced to two: black and white. The reason was that German dyes were no longer available in China on account of the war. An American chemist in New York told me that in Germany several specialists worked on one color, whereas in America one chemist dealt with many colors. This was some twenty years ago. Conditions have changed by now, since Americans have acquired so much of the German thoroughness during the last two or three decades.

Thus on the American side of the water English democracy and German science have gone hand in hand. With her rich natural resources, her power of organization and love of great projects, America may now easily be ranked as first of the democracies of the world. Just the other day at a party in the American Embassy in Chungking, a British diplomat remarked to me that "England is Americanized, Russia is Americanized, and China is Americanized."

"In what way is England Americanized?" I asked.

"Hollywood, for example," was the reply.

"Russia—in the sense of great industries?"

"Yes."

Meanwhile flashes of pictures passed rapidly through my mind, in which I saw that Chinese political and educational systems, social changes, and industrial developments were richly tinged with Americanization. At the same time I was not unaware of the fact that China colors all the sea that washes her shores.

Pointing at the six rows of eight stars each on the American flag, the same diplomat turned to a high-ranking American military officer standing by and asked with a touch of humor, "What are you going to do when you add one state more?"

"Well, we'll make it seven rows of seven, but what new state do you have in mind?"

"England," replied the diplomat. We all laughed. It was only a joke, but in jokes one may see the temper of the times.

In days of old, when the West fought for colonial empire in the East, all the important Western Powers except America at various times wronged China. Even Portugal bit off a tiny piece of land called Macao, in the province of Kwangtung. The only thing America got from China was extraterritoriality, but what she has done for China is far more and will be remembered for generations to come. As everybody knows this, I need not elaborate here. Now both America and Britain have abolished that system and Britain has returned all the settlements, which were an anachronism—though Hongkong remains in British hands. In spite of terrible wars all over the world, much encouraging light has shone through the international clouds. Let us hope that, with victory achieved, it may grow into brilliant sunshine in a cloudless sky.

America has definitely joined the coming international peace organization. She has fought the war. She is to fight for an enduring peace. A new epoch in history is in the making. The combined resources of America, Britain, Soviet Russia, and China are so great that if they desire peace, with an effective world organization backed up by an international defense force to enforce it, peace will indeed be enduring.

For China's part, she will have to redouble her effort of reconstruction and regeneration for the coming twenty or probably thirty years. This will be a critical period for China. Success depends upon foresight and leadership, and the extent to which our Allies will co-operate. The extent to which co-operation is given will also depend upon our political developments and how sound a policy we adopt regarding international investments. Our difficulties are enhanced by the devastations of war and wanton destruction in all the once-prosperous provinces where the heel of the enemy has trodden.

On the other hand, China has a double duty to perform. First, it is her duty to herself to become strong and prosperous. Second, it is her duty to the world to help make world peace secure. In the political philosophy of the Confucian school, peace for the world is the ultimate aim. On the basis of the Confucian philosophy Dr. Sun Yat-sen aimed at world peace in his Three Principles of the People.

If we can bridge over this critical period of twenty or thirty years the momentum thus gathered will carry reforms and reconstruction forward, ever increasing and ever widening, into a glorious future in which China will be in a position to help the world in assuring a more permanent peace.

From the West China has still much to learn. Ever since the downfall of the great dynasty of the Tangs she has been overrun from time to time by peoples from the immense outlying territories of Asia. The decline of Chinese civilization after the fall of that dynasty was due to the invasion of barbarians who at intermittent periods devastated the country and turned it into a stretch of ruins. The successive invasions, together with famine, disease, and internal dissensions, sapped the energy of the Chinese people and thus weakened their creative power. When Western influence began to come into China, therefore, she met it with her civilization at the lowest ebb.

People in China now talk of the Tang civilization as if in hopes of restoring the glories of that era. It is a good thing, so far as we can, to draw inspiration from the Tangs and be stimulated by their more humanistic civilization as contrasted with the ascetic type of the later Sungs. In Tang paintings we admire the strong physique of the people. Music, dancing, poetry, painting, and calligraphy were developed to a very high level, which finds no equal in later days.

But for China to go back to this brilliant period of her history is next to impossible. For centuries we have tried to recover our past glories, yet our civilization slid progressively downward in steady decline. For conditions had changed. The fertile soil in which the Tang civilization grew had been washed away by the tides of long years of devastation. If, however, we can get rid of the cause of the Tang downfall by learning from such modern Tangs as America and other countries where arts, science, political and military organization, health and wealth, are on a very high plane, we shall then perhaps find the glories of the Tangs redescending upon us.

In making the peace China's part will be by no means small. Throughout her history she has had many wars. But they have been wars more in the nature of internal revolution than external aggression—internal conflicts generally caused by the rebellion of oppressed farmers and suffering people against a rotten official-dom. Even her external wars have been more defensive than of-fensive in nature. China has been oppressed much more than oppressing. Ever since the time of the first emperor of the Chin Dynasty who built the Great Wall—symbol of a defensive men-tality—China has wished to be let alone.

Confucius' teaching of proper human relations and world peace, and the democratic ideas of Mencius, will fit China to be a modern democratic state which wishes to do no wrong to other peoples. What China must emphasize after the war is modern science with its applications to means of production; and democracy in its or-ganized form, with emphasis upon unification of the country. Sci-ence and democracy, twin instruments of a progressive modern state, are the key to power, prosperity, and a more lasting peace.

With the practical wisdom of her people, in its special emphasis on human relations and democratic ways of living and thinking, China has the solid foundation for a modern democracy. As we have seen, her democracy is loosely organized. Her intense love of individual liberty has not kept step with modern social conscious-ness. Strong family ties have been partly responsible for retarding the organization of individuals into a broader society. But these ties are rapidly loosening; modern institutions have appeared in the larger cities, and further industrialization will mean a further loosening of family bonds and socialization of individuals.

In the field of knowledge China's way of looking at things has given her a practical wisdom but made her neglect the importance of generalization and abstraction. Her love of nature in poetic, artistic, and moral ways has given her breadth of mind, as exem-plified by great scholars and statesmen, and a harmony of feeling, as revealed in the arts and in conduct; it has not extended to the investigation of natural laws, which are the indispensable weapon of man in controlling nature. With the assimilating power of Chi-nese civilization, the Western contribution of science will be ab-sorbed in due course of time, and with the rich natural resources of the country and high intelligence of her people, the integration of science into her life will open up wonderful opportunities in the future. Chinese morals and arts will prosper in the material wealth thus developed, while Chinese thought and the rich store of literature and philosophy will tend to be clarified and systematized by modern logical and scientific ways of thinking.

On this new basis of initial peace and prosperity, China will be in a position to build up a new defense force to preserve and sustain peace. No country would be a worthy partner for peace that was not a worthy partner for war. The attention of the world has already been drawn to China by the contribution she has made to the world in a war of resistance for eight long years, in spite of weaknesses and shortcomings in some aspects of her national life during the war.

Modern science, with special reference to inventions and industry, will fuse with China's rich treasures of art and sound morals. A new civilization is in the making; perhaps it, too, can contribute to the world's progress.

INDEX

Abbott, Lyman, 78
Academia Sinica, 146, 156
Actors' make-up, 19 f.
Adirondacks, 88
Ah Yi, dream of, 15
Air lines, 154
Altar of Heaven, 258
America, education in, 267 f.; world influence of, 268 f.; benefactor of China, 269; returns the Boxer Indemnity, 90
American Air Force, 235
Americanism, 88
Americans in the Philippines, 218
Amoy, 5
Ancestor worship, 12, 102
Ancestral Hall, 12 f., 39
Anhuei, 190
Anking, revolution in, 64 f.
Annam, 217, 219
Annamese language, 217
Architecture, 240
Aristotle, 74, 245 f.
Army, problem of in China, 106 f.; Japanese, copy of German, 231
Art, Chinese, 178 f., 256
Art treasures, in palace, 177 f.; saved, 152
Artisans, place in society, 38
Assembly. *See* National Assembly
Astronomy, 3, 238
Atrocities, Japanese, 223
Automatic writing, 14
Automobiles, 262

Bamboo shoots, 11
Banditry, 43-45, 95, 194
Banking, 168
Barn dancing, 88
Beauty, East and West, 116
Beetles, 27
Black Dragon Pool, 228
Boating, 54
Bombing by Japanese, 210, 223-226
Bookstores, 56
Borodin, 142
"Borrowing," 37

Boxer Indemnity, America returns, 90
Boxer War, 44, 46, 50, 241, 262
Britain, refuses to protest Japanese invasion of China, 200
British, shoot Chinese sympathizers with labor movement, 132; feeling against in 1925, 132; as colonial administrators, 218 f.; modern traits of character, 266 f.; keep Hongkong, 269
Buddha, power of an image of, 235
Buddhism in China, 105, 228, 239
Buddhist monk, story of, 26
Burma, 2; British in, 218 f.; fall of, 226
Burma Road, 1 f., 156, 225
Bushido, 231

California, 76 f.
Candle tree, 27
Canton, 4 f., 86, 154; fall of, 226; university at, 221
Cantonese dialect, 170
Catholicism, Roman, in China, 238
Central Aviation School, 130
Central Daily News, 207
Central Research Institute, 156
Chambers of Commerce, 172
Chan Yuan-yuan, 142
Chang Chi-tung, 163, 241
Chang Chung-hsiang, 120
Chang Hsun, 138
Chang Pin-ling, 49
Chang Tso-lin, 191
Change, value of, 89
Changkaofen, 210
Changsha, life in, 215; monastery at, iii; University at, 211, 213-216, 221-223
Changsha Bible School, 213
Charms, carried by Japanese soldiers, 234 f.
Chekiang, Province of, home of Chiangs, 10; Hangchow capital of, 46; gentry of opposed railroad, 64; agrarian problems in, 148; peaceful, 170
Chekiang, Provincial College of, 47-53, 58 f., 103; National University of, 149, 221